The Step-Father's
Step-Son

BARBARA M. COX

The Step-Father's Step-Son

Copyright © 2021 by Barbara M. Cox

All rights reserved. No part of this book may be reproduced or transmitted in any form or by any means without the written permission of the author.

All biblical references are from the King James Version of the Bible.

Family Matters Publishing
614 S Business IH35
Ste C
New Braunfels, Texas 78130

www.stepfathersstepson.com

Library of Congress Control Number: 2021921073

ISBN: 978-0-9969537-1-9

This book is dedicated to the mothers, fathers, and children that have been affected by divorce and adultery.

It has taken me forty years of marriage and some very difficult challenges to reach this point in my understanding. This book is the product of that journey.

We are Homeward bound!

Acknowledgments

I would like to thank each and every one of you that have been a part of my life. I have worked with and learned from the educated and the uneducated, the rich and the poor, the arrogant and the humble. Each life is unique and different, and everyone knows something that I don't know. We are all important in God's eyes. You have all taught me something! Thank you!

Foreword

On Earth, every child has a father. But unfortunately, just because the child has a father does not mean that he will be raised by his father or that his father will be a part of his life. This is the truth of a world run by men. A man's world is based on laws—laws for everything from marriage, divorce, children born out of wedlock, test-tube children, abandoned children, and aborted children. It is a world in which men and women desire to control their own destinies by using laws and pieces of paper.

But on the opposite side of our world is a world about love that rises above laws and men. It is God's world. Every minute of every day, we are given the freedom to choose between the two.

We can physically see our earthly fathers, but it takes faith to believe in the unseen: our Heavenly Father, whose evidence is all about and around us.

Table of Contents

Introduction 1
1 The Garden of Eden 5
2 Man's Kingdom on Earth 23
3 Marriage and Family 49
4 Abraham, Isaac, Jacob, and Their Families 61
5 The Lost Children of the House of Israel 99
6 Our Founding Fathers 121
7 Who is the Greatest? 133
8 What About the Step-child? 169
9 What Happens to Painful Emotional Memories? 179
10 How Does Abuse Affect Us? 191
11 The Old Law Is No More! 203
12 The Brain and Our Nighttime Dreams 209
13 Human Development 215
14 The Origins of Narcissism 225
15 The Shift from Love to Fear 245
16 The Betrayal 255
17 How Is Eye Dominance Determined? 261
18 Methods for Shifting Eye Dominance and Perception 269
19 Jesus Is the Way, the Truth, and the Life 275
20 Are You a Son or a Daughter of Men, or Are You a Son
   or Daughter of God? 279
Index 281
Endnotes 287

Introduction

There is an old saying that an ounce of prevention is worth a pound of cure. But as I look around me, I mostly see cures for everything from the common cold to law breakers. It seems that we are continuously busy trying to create more cures. As a result, more laws will be created to justify the cures, and cures require a lot of research and money. Much money will be invested up front, and then a much larger payout will be expected in the end as the victims flock to the creators of our proposed cures for help—some forced, others coming freely.

But is there any evidence that any of these so-called "cures" actually do what they are supposed to do? Speeders get speeding tickets, but does that really keep them from speeding again? Thieves get jail time, but does that really help them to stop stealing? The sexually promiscuous sometimes end up with venereal diseases that doctors and pharmaceutical companies can cure with a pill, but does that really stop them from repeating the same behavior? People that buy a car and don't make their payments loose the money that they invested and the car for forfeiting on a paper agreement. People that fail to make their credit card payments get late-payment fees tacked onto their debt plus a double-digit interest rate. Does a speeding ticket, prison isolation, a poor credit rating, a high interest rate, or a late-payment fee really put them in a better position to pay off their debts to society? In many cases, it looks as though the cure is a way for someone to make money off of someone else. I don't think that many of these cures are worth what they cost.

The Step-Father's Step-Son

The majority of Americans pop pills daily to improve their health, vitality, and sexuality and to try to correct health problems. We have thousands of people locked up behind bars in our jails, prisons, and mental hospitals to try to make our world a safer and more peaceful place. We have nursing homes so that we can be relieved of the burden of caring for the aged in our homes. We have adoption services, day care centers, and boarding homes so that we do not have to provide care to our children in our homes.[1]

Most of us don't even understand how a pill is created or how our prison system is run. Even worse still, we know little about the laws that govern either. We have placed blind trust in the creators of the systems that oversee all of our cures. As a result, there is a lot of waste, abuse of power, and greed. In many cases, the side effects of the cure are worse than the actual illness.

Looking deeper still, I wonder about our economy. How many of our jobs are about prevention and how many are about cures? Our police, jails, and prisons are our "cures" for lawbreakers. Our doctors and hospitals are our "cures" for the sick. Our preachers and churches are our "cures" for the ones that have been beaten down by our cures. We spend our money, buy their books, and attend their special services. We buy insurance so that we do not have to ask for help from God or others. I think that most of our jobs are about a cure rather than prevention.

But how can this be so? We call ourselves Christians. We claim that we believe in God. On the surface, that is great. But God is about the unseen. He is about faith. He is about love.

The truth is that most of us find it easier to believe in the physical rather than the spiritual. We can see the prison. We can see the pill. We can see the insurance contract. We can see the doctor. We can see the preacher. We can see the police. We can see the military. We can see the guns and war machines.

Our man's world is based on what we can see—the physical. That is the world that most of us live in every day of our lives. It is something that we are taught early in our lives. If we make a mistake, something will be taken away from us—maybe a toy, a radio, money, or love. It could be an

Introduction

even bigger payoff—our freedom, a house, or a car. One thing is certain: we will be punished in some way.

And it is a world that causes a lot of people to feel a false sense of security and safety. Any of the systems can fail at any time. They are not necessarily a deterrent for anything. If we cannot put our faith in the physical, then what options do we have?

What if we all chose the ounce of prevention rather than the pound of cure? What would our world be like? Would there be any jobs left? What if we loved others and did the right thing because we loved them and ourselves rather than because of a law or a piece of paper created by a man? What if our "yes" really meant "yes" and our "no" really meant "no"? (Matthew 5:37) If that were the case, we would not need the police; we would not doctors to treat venereal diseases or to abort an unwanted child; we would not need a lawyer to break up our family or to sue someone; we would not need our government or large corporations to dole out our money to charities; we would not need a church building on every street corner; and we would not curse our children with lives of confusion and uncertainty by breaking the family ties between wife, husband, and God, which is the focal point of this book.

We all need to be reminded about God's role in our creation. He is the Father of all of us. He gave our mothers a womb for our protection and development. He gave our mothers two breasts for milk production. Our mothers are the ones that provide our first shelter and our first food. Our fathers, with their muscles and facial hair, are like umbrellas—they provide shelter from the elements and food for our nourishment. God cares for our mothers and for us through our fathers. All of this was created with "love" in mind. We can see our mothers and fathers, but quite often, we forget about God and His role in our creation. As a matter of fact, we must give God credit for our very existence.

Women were created by God for a very important reason. We are the mothers that give life to each new "living soul." For this reason, we must be active participants in the rearing of our children. Our children are not the property of our men—they are the ones that will carry our families into the future. It is imperative that we do our very best to ensure that they grow up on fertile ground for the maintenance of their souls and their relationship with God. Love is the ingredient that is missing in our man's world. More people than ever before are embracing and practicing the laws of this land. This is the reason that our country is on the brink of failure, both at home and abroad. Our children are not the problem. We blame them in most cases for almost everything, but we must take the time to look deeper to find the root cause.

Our society and the way that we treat our children are directly responsible for this shift away from love. We have reached the point in our human evolution where the soul has been diminished to the size of a tiny mustard seed. Many of us are no longer aware that we have a soul. We have become living bodies instead of "living soul[s]" as God created us (Genesis 2:7). As a result, illness will abound and a doctor's role will become first and foremost in our lives and the lives of our children. But I do propose that the less that we love others and ourselves, the more laws will be created to govern us and the less freedom that we will have. Freedom is a very fragile thing. When we do not love others and ourselves as we should, our freedoms are taken away by greedy and controlling individuals. It gives others the opportunity to dominate us. This book is about the ounce of prevention.

The Garden of Eden

In the beginning, God prepared a special place for man. He called it the Garden of Eden. He planted many trees there—beautiful trees of different types and some that produced fruit for food. But He gave very specific instructions concerning one particular tree: the tree of the knowledge of good and evil. He said not to eat any of the fruit on it! God said that if man did eat of the fruit of that tree, he would die (Genesis 2:16, 17). Death was not a part of God's plan for us in the beginning.

"And the LORD God formed man *of* the dust of the ground, and breathed into his nostrils the breath of life; and the man became a living soul" (Genesis 2:7). He did not create man as male or female in the beginning but as "male and female" (Genesis 1:27; Matthew 19:4–6). "Male and female created he them; and blessed them, and called their name Adam, in the day when they were created" (Genesis 5:2). He did not create only one man; instead, He created them! Furthermore, He called them all "Adam" because they most likely all looked alike in the beginning. "And God blessed them, and God said unto them, Be fruitful, and multiply, and replenish the earth, and subdue it" (Genesis 1:28).

A penis was not needed for reproduction in the beginning because we most likely reproduced asexually. God played the role of Father exclusively. Adam did not go around having intercourse with Adam for reproduction. It all happened inside Adam's body just as Mary gave life to Jesus! There are female creatures that reproduce without a male and the product is always a male.[2,3] This is called parthenogenesis. Eve was the mother of all living—even Adam said so himself (Genesis 3:20).[4] A womb was a requirement for giving life to each new "living soul" (Genesis 2:7).

Even Christ said that they were both male and female in the beginning (Matthew 19:4, Mark 10:6). Following the separation of the genders, it now takes one male and one female to equal one reproductive unit. It is through intercourse and conception that we again become one flesh as we were in the beginning—through our children. He also told us that no one, male or female, is to separate what God has joined together (Matthew 19:4–6, Mark 10:5–9).

God brought the creatures of the land and sky to Adam, and Adam named them all (Genesis 2:20). Then, God said that it was not good for man to be alone, so He put Adam into a deep sleep and took one of Adam's ribs to create a human of the opposite sex. In the beginning, Adam was male and female within the same body. And since man was woman and woman was man, either of them could have claimed to be first in God's creation.

In Genesis 4:1, Adam, who had been driven from the garden and was no longer a son of God because of his failure to keep God's commandment and to repent, claimed the title of "man" when Cain was born. He said, "I have gotten a man from the Lord." This is when the word "man" began to be used to describe "men" and "woman" to describe "women" (Genesis 2:23). No longer were male and female both man. It was only the male that was referred to as a "man."

> And Adam said, This *is* now bone of my bones, and flesh of my flesh: she shall be called Woman, because she was taken out of Man. Therefore shall a man leave his father and his mother, and shall cleave unto his wife: and they shall be one flesh. And they were both naked, the man and his wife, and were not ashamed. (Genesis 2:23–25)

The Garden of Eden

If we stop to think about it, men and women both are made from the same flesh. Our bodies are basically the same. We both have hair in the same places—some of it is coarse, and some is fine. We both have genitalia—comparable and with small differences. Men can see their sex organ. Women's ovaries, which are inside of our bodies and produce eggs, are the equivalent of the male testicles that are outside of their bodies and produce sperm. Men have a scrotum to hold the testicles. Women have labia (empty scrotum) since the ovaries are inside and not outside. We both have breasts, although women's breasts are larger for milk production. Men have a penis; women have a small penis, or clitoris as it is called. Some men have testicles (ovaries) that do not migrate outside of their bodies but remain inside. The seminal vesicle may be the male version of the female uterus. The prostate gland may be the male version of the female vagina. On some male children, the line can be seen where the vaginal opening was closed during fetal development. The prostate gland produces fluid to help neutralize the acidic secretions of the vagina. Conversely, the vagina produces fluids that can impede the movement and survival of some sperm. Hence, the woman can determine the sex of the child by limiting the passage of certain sperm. This is why some women produce only girls, while others produce only boys. With a neutral or fluctuating pH, a woman can produce male or female children.[5, 6]

It is obvious that we are all made from the same body. Man is woman, and woman is man—male and female are we (John 16:21). Estrogen with a little testosterone develops a body with female characteristics, and testosterone with a little estrogen develops a body with male characteristics. A man's sex organ primarily is on the outside of his body; ours is primarily on the inside of our body. They can see their sex organ and observe its function, while we cannot. Men have short orgasms, and, conversely, women can have long orgasms.

If our bodies are basically the same, why should our minds be any different? When God gave us the Ten Commandments, He did not specify that they were for women only to obey (Exodus 20:1-17). When Jesus commanded us to love, He was not referring only to women. Never did Christ refer to intercourse as love, yet today it is known as "making love." This is a commandment of physical man. He desires a physical kind of love that does not involve the melding of souls. Genuine love is spiritual and without boundaries. It is a partnership.

It was after God separated the genders that Eve made a life-changing decision. She knew not to eat the fruit of the tree of the knowledge of good and evil because God had told her not to eat of it when male and female were in the same body, but she thought about Adam and how the beautiful tree was good for food and could make them both wise. She made the decision to pick the fruit of that tree and give it to Adam, her husband, who was with her, and he ate also (Genesis 3:6). "And the eyes of them both were opened, and they knew that they *were* naked, and they sewed fig leaves together, and made themselves aprons" (Genesis 3:7). This is when they experienced fear for the first time!

> And they heard the voice of the LORD God walking in the garden in the cool of the day: and Adam and his wife hid themselves from the presence of the LORD God amongst the trees of the garden. And the LORD God called unto Adam, and said unto him, Where *art* thou? And he said, I heard thy voice in the garden, and I was afraid, because I *was* naked; and I hid myself. And he said, Who told thee that thou *wast* naked? Hast thou eaten of the tree, whereof I commanded thee that thou shouldest not eat? And the man said, the woman whom thou gavest *to be* with me, she gave me of the tree, and I did eat." And the LORD God said unto the woman, What *is* this *that* thou hast done? And the woman said, The serpent beguiled me, and I did eat. (Genesis 3:8–13)

I looked up the word "beguile" in the dictionary, and it means to trick or cheat by deception. The serpent was not trying to help her but, instead,

The Garden of Eden

to trick her into something that was against God's plan. In that day, the serpent was a reptile. In today's world, that creature could be a pimp luring a young woman into prostitution, a lawyer offering a quick solution to a problem with one of our laws, a man luring another man's wife into bed with him, a woman luring another woman's husband into her bed, or a drug dealer selling drugs along with their addictions. All of these deal with cheating someone. It was Adam's responsibility to protect his family, but Adam did no such thing—he became a participant himself and bought into the deceit and trickery of the serpent! Eve already was like property to him, much like we blame a pet goat for eating the flowers.

> And the LORD God said unto the serpent, Because thou hast done this, thou *art* cursed above all cattle, and above every beast of the field; upon thy belly shalt thou go, and dust shalt thou eat all the days of thy life: And I will put enmity between thee and the woman, and between thy seed and her seed; it shall bruise thy head, and thou shalt bruise his heel. (Genesis 3:14–15)

To this day, the snake is one of the most feared of all reptiles. When a snake appears, most people prepare to kill it. We strike its head, and it strikes our heel.

Eve was caught in the middle. She could either keep God's commandments or give everything to Adam, her new helpmeet. Many women today give everything to men without considering God in the decisions that they make. All we need to do is look around us in strip clubs, in porn magazines and movies, on football fields, in movie theaters, in magazine advertising, and in restaurants to find partially clad waitresses and see their bodies on display. We are all called upon every day to make those choices. Do we choose to serve God, or do we choose to serve men? Were our bodies made for men, or were our bodies made for our children? Which is more important? God has given each of us the freedom to choose!

Furthermore, they did not consider intercourse to be love as we do today. The one tree that they were told not to eat probably changed the way that they looked at their existence. The very act of disobeying God's commandment and failure to accept responsibility caused them to experience guilt; hence, they awoke and became like God: aware of good and evil. The failure to accept responsibility caused them to lose touch with their conscience—their soul—because they were guilt-ridden. Spiritual death was brought into the picture. No longer could God say that His creation was good, because sin was beginning to stain everything.

God's admonishment to Adam was different than Eve's. Adam's job was to maintain the garden and protect his family. He did not seem to have a problem with this responsibility, at first. Following his "shift from love to fear," work became drudgery, and it would be by his toil and sweat that he would earn the food to feed himself and his family (Genesis 3:17–19).

Once they started focusing on their physical form—their bodies—sexual intercourse became frequent. Woman's conception was increased, and she began producing children in sorrow. Her labor pains were also increased because now her physical form was ruling instead of her soul. Her desire was now for her husband. She began doing things to get him to notice her body and to please him instead of God. This could also have been her way of ensuring that he would be there to help her with the family, especially the children. Unfortunately, she and Adam were no longer a part of the Garden of Eden (Genesis 3:16).

As I consider these verses, what emerges as the real problem is not that Adam listened to Eve. The real problem is that Adam knew better but went on and did it anyway. Eve was not a very good helpmeet when she persuaded Adam to do something that was against God's plan. But God went to Adam first to address the problem. Neither Adam nor Eve took a stand to protect their family and future generations—worse still, neither one of them accepted responsibility for their choices. Their decisions affected their future generations and led God to make the decision to flood the earth in that region.

Adam's job was to protect God's family, but Adam failed to do so. Adam put himself first. This reminds me of a farmer that told me a story about his herd of goats. Coyotes attacked the herd one night, and when the farmer arrived on the scene the next day, all of the females were dead. The only survivor was the ram. The ram protected himself with his horns but let the females die.

What would have happened if Adam had spoken up, reminded Eve about what God had told them when they were in the same body, and stopped the sin from being committed? Furthermore, what would have happened if Adam had accepted responsibility for what he had done instead of blaming Eve? What if Eve had accepted responsibility for what she had done instead of blaming the serpent? I believe that if Adam had accepted responsibility instead of blaming and dominating Eve, their oldest son, Cain, would have been spared.

Victims of Sin

Adam   Cain

Unfortunately, that is not the way that it happened, because Cain became the victim of his father's failure to accept responsibility. Abel paid the price. Cain's countenance (or ego) fell because his gift was not pleasing to the Lord and, most likely, because he was underappreciated by his father and other men. Abel received much recognition.

In a similar way, God gave instructions to our grandfathers pertaining to the care and nurturing of our families and God's children, but grandfathers failed to listen, much like the Pharisees failed to listen to Jesus. Their sons have become the victims of their fathers' failure to accept responsibility. Jesus paid the price with His life, like righteous Abel, over two thousand years ago. Very little has changed since that time. As a result, our children, especially our sons, are paying the price for their grandfathers' unwillingness to accept responsibility even to this day (Exodus 20:5).

God tried to boost Cain's faith by talking to him about his feelings. But instead, Cain's faith was too shallow to overcome the temptation to take his revenge out on his brother. Cain became the victim of Adam's unwillingness to accept responsibility for what he had done. God tried to keep Cain on the right path, but he fell hard for sin.

I believe that there is no such thing as original sin. The true "original sin" that we have in our lives is what has been passed down to us from our parents and their second, third, or fourth spouses and our grandparents and their second, third, or fourth spouses, not Adam and Eve's first sin. Then, that sin manifests itself in our adult lives and is passed on to our children.

But despite poor parenting, we can still remain in the Garden by maintaining faith in the Lord, obeying the commandments, forgiving, accepting responsibility, and repenting of our sins. Each one of us starts out in the Garden of Eden—the kingdom of God—because Jesus told us that unless we "become as little children, [we] shall not enter into the kingdom of heaven" (Matthew 18:3).

The only question that remains is this: will we stay there? Most don't even try. It is as though sin is an entitlement for them.

The Garden of Eden

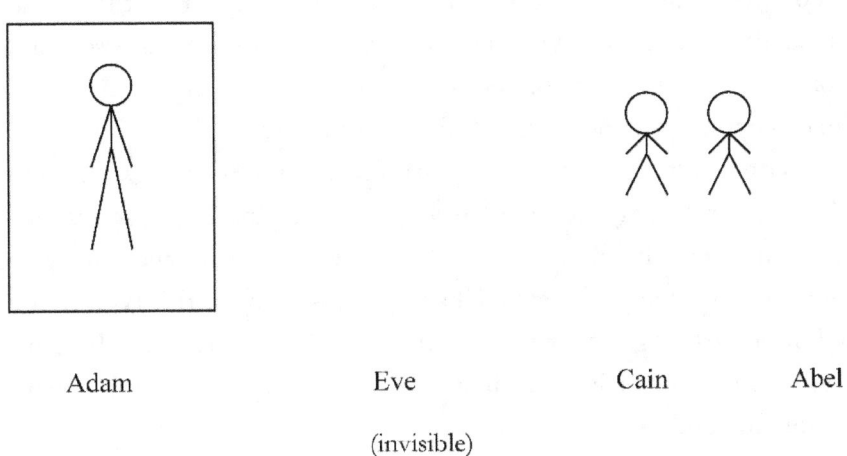

We have two extremes in this relationship. There is not a balance of power. There is not a relationship or a partnership. There is not love. One dominates and the other submits in every way. Children are very vulnerable in relationships such as this.

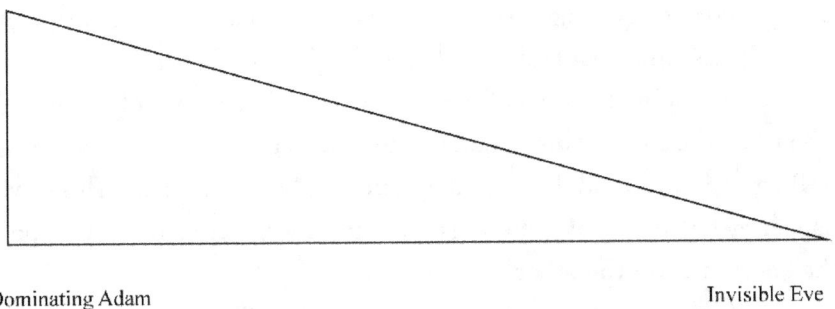

Cain, like his father, gave in to sin rather than mastering it, even with God's intervention and offered assistance. But Cain did one thing that his father never did. Cain accepted responsibility for what he did and regained some favor with God. He did not blame his dominating father or his silent mother. God protected him from being killed by others as he had done to

The Step-Father's Step-Son

his brother. After Cain killed Abel, Adam and Eve had another son and called him Seth. It took two generations to recover from Adam's separation from God with the birth of Seth's son, Enos. It was then that man began "to call upon the name of the LORD" (Genesis 4:26).

With a dominating father, it must have been difficult for Cain to find himself. Most likely, he grew up desperately trying to please his father as his main priority. Later, he was concerned about what men thought of him and his accomplishments. Children growing up in this type of home will have little respect for their mother or other women. They have been taught to fear the male in the household and to please men rather than to please God and to love.

Just as Adam tilled the land, so did Cain. From early childhood, Cain probably imitated his father in all aspects. As a result, he never had the opportunity to work through issues, such as jealousy and failure, because he had been as perfect as he could have been in his childhood. This helped to ensure that he would not be punished or ridiculed for making a mistake. Then, at the very moment when God and most likely other men were not pleased with his offering, he lost control. As an adult man, he was finally big enough and strong enough to dominate another human being. No longer was he a helpless child that had to submit to his father's domination over him.

Abel did something out of the ordinary—he had a flock of sheep. Cain, who tilled the soil like his father, was unable to resist the jealousy that was welling up in his mind. He ended up killing Abel, his brother. This is what happens when men make offerings that can be seen before men. Men praise the one and curse the other.

Just think of the poor widow mentioned in the Bible that gave everything she had, even though it was less than everyone else gave. Even today, her story is told because she did such a great thing. She was the least among all of the men there, and yet she was the greatest. But she never went around boldly parading what she had done. She never suggested or demanded that a building or a street be named after her.

The Garden of Eden

Just think of the number of buildings that have been named for men that make huge contributions. Most of these donations are tax benefits for these individuals. They did not have to alter their lifestyle at all, and yet we honor them over someone who has made a meager but substantial offering. Many of our women have given more than any of these men. You will never find a building or monument to honor any of them! But still, they are greater in the eyes of God than any of these men.

men	Sons of God
Want and desire greatness and recognition.	Serve God and do his will because they know it is expected of them.

How many of our oldest sons and daughters try to dominate their younger brothers and sisters? They were born first and want to do everything first and best. Then, when one of their younger brothers or sisters has an opportunity to succeed, the oldest will stand in his or her way. Fathers do the same thing when they dominate their children. They want to be greatest, and they will take from their wife and children in order to make themselves look even bigger and greater than they actually are. What the father, mother, brothers, and sisters need to realize is that they will have other opportunities to excel and that they do not need to win all of the time. Life is not about "winning." They need to let their sons, daughters, sisters, brothers, and even their wife achieve important goals in their lives. There should not be competition between father and son, or oldest brother and younger brother, or husband and wife. Each will have plenty of opportunities to excel during their lifetime if they put forth the effort and try. We should encourage each other and swallow our pride. Our turn will come.

In today's world, our men want their wives to cleave to them and follow them. It is sinful for men to force or expect women to serve them. Women are naturally made to serve God. We are God's servants and not men's servants. But when the women grow tired and weary of caring for family, home, job, and husbands by themselves, their husbands, in many cases, will leave home for another woman. Also, if the woman commits a sin, as Eve did in the Garden of Eden, the man will blame her exclusively, leave her, stone her, beat her, divorce her, or kill her.

A double standard exists for men. They can commit the same sin but expect to be forgiven as though it never happened. This is what happens in a world where the man expects a woman to cleave to him. The man wants to rule over us. The man does as he pleases but expects the woman to keep all of the commandments. A woman should never cleave to a man that does as he pleases without considering the needs of his family. In a situation such as this, the woman must use her head, mouth, and brain to make decisions independently of the man. She must accept the fact that she and her spouse are spiritually and physically separated.

Sometimes, women take matters into their own hands and commit great sin. Statistics show that women do kill their husbands. The only difference is that they don't do it as frequently.[7] Women have options to consider that exclude sin. We can leave him! We will only make matters more difficult for everyone involved, especially our children, when we add more sin to the equation. The more understanding that we have, the clearer our path will be. We must think of our future generations.

Following Abel's death, Adam and Eve produced Seth. Seven generations from Seth, Noah was born. "The earth was also corrupt before God, and the earth was filled with violence. And God looked upon the earth, and, behold, it was corrupt; for all flesh had corrupted his way upon the earth" (Genesis 6:11–12).

Noah, a son of God, had only one wife (Genesis 7:13). Each of Noah's three sons only had one wife each. "Noah was a just man *and* perfect in his generations, *and* Noah walked with God" (Genesis 6:9). He and his sons maintained their loyalty to their first wives and to their first families. This entire family was spared in the flood. We can already see from scripture that, in the beginning, it was God's intention to have only one man and one woman in the family unit (Genesis 7:1).

The Garden of Eden

God considers intercourse to be marriage. It is a bonding between the mind and body. When a child is conceived, man and woman again become one flesh. A piece of paper, a ceremony, a marriage license, a wedding ring, and a man's last name do not matter in God's eyes—that woman and little child matter most!

> And it came to pass, when men began to multiply on the face of the earth, and daughters were born unto them, That the sons of God saw the daughters of men that they *were* fair; and they took them wives of all which they chose. And the LORD said, My spirit shall not always strive with man, for that he also *is* flesh: yet his days shall be a hundred and twenty years. There were giants in the earth in those days; and also after that, when the sons of God came in unto the daughters of men, and they bare *children* to them, and the same *became* mighty men which *were* of old, men of renown. And GOD saw that the wickedness of man was great in the earth, and *that* every imagination of the thoughts of his heart *was* only evil continually. And it repented the LORD that he had made man on the earth, and it grieved him at his heart. (Genesis 6:1–6)

In the beginning, God created "them," so we know that there were others. The ones that remained "living soul[s]" were the sons of God that grew to become giants and lived for one thousand years. But greater problems developed for mankind when the sons of God started looking upon and having intercourse with the daughters of men. The offspring of this union were also giants that lived for one thousand years.

"[T]he sons of God saw the daughters of men that they *were* fair; and they took them wives of all which they chose"(Genesis 6:2). This is the first time that the word "men" is described as a dirty word. The scripture illustrates the fact that "sons of God," men who keep God's commandments and remain loyal to their first families, should never marry the daughters of men who have gone from woman to woman and abandoned their first wives and their children with their first wife! This was when God made the decision to shorten man's life from almost 1,000 years to 120 years (Genesis 6:3, 5:5, and 9:29).

"And the LORD said, I will destroy man whom I have created from the face of the earth; both man, and beast, and the creeping thing, and the fowls of the air; for it repenteth me that I have made them"(Genesis 6:7). But God loved Noah because "Noah walked with God" (Genesis 6:9). Noah's sons—Shem, Ham, and Japheth—also only had one wife each.

Following the flood, we can see a remarkable decrease in life spans.

FATHER	Age at birth of 1st son	First son and other children	Age at death
Noah	500 (Gen 5:32)	Shem, Ham, Japheth	950 (Gen 9:29)
Shem	100 (Gen11:10-11)	Arphaxad, sons, daughters	600
Arphaxad	35 (Gen 11:12-13)	Salah, sons, daughters	438
Salah	30 (Gen 11:14-15)	Eber, sons, daughters	433
Eber	430 (Gen11:16-17)	Peleg, sons, daughters	860
Peleg	30 (Gen 11:18-19)	Reu, sons, daughters	239
Reu	32 (Gen 11:20-21)	Serug, sons, daughters	239
Serug	30	Nahor, sons, daughters	230
Nahor	29 (Gen 11:24-25)	Terah, sons, daughters	148
Terah	70 (Gen 11:26-27)	Abram, Nahor*, Haran	205
Haran(Gen11:27)		Lot, Iscah (Gen 11:29)	>135
Abram**	86 (Gen 16:16)	Ishmael	175 (Gen 25:7)
Abraham**	100 (Gen 21:5)	Isaac, sons, daughters	175 (Gen 25:7)
Isaac	60	Esau and Jacob	180 (Gen 35:28)
Ishmael		Nebajoth, sons, daughters	137 (Gen 25:17)
Jacob		Joseph, sons, daughter	147 (Gen 48:28)

Notes:
*Nahor married his brother Haran's daughter. Her name was Milcah.
**Abram and Abraham are the same person—God changed his name after he became a son of God.

Today, we see many women tending the garden and caring for their families, much like it was in the beginning when Adam did not have a helpmeet (Genesis 2:20). Adam had the responsibility of dressing and keeping the garden (Genesis 2:15). But Adam also reproduced alone (Genesis 1:28). Many of our husbands leave their families and go on to another woman. This puts a lot of stress on the woman and her children because there is no helpmeet to help her care for the family. She is tending the garden and raising children by herself because of her wandering spouse. This is something that God never wanted to happen!

But when any man or any woman does eat of the forbidden fruit of the tree of the knowledge of good and evil, their eyes will be opened, their lives will be changed, and they will know good and evil. Many will refuse to accept responsibility for what they have done, just as Adam and Eve hid their nakedness with fig leaves. Jesus said, "[f]or out of the heart proceed evil thoughts, murders, adulteries, fornications, thefts, false witness, blasphemies: These are *the things* which defile a man: but to eat with unwashen hands defileth not a man" (Matthew 15:19, 20).

Adultery is the most protected and sacred sin in this country. The reason we have so much chaos in this country today is because more and more people are practicing the religion of this land than ever before. God has instructed all of us not to commit adultery, and yet I doubt that there is a single family in this country today that has not been damaged by adultery in one way or another. But I will say that once adultery has been committed, the adulterers' eyes will be opened. For those that refuse to accept responsibility for their actions, excuses will be made to justify their decisions. Their excuses will be like the fig leaves that Adam and Eve used to hide their nakedness. These men and women will victimize their own children until someone ends up paying the price for their great sin.

Our country's definition of adultery is to have intercourse with someone other than the person to whom we are currently married. Many people would most likely consider intercourse with an ex-spouse to be adultery. When a couple divorces and then remarries, most people readily accept the new mates without hesitation. There is little to no stigma attached for abandoning a first family as long as child support is paid regularly. It is even easier if this "new" couple keeps the first family a secret and eliminates this family from their lives. They appear to be a normal married couple. The magic word is "married." This is the fig leaf that most use to cover the adultery. Adultery is legal with our laws and lawyers.

Our young men and women have intercourse with any consenting body of legal age that they choose prior to "marriage." This is much like the beginning when men took as many women as they chose. We have definitely returned to our roots, because we learned nothing at all from Jesus and His life on Earth! Our men are taking as many women as they can get. Our women are taking as many men as they can get, too.

We now know that diseases like breast cancer and diabetes run in families. Could it be that we are focusing too much on the breasts of women instead of their whole body and mind? The whole is more important than the part. Breasts do not make a woman any more than a penis or muscular build can make a whole man. They are a part of our body but not the whole. The part should never be more important than the whole. The same is true for our families—one part of the family should never be more important than the entire family. But with divorce and remarriage, it often seems that the second family is more important than the first family. In most cases when a man divorces a woman, he also divorces his children.

If we can transfer talents, I think that it is certainly possible that we can transfer illnesses like cancer and diabetes. We pass along dysfunctional traits to our children. The Israelites went forty years without illness. If they could do this, we can, too. But we must love the Lord God enough to obey His commandments and to walk by faith.

If our men truly loved us, they would not be doing any of these things. They would keep their penises where they belong!

In the beginning of time, we did not divorce—Christ said it was not so in the beginning (Matthew 19:8). But it has become commonplace today. Violence has been prevalent since man was driven from the Garden of Eden. Studies show that wives are killed in the United States at a rate that is much higher than in Western Europe.[8] In many countries, it is considered normal and acceptable to beat a wife. Countless women have been killed, raped, or beaten at the hands of men since Adam's time.

It amazes me the lengths to which some men and women are capable of going and that they are willing to cheat themselves out of something so wonderful in an attempt to control their spouse in such a sinful way. God never said that woman was less than man or that man was less than woman. He created someone that was "comparable," "equal in dignity and complimentary in nature," as I once heard a Catholic priest explain it to me. Man is a part of us, and we are a part of him. We are inseparable! We stand side by side in this world that God created. "So God created man in his *own* image, in the image of God created he him; male and female created he them" (Genesis 1:27). We are all "man," as in "human," and we are male and female humans. We are all created in God's image and likeness (Genesis 5:1). I doubt that God has a penis or a vagina. These were created by God for the reproduction of the flesh. Our job is to help Adam tend the garden and our families properly. And Adam's job is to help us to tend that same garden and family properly. Considered in that image, our family is a part of Jesus' vine within the garden, with branches of children and generations of families running through time. He expects us to keep our generations perfect.

Jesus said, "Take heed to yourselves: If thy brother trespass against thee, rebuke him; and if he repent, forgive him" (Luke 17:3). Men and women need to be corrected. It is a test—men and women are to humble themselves before children just as Christ humbled Himself! Adam's responsibility was to speak up and remind Eve of the commandment which God had told him when he was male and female. He failed to do so and blamed the female Adam, Eve. He failed to protect his wife and his future offspring. Each one of us begins our life like little children, just as Adam and Eve started their lives in the Garden of Eden. We are free from sin. Through our parents, our eyes become opened to sin but with little to no understanding of laws. Then, these little children grow up to transfer their sin to others just as their parents did to them. Adam victimized Cain, and Abel paid the price.

Since abortion was approved by our Supreme Court, women have chosen to abort an unborn child at least 50 million times rather than give birth to the child. Could it be that these women are entering into a "relationship" with a man that is in a sinful state? Do these women think of themselves as the victim of a man who has abandoned them for another woman and left them with a child? Are they the victims of our nation's laws regarding family? I believe that this is a very real possibility because the laws of this land are hostile to our families. Through a writing of divorcement, a man can legally abandon his wife and children for another woman. Without a marriage license, these women and children have little legal standing. This man is only responsible for these children born outside of marriage and of the first family until they reach the age of eighteen. He has no obligation to his children other than money. As a result, our children suffer for our sins, just as Cain and Abel had to suffer for Adam and Eve's omission. And so, too, does the unborn child pay the price for their parents' sins. Woe to us for passing the burden of our sin onto our little children by abandoning and aborting them.

Today, very few of our men and women feel any obligation for their wives, husbands, children, grandchildren, and great-grandchildren. They divorce their wives or husbands, and their children cease to exist, along with all of the future offspring that have not yet arrived. They seem to erroneously believe that they can erase an entire generational branch from themselves and create a new one. It is as though they think of themselves as "God" and that they are the family.

Man's Kingdom on Earth

After the flood, Noah's sons—Shem, Ham, and Japheth—all had children. Each family grew in number and spread across the plains. Again, the "children of men" among Noah's family began to anger God.

> And they said to one another, Go to, let us make brick, and burn them thoroughly. And they had brick for stone, and slime had they for morter. And they said, Go to, let us build us a city and a tower, whose top *may reach* unto heaven; and let us make us a name, lest we be scattered abroad upon the face of the whole earth. And the LORD came down to see the city and the tower, which the children of men builded. And the LORD said, Behold, the people *is* one, and they have all one language; and this they begin to do: and now nothing will be restrained from them, which they have imagined to do. Go to, let us go down, and there confound their language, that they may not understand one another's speech. So the LORD scattered them abroad from thence upon the face of all the earth: and they left off to build the city." (Genesis 11:3–8)

children of men	Sons of God
They built the tower of Babel to make a name for themselves.	They served the Lord without seeking greatness.

The sons of God reserved their strength and energy to support and provide for God's children. The sons of men used their talents and energy to build a tower to heaven. This one particular tower was called the tower of Babel. Today, we have many of these towers in the midst of our cities around the world.

The children of men built the tower. The children of men wanted to be famous—they wanted to make a name for themselves. Our country is founded on this premise today. Men are the ones with the family jewels, and they are the ones that carry the family name from generation to generation. I think that they actually think that they are the family. They also have the power to give their family and the family name to another woman. Men of today divorce their wives and their children at the same time.

Our country is set up for the breakup of the family, not the maintenance of the family. A man is only responsible for supporting the children of the first marriage, the ones that he divorced, until the children reach the age of eighteen. Many men will abandon their children from the first marriage even earlier and never send birthday presents or pay child support at all. The first wife may be forced to adopt the children of the first marriage out to another man. Many will be forced to go on government subsidized welfare.

In our culture and society today, it is acceptable for men and women to have multiple sex partners during their lifetimes and, especially, prior to "marriage." Birth control has encouraged this movement because there is little evidence of a relationship without the presence of a child.

> "Daughters of Jerusalem, weep not for me, but weep for yourselves and for your children. For, behold, the days are coming, in the which they shall say, Blessed are the barren, and the wombs that never bare, and the paps which never gave suck. Then shall they begin to say to the mountains, Fall on us; and to the hills, Cover us. For if they do these things in a green tree, what shall be done in the dry?" (Luke 23:28–31)

These women and men have never been toughened and tested. They are childless and have not made any sacrifices. They have had everything that they wanted and did not have to spend a dime or any of their time on any children. They will yearn for trials and to die. We have many young men that climb Mount Everest and do many other ridiculously dangerous things. The ultimate test could have been to be a parent—but instead that choose a mountain that could fall on them with an avalanche or rock slide.

But when he does have intercourse, there is always a "first woman." Then, he finishes with her and goes on to another woman . . . and another . . . and another until he finally finds the one woman with whom he chooses to spend the rest of his life.

Most of our men begin their adult lives in this manner. They have "casual" recreational intercourse with one young woman.

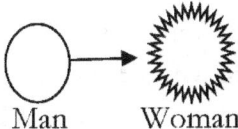
Man   Woman

Then, he puts her aside for the next young woman and then the next.

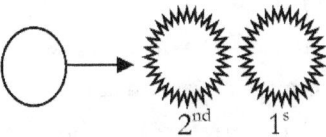
2nd 1^{s}

Without a marriage license, none of these women has any legal standing in our current society. The most that they could ever expect to receive, if conception did occur, is child support until the illegitimate child reaches the age of eighteen. At that point in time, the mother and child, or children, can expect to receive nothing further.

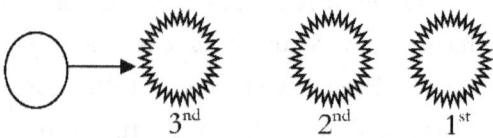

Finally, after much ejaculation, he finds the woman that he truly "loves" and decides to marry her while putting aside all of the other women with whom he was sexually active. He gives up his "old" way of life and decides to turn over a new leaf and become a responsible "man."

A true marriage is not recognized in this country unless there is a marriage license. A man, in most cases—a minister, priest, or justice of the peace—administers the rite of marriage. This man is like God because he has the ability to discern who has a state sanctioned marriage license and meets all of the state's qualifications for marriage. Furthermore, he does not look deeper to see just how many women this man has had in his past. It is as though none of these women from his "past" ever existed.

But if children are born without the official rite of passage, they are considered to have been born out of wedlock. Our laws put all of the responsibility upon the child and the mother. The father may have the responsibility of paying child support, but child support money is not a suitable replacement for his physical presence in the child's life. But neither is welfare from our government.

Our government is more than willing to accept responsibility for these children. It actually encourages irresponsibility of both the mother and the father. It leads to dependency, and there are many politicians that use this tool as a way to stay in office. Hence, our government replaces the father and becomes a substitute. Receiving a monthly check in the mail cannot replace a father that uses his own head, two hands, and two feet to earn money to support his family.

There can be complications in a marriage even when he marries the first woman with whom he loves and has intercourse.

Man's Kingdom on Earth

Minister or Judge

Traditionally, the woman abandons the name of her family and takes the man's last name. But I think that his importance is greatly exaggerated in this country. I think that it is God, the "first wife," him, and the children of the "first marriage" that are the actual core of the family and not him alone.

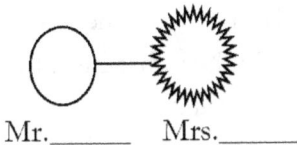

Mr._____ Mrs._____

Then, this couple produces a child.

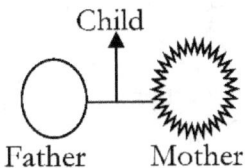

Father   Mother

Now, let's get on with the second round in the kingdom of men. Mr._____ decides that he is not "happy" and lusts after another woman. When a man is alone without his wife and during his most vulnerable of times, there are many women that will take advantage of him if he is willing to give them everything that he has, including his soul. These women do not truly love him, his family, or his wife. They do not love the child. They are interested in what they receive.

As time progresses, the adulterous lust becomes physical. He refuses to come home to his wife and child. He turns his back on his wife and child. He moves in with the other woman.

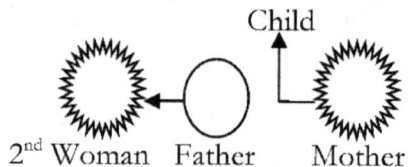

His wife either catches him in the very act of adultery with another woman, or someone tells her about what they have seen. As a result, she consults with a lawyer and draws up the necessary paperwork for a divorce. At this point in time, the child still has his father's last name.

Now, she finds another man and proves to her husband that she is equally as physically attractive to another person. Then, she decides to marry him, realizing that her husband has abandoned her and the child.

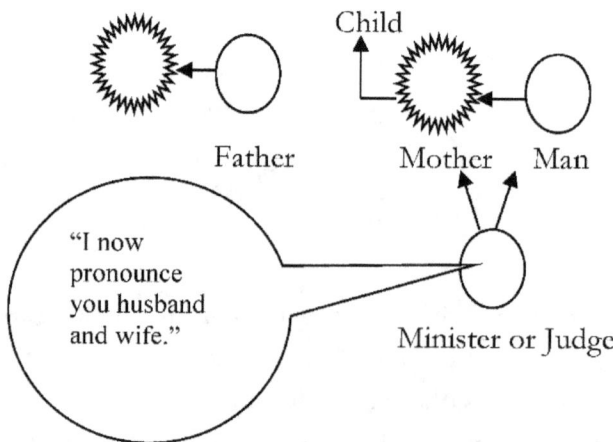

Then, he marries the woman that he lusted after, gives her his last name, and makes her a part of his family, eliminating his former wife and child.

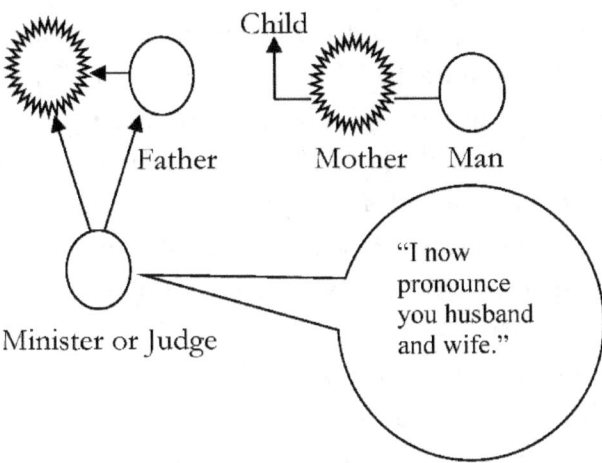

The holy union has been split asunder. A man and woman have separated the husband and wife. At this point in time, the situation becomes very serious and there are some very difficult decisions that must be made.

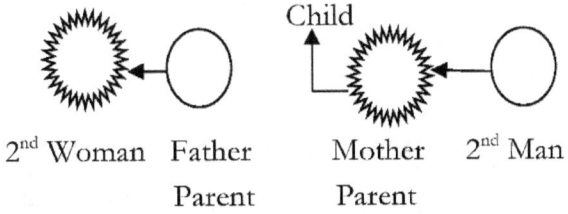

Jesus said in Matthew 5:31, 32,

> It hath been said, Whosoever shall put away his wife, let him give her a writing of divorcement: But I say unto you, That whosoever shall put away his wife, saving for the cause of fornication, causeth her to commit adultery and whosoever shall marry her that is divorced committeth adultery.

According to this scripture, both my husband's father and my husband's step-father committed adultery. My husband's step-mother committed adultery by separating my husband's father and mother. She also committed adultery by separating my husband's father from his firstborn son. My husband's mother committed adultery by marrying another man. All of them committed sins against my husband and my children.

Jesus also said in Mark 10:11, 12, "Whosoever shall put away his wife, and marry another, committeth adultery against her. And if a woman shall put away her husband, and be married to another, she committeth adultery."

Each new spouse is going to want to be the significant other. They will want to be treated like the parent's first and only spouse. This will be especially true with the father's second wife. This woman will see the child of the first marriage as a threat because she knows that this child is technically this man's heir. She will compete with this child in an attempt to gain control of everything that belongs to this child. She will desperately attempt to separate the man from his child or children. She will welcome the opportunity to relocate to another state or foreign country in order to distance her "new husband" from his first family so that she can strengthen her relationship with him. This will help to broaden the separation when he returns back to the area where the adultery began.

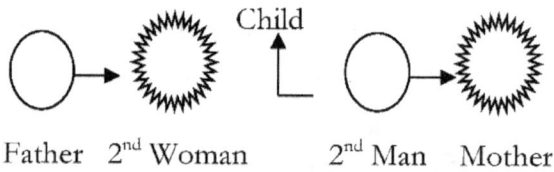

Father   2nd Woman   2nd Man   Mother

The "second husband" of the child's mother will also want to gain control, especially if she has money and property. The child's mother will take his last name and later may change the abandoned child's last name to that of her "second husband." This man will compete with the child of the first marriage in order to eventually get control. This little child is doomed, even from the beginning. He will be bullied for everything that is rightfully his. This is the reason that it is called "adultery"! These bullied children, the victims of their father's unwillingness to accept responsibility, will become bullies themselves because they never knew the genuine love of a mother and a father. The "step-father" will want his oldest child to be the oldest child. The "step-mother" will want her oldest child to be the oldest child. This child will be stripped of everything by the "step-father" and "step-mother," if the child's parents permit it.

When my husband was quite small and his half-brother was a toddler, he had a teddy bear that he loved. One day, his step-father gave a teddy bear to his oldest son, my husband's younger half-brother. My husband asked only a question and nothing more. He asked his step-father why his brother's teddy bear was larger than his teddy bear since he was the older "brother." He never got an answer. His step-father took his bear away from him and never gave it back. His step-father was placing his firstborn son with my husband's mother first in "his family." He was replacing this little child with his son.

A woman should never marry for a second time. This second man will take everything that she has and make it his own. He becomes the legal heir while our children from the first family are the natural heir. With laws and lawyers, legal heirs are more important than natural heirs. A woman will not normally give away her firstborn child's position in her family, but men in this country have no problem giving this firstborn child's position and all property to the other woman and her children. This will make him a much better catch because he still has a lot to offer, even though he has been married before. Our laws make him a very desirable prospect.

Jesus said in Matthew 18:10, "Take heed that ye despise not one of these little ones; for I say unto you, That in heaven their angels do always behold the face of my Father which is in heaven." The children of the first family are at great risk in homes with a step-mother and/or a step-father living there.[11]

Now, let's get on with the third round in the kingdom of men. "Children of the kingdom" will be born to the adulterers.

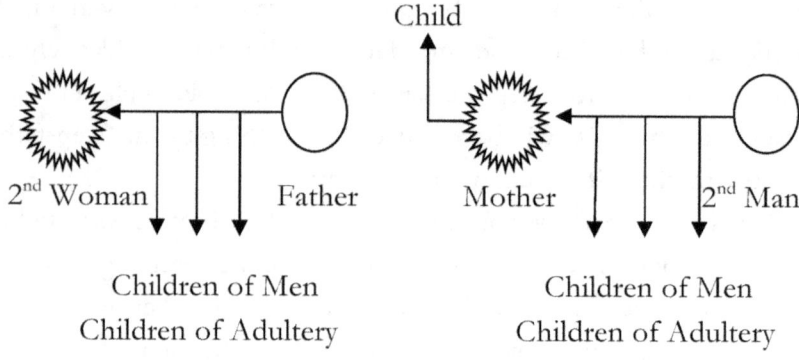

Jesus said in Matthew 8:11, 12, "And I say unto you, That many shall come from the east and west, and shall sit down with Abraham, and Isaac, and Jacob, in the kingdom of heaven. But the children of the kingdom shall be cast out into outer darkness: there shall be weeping and gnashing of teeth."

In the above diagram, the father is looking away from his first wife and child. Men usually look in the direction that their penis faces. In this case, the penis is pointing away from the first family and to another woman and her children.

The mother still has ties to the child's father because she is the one that will bear the responsibility of raising this child. She forever will be tied to two men because she has children with two different men. She will have the difficult decision of deciding whether her first child has priority or whether her "second husband's" children have priority.

On both sides of the diagram, the child from the first family is outnumbered, will be bullied by both adulterers, and will eventually be dominated by the children of men . . the children of the second family. I will demonstrate how this happens in the next few diagrams. Let's start with the child's mother. She declares her second husband to be her legal husband and gives everything to him, including her child with her first husband. This man is not this child's father and never can be. He may try to substitute for the father, but that is about it.

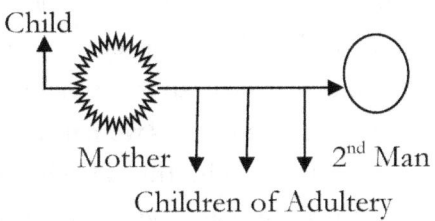

Children of Adultery

When she dies, he becomes the legal heir of the family property. Then, when he dies, his oldest child will be given control.

The next thing he will do is marry another woman. Perhaps, he will marry the woman that he was "looking for all of his life," even while he was married to the child's mother – these were the actual words used by my husband's step-father. This man indeed, was looking for another woman because he would look at every woman that came through the door, even with his wife and daughter present. He kept *Playboy* magazines in his office. He married for money, power, or status the first time when he took the child's mother for his wife; now, he will be looking for someone to marry for love.

When the step-father dies, things will get really complicated. The children of the kingdom will want the child of the first family to help support the step-father's second wife. When the child refuses to accept responsibility for this woman, they will leave the child out of all matters pertaining to the family property. They will make decisions without him while blaming him for being callous and unloving.

Now, let's venture out of this dilemma and look closely at what happens on the father's side of the family.

In full-blown adultery, the child's father will find himself in a very difficult situation, one that will be very difficult to escape. Long ago, he eliminated the child of his first marriage from his life. Abandonment is about as close to death as one can get without actually killing the child.

His oldest child of the second marriage, male or female, will have to be in control of his estate—the adulteress will have it no other way. My husband's father and step-mother had a girl first. This girl was the one that replaced my husband as the oldest child in his father's family.

This daughter had to be first. This is the only way the adulteress could keep this child from the first marriage out of the picture. She had to ensure that her oldest child had total control. This woman and her daughter knew that my husband was his father's heir. This daughter never talked about family property with my husband. She and her mother both spoke to me instead. Her daughter came to me first, asking about the things that my husband had received when his mother and step-father had both died. Then, my husband's step-mother came to me and told me that she had worked for fifteen years. It was as though she had bought her way in and deserved to receive all of the family property herself. Both of these women were indirectly trying to explain that there would be nothing left for my husband or our sons. These women were planning the distribution of property even before my husband's father had died. All of this was being done behind his back.

It is ironic that my husband's step-mother was angry about having to work for fifteen years to help support her family. My husband's mother would have loved to have had the opportunity to work. It was the step-father that did not want her to work. It was also ironic that my husband's mother was an amazing gardener. She grew orchids and all sorts of beautiful plants in her green house. I remember the step-mother saying that she demanded that the builder remove a greenhouse that was built into their last home. You could see the ugly scars that were left behind after the walls to the greenhouse were removed. My husband's mother loved, but my husband's step-mother did not appreciate her opportunities. They both seemed to be jealous of each other. It may have been that my husband's mother found the perfect husband for my husband's "step-mother" and my husband's father may have found the perfect wife for my husband's step-father. I also believe that my husband's mother and father were a better team than the people that they married the second time around.

The adulteress will demand the child's father's allegiance to her. He will serve her and not God. She will establish rules that he will have to follow. She will decide what he likes and doesn't like. He has become property and will live his entire life in bondage unless he wakes up and kicks this adulteress out! This woman must never be the heir of this man's property. Our children are our natural heirs, not the other woman or the other man. Legal heirs must never be permitted to replace natural heirs – our children. If this woman becomes heir, as do most second and third wives in this country, the family will be split asunder and there will be little to nothing for the children of the first family, especially our sons.

This other woman will do everything that she can to separate the father from his first child. If the father likes the gifts that his son has sent, she will declare to the child that his father doesn't like the gift. My husband bought dates for his father, and his father loved the gift, but his step-mother made a point to tell my husband that his father did not like the dates that he sent. Her world is an upside-down world, and she will have to continue to confuse everyone so that her fantasy can become reality.

This woman will declare that her children are superior to the child of the first family, even after doing her part to break up the family and destroy the child. She will declare herself to be selfish and a rebel. My husband's step-mother took me aside to the pantry and told me these things. First, she told me that she was "selfish," and I could not answer because I am not selfish. Then, she called me away again to the pantry and said that she was a "rebel." I said, "I am a rebel, too!" This woman was competing with my husband. The only problem is that the child is not selfish—the child only wants what is rightfully his. She will do her dirty duty to ensure that the child gets nothing that is rightfully his. She will want everything for herself and for her own children. She will do everything in her power to separate father and son. She has become a dominator and a manipulator.

At this point in time, there was nothing left for my husband, and he never asked for anything from any of them. His father's life had been spent with someone else. When we visited this old man, it was like going to a museum. We could see him, but we could not really touch. He was the property of another family. We never saw him use his hands or his feet to accomplish anything. We knew little about his life or the kind of man that he was. But we do know about him because of the way that he treated his firstborn son, my husband. That speaks volumes about his character.

My husband's father compromised with his second wife. They did not celebrate birthdays. I honestly believe that his father wanted to remember his firstborn son on his birthday, but the step-mother most likely objected. Their compromise was to not celebrate any of the family members' birthdays. She was willing to do this because of her perceived necessity of eliminating my husband from "their" family in every way possible. This was another way that she could keep my husband and his father separated. Manipulation and control were the tools that she used to create "her" family, and my husband's father was the helpless pawn. Some believe that this is what witchcraft is actually about: twisting the truth for your own advantage.

Just as Jesus had no place to lay his head (Matthew 8:20), this child of the first marriage or his children may very well end up homeless and on the streets with alcohol and drug problems, mental health issues, or in jail or prison because of the mass confusion of growing up in a progressively adulterous family. The children of the second family will grow up as though nothing happened. To them, they have grown up in a healthy normal family. They actually want to believe that they are the FAMILY!

Only when one looks deeper than the surface can one see the damage caused by putting a child of any age into such a difficult situation. The earlier it happens, the more damaging it is. The children of the second family will be the type that believes that if a limb falls in the woods and they weren't there to hear it, no sound was actually made. If my husband cried out and they were not there to hear him, then he never really cried out. They will be so hard-hearted that they will be enemies to the child of the first family. They and the "step-parents" will be like hogs at the trough, gradually rooting out the child of the first family. Furthermore, they will justify their actions by finding flaws in this child.

The father may have abandoned his child by delaying his arrival at the hospital after his birth. My husband's father sent a telegram four days after his birth that said, "I am fine. I love the two of you." Then, he may abandon him the second time because he went to a far-off land to make a lot of money. My husband's father went to Venezuela with his second wife for four years. He may later abandon him because his last name is no longer his last name. My husband's mother changed his last name to that of his step-father while his father and "step-mother" were in Venezuela. He may have abandoned him because he was scared of an attorney. My husband's uncle was an attorney. He may have abandoned him because his "step-mother" decided that it was too confusing to have him around. His "step-mother" actually said this. Now, they will justify the further abandonment because he has become an alcoholic or a drug abuser and never finished college. I am writing this not only for my husband but also for others who have experienced similar circumstances. My husband did not use drugs, but he did drink and chew tobacco. This small child has carried the price of adultery for his entire life. This child has never known the genuine love of a devoted mother and father. This child will never have the opportunity to experience emotional balance in his life.

These children of the second family will continue taking until they have acquired anything and everything of value to them. They will feel entitled since they think of themselves as "the family." They have a biological mother and father, whereas the child of the first marriage does not. This small child is at a definite disadvantage. He will be taken advantage of for his entire life until he dies unless this cycle is stopped by one or both parents.

A relationship of this type must never be permitted. Women like this must be given their walking papers. She should not be permitted to receive anything. If she becomes the heir instead of the children of the first family, she will rule over the family and gain control over the family. The children can come back to the family but only as second under the child or children of the first marriage. Otherwise, the child of the first marriage will be treated as though he is dead or was never born. It is a legal live abortion. There is no other way—she and her children must be sent away immediately! They must never ever be permitted to replace the child or children of the first family!

There are some men that will take a second wife and have children with her without mentioning that he already has a wife and/or children. One thing is certain: he will be accountable to God because He knows everything. He may not think that he is accountable and may get away with it here on Earth, but God does not ignore the sins of man. Jesus knew about all of the men that a woman had been with, and He also knew that she was not married to the man that she was living with (John 4:15–18). God loves His family of souls very much. So, we can know that God knows all of these details. The man had better tell the truth. But even in a situation such as this, the woman does not have the right to take over the family so that she can pretend to be a man's first wife. If that were the case, Hagar would have been permitted to replace Sarah. Abraham did not let it happen.

When my husband and I found his eighty-year-old father the second and last time, my husband told me to be very careful about what I did and said. He knew that he was on shaky ground with them, even before they were briefly reunited. He would have had to embrace adultery in order to be accepted and even then, it would have been minimal. But there were things that I said anyway because I refused to participate in the fantasy that the "step-mother" had created. The truth is more important than living a lie. Furthermore, there was little hope for reconciliation because of all of the terrible things that had transpired. He was truly treated as though he never existed—he was abandoned. He was totally eliminated from his father's family. This woman wanted everything that was his for herself and her offspring, and my husband's father permitted it all to happen.

A man cannot fight with a woman, but a woman can fight with a woman. Many of our fathers do not love their firstborn children enough to take a stand for them. They put their trust in the laws of this land and their second wives to ensure that everything is done properly. They put the legal before the natural. I am going to take a stand for our children. These women need to be put in their proper place.

Let me give you some examples of how my husband was excluded from his father's life. My husband's mother had a serious medical condition. She was Rh negative, but the child that she was carrying (my husband) was Rh positive. For that reason, she had to spend the last four months of her pregnancy near a Fort Worth hospital in case complications arose. My husband was born prematurely on October 11. On October 15, my husband's father sent a telegram that read like this: "I am fine. I love the two of you." There was no mention of when he would be coming to see his firstborn son! My best guess is that he had already been with this woman and was ashamed of what he had done to his family.

Later, my husband's father broke the windows out of the family car. This was a strong indication that he had some unresolved issues. He had accumulated some debt. He bought a very large platinum diamond ring for my husband's mother. He had a hard time paying off that debt according to a family member. This is the ring that I wore when I was in Iraq. The only thing that was missing was the diamond because it had been replaced with a fake diamond that scratched easily. (The original diamond most likely was placed onto the setting of my husband's mother's ring given to her by her second husband.) I found out later that I was known to many as "the ring." This ring helped to protect me. The guys associated this ring with the amount of love that my husband had for me. After returning from Iraq, I no longer wear a ring. I am free of the tradition and I understand and respect my position and role within this family.

Furthermore, life gets complicated when we bring additional relationships into a family, even more so if those relationships are based on adultery. In this case, my husband's mother was not involved in the decision to bring this other woman into the family. My husband's father made that decision when he was alone. This is the perfect time for another woman to take advantage of a man, his wife, and their child.

I do not know all of the details of when they divorced or when they both remarried. My husband's half-brother is around my age. I am two years and three months younger than my husband. All that I know is that the divorce and remarriage happened very quickly.

My husband's father waited for my husband, his firstborn son, to ask about him before he scheduled the first meeting between the two of them. The meeting happened approximately twenty-four years after my husband's birth in a small, dark motel room in Knox City, Texas. My husband, our oldest son, and I arrived and knocked on the door. Inside were my husband's father, his second wife, and their children. Very little was said. My husband took us and we left. That was the last time that we saw him or heard from him until I accidentally found him fifty-plus years later.

I doubt that this man ever acknowledged the existence of my husband to anyone. He and his second wife treated him as though he never existed. My husband's father completely abandoned him for his second wife and the children that he had with his second wife. The one way that he could keep from telling a lie was to say that these are "our children"—meaning his and his second wife's children. In this manner, he was able to exclude my husband. This is the way that he worded his will. He gave everything to "our children." My husband was not her son, so he was not included.

It is ironic, but our first two sons were born at the Knox City, Texas, hospital. This is where my husband's grandfather had worked as a medical doctor himself. My husband told them that Dr. Frizzell was his grandfather, and they moved us to the best room in the hospital. My oldest son was born there, and my second son died at that hospital—Theodore lived only a day and a half. We did not know any of the Frizzells before this time. It was later that we met my husband's father in that dark Knox City motel room.

Our family tree is split and we don't have any roots because my husband's parents gave everything away to another man and another woman. We are starting this family new from this generation forward. We have loved the other two families enough to let them have everything without a big fuss. They all got almost everything they wanted. Since they did not love the firstborn child of the first marriage enough to come to him, I doubt that anything will ever change with the remaining years of our lives. We are both gray now and a little wrinkled, but we are a cute couple. We have weathered the storm created by adultery and are doing everything that we can to set our children on a course in the right direction.

Since neither of the two families honored the cornerstone of the family, they felt entitled to do what they did. Without the child, they looked like every other normal family – one man and one woman. Just think of all of the men and women that have aborted a cornerstone. The mother looks like a single woman that has never had children. He looks like a single man that has never had children. Most would never know her secret or his secret. Most would never know that they did not love the child enough to keep from killing it. But one thing is certain, God knows!

> "And ye shall be betrayed both by parents, and brethren, and kinsfolks, and friends; and some of you shall they cause to be put to death. And ye shall be hated of all men for my name's sake. But there shall not an hair of your head perish. In your patience possess ye your souls." (Luke 21: 16–19)

I knew that there was something wrong in my husband's mother's house, but I did not understand how adultery affects people. All that I knew were my family's problems. I did not understand my husband's family's problems. My husband never talked about his father. The only man that I ever saw was his "step-father," and I could see that they were not close.

When I found my husband's father accidentally for the last time, he was living in the Abilene, Texas, area. I had tried to find the man and assumed that he was deceased. In my search, I did locate a "Frazzill" (at the time I did not know how to spell my husband's father's last name. I had seen it only once before on a silver platter with the name engraved that my husband's mother had temporarily given to us. She later took it back without us knowing. I had not spent much time in my husband's baby book because I did not understand what was going on.) on the internet and he said that he had been adopted and that his step-father had abused him. He said that he had heard about my husband. He warned me not to go to my husband's father. He said that they would only abandon him again. My husband's father never made any effort to come his son. He wanted my husband to come to him. My husband's step-father did tell my twenty-plus-year-old husband years earlier that his father's health was poor and that he should go to see him at the Petroleum Club. My husband did not go to this man.

It is odd that the adults communicated with each other and shared common threads, but his father still omitted his oldest son from his own life. I think that I know why. He used the adoption as an excuse to abandon his son even more than he had already done before. He and his second wife did not want to pay child support, and this was his excuse. He refused to accept any responsibility for this child. His second wife must have been delighted that my husband's mother married for a second time. It took the pressure off of them to be involved in the child's life. This child was just an "ejaculation."

This man waited for his abandoned son to come to him. It was as though my husband had committed adultery and abandoned his father. Who was the grown-up here? My husband was the better man. During all of these experiences, I did not fully understand what exactly was going on because I did not understand full-blown adultery. But now that I do, I know that my husband made some very wise decisions. My husband is very hurt by what his father, mother, step-father, and "step-mother" did!

The first Christmas that my husband had with his father, who was now an eighty year old man, his father wrote out a check to him for $500. Shortly after this, his father's oldest daughter from his second marriage got power of attorney over his father. The second Christmas—and our last with them—my husband received a check for $500 signed by his oldest half-sister from the second marriage. My husband and I both objected.

When my husband's father died, his second family mentioned no details about my husband's father's life in his own obituary—they only offered two poems to ponder. They waited to mention family details, which excluded my husband, until his step-mother died and her obituary was published (this gives another strong indication that my husband's father had become property and my husband's step-mother was, indeed, the head of the household). In my husband's "step-mother's" obituary, they mentioned their youngest family member, their brother, first and gave him my husband's father's first name. It was only after they had successfully taken everything from my husband that they could finally let their younger brother have his proper place within "their" family. This could only happen after my husband's father died. The oldest daughter could now give up her dominating position because both their father and mother were deceased.

I recall sitting at a table with my husband's half-brother on his father's side during one of our last visits and him asking aloud why his father had never let him manage the family's assets like he had his older sister. (No one answered his question.) He, like my husband, had distanced himself from the "core" family—his half-brother by choice and my husband because his father had eliminated him from his family. Both sons had to take the backseat so that the adulteress and her oldest daughter could maintain control of "their property."

> "For I am come to set a man at variance against his father, and the daughter against her mother, and the daughter in law

The Step-Father's Step-Son

against her mother in law. And a man's foes shall be they of his own household" (Matthew 10:35, 36).

This step-mother and daughter worked against my husband's father, against his firstborn son, and against her own brother. This daughter loved her mother more than all of them, and that includes my sons.

When my husband went to his father's funeral, he sat on the back row with the visitors. The geologist that sat next to him asked my husband who he was. My husband told him that he was the son of the deceased man's first marriage. The man said that he remembered "that marriage." I doubt that this man ever knew that my husband existed until that moment. I wonder how many lies my husband's father and step-mother had to tell during their life to hide the truth. It is awkward and awful for a child to have to introduce himself as a son because his father failed to do so! When my husband approached the "step-mother" to express his condolences, she denied knowing him. (I told my husband that there was no doubt in my mind that this woman knew who my husband was.) This man had his entire life to correct the problem. I guess that he wanted to save face instead of claiming two failed marriages. He would have had to kick his adulteress out in order to make things right and give his firstborn son his rightful position within the family.

This is their family.

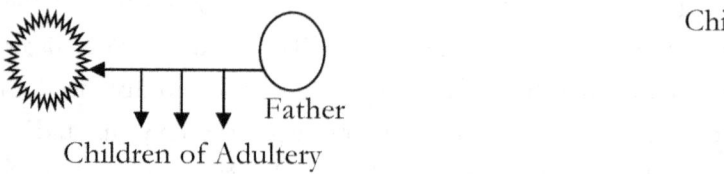

Child

Father

Children of Adultery

I had the opportunity one day to talk to a woman whose father had married for a second time. When her father died, the second woman did some very strange things. She buried this woman's father at the cemetery of her choice. Beside him, she placed a tombstone for herself, as though she planned to be buried beside him when she died. This daughter had requested that her father be buried beside her mother, his first wife when her father died, but this woman had refused. Finally, when this woman did die, she chose to have her remains buried beside her first husband. Her second husband had an empty grave beside him. This is what can happen when a man abandons the family and marries another woman.

> "The children of this world marry, and are given in marriage: But they which shall be accounted worthy to obtain that world, and the resurrection from the dead, neither marry, nor are given in marriage: Neither can they die any more; for they are equal unto the angels; and are the children of God, being the children of the resurrection." (Luke 20: 34–36)

The mistake that this man made was to marry for a second time! The children of the kingdom marry. Children of God do not need laws to govern and define their families—they know where their families are located and who the members of their family actually are. They don't need a lawyer, priest, pastor, or doctor to tell them.

I talked to another woman who had married a man that had been married previously. She told me that they had combined their assets in their will and were going to distribute the property equally between her children and his children from their previous marriages. It seems that before this man married this woman, he had been generous with his children. But now that he was married again, this other woman was making financial decisions for this man and his family. This woman said that this man's oldest daughter was no longer speaking to him. I told this woman that she was not a member of this family.

This woman was actually a member of the second family, and she could never move in and replace the first wife or her children. The mistake that this man made was to marry this woman.

The Step-Father's Step-Son

There are several problems with this situation. First of all, this woman cannot be his heir nor should this woman's children from her first marriage be his heirs. Second, this woman should never be permitted to separate this man from his daughter nor should she have any say about what the father gives to his daughter and her brothers and sisters. These children are his rightful and natural heirs—unless, of course, you talk to one of the "attorneys" in this country. If you talk to these people, they will tell you that this second woman is his heir because she is married to this man. Our laws are not structured for the children's benefit. They are structured to benefit the adulterers and adulteresses. The laws of this land put the second woman into the position of heir. If he dies before she does, she will be his heir. Then, she can rewrite her will to exclude his children from his first marriage!

This is my husband's FAMILY. He is the "cornerstone."

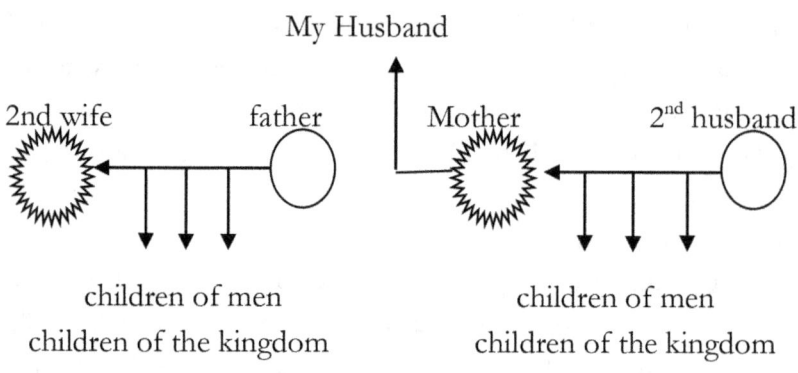

And now, we wonder with curiosity how our children could experience mental illness. Don't be fooled, because this woman will not only affect this generation, but she will also profoundly affect future generations. She has replaced the child with her children and taken the child's father to raise her children.

The children of the first family have nothing, and there will be nothing to hand down because the adulteress will take everything that she can get her hands on. There will be no family pictures, no family tree, no family memories other than those of abandonment, and no heirlooms. The ones that will suffer even more are the children of this child of confusion and abandonment. There will not be a grandfather to bless his grandchildren. Oh yes, he will bless her children, but he will do no such thing for the child of his first marriage or for the children of that child. Neither the father nor the "step-mother" ever accepted the child; therefore, they will be incapable of accepting the fact that he has a wife, children, or grandchildren. It will again be as though these children never existed, and the lie continues on for another generation.

I have personally witnessed one instance where a step-daughter was used as a babysitter for her three half-brothers and half-sisters. It was obvious to me that the three small children had been forced upon her and that she cared little for them. She was expressionless in providing care for these small children as their "parents" went through the fast food line together. It was only when I approached this young girl to exit the building that she raised her slumped shoulders, sat up, and smiled at me.

Why is it that the "parents" could not or would not see what I saw that day? After forced servitude, what sort of mother will she be? What kind of servitude did she have to provide early in the marriage when these children were conceived? Did the natural parent and step-parent spend a lot of time away from her or in the bedroom with the door locked? How many times did she have to get up during the night to care for a crying baby and then go to school the next day?

Who will be responsible for her sins? Will it be her, or will it be her "parents"? She was being used to serve the purposes of the "parents." She was the oldest child, but it was obvious that she had no social standing within the family. The three young children were the only family that mattered in the eyes of these two lovers. The parents' adultery has led them to other sins—sins against the child of the first family!

> And he spake this parable unto certain which trusted in themselves that they were righteous, and despised others: Two men

went up into the temple to pray: the one a Pharisee, and the other a publican. The Pharisee stood and prayed thus with himself, God, I thank thee, that I am not as other men *are*, extortioners, unjust, adulterers, or even as this publican. I fast twice in the week, I give tithes of all that I possess. And the publican, standing afar off, would not lift up so much as *his* eyes unto heaven, but smote upon his breast, saying, God be merciful to me a sinner. I tell you, this man went down to his house justified *rather* than the other: for every one that exalteth himself shall be abased; and he that humbleth himself shall be exalted. (Luke 18:9–14)

My husband's father said that it was his first wife's mother who caused him to do "it." My husband's grandmother was dominating and overbearing or so many of the men thought. For this reason, he used this as one of his excuses for leaving my husband's mother for another woman. The "it" most likely meant that he put his penis where it did not belong. The odd thing is that this man created exactly what he said he was running from: an adulteress. The most common trait that I see among adulterers and adulteresses is selfishness. He had described my husband's mother's mother as very selfish. My husband's father did exactly as Adam and Eve did—he blamed someone else for his decision!

Adultery is the most sacred sin in this country. Many of our children serve jail and prison time for lesser crimes. The only punishment for abandoning a wife and children is to have to pay child support until the child reaches the age of eighteen. Our laws are written to protect the adulterers and the children that are born from the adultery. Divorce severs all ties with the first wife and in many cases her children also. This second woman is a concubine whose status has been forcefully elevated to that of "wife" with a writing of divorcement and laws that are nothing but the commandments of men. This woman is not worth what she has cost.

Marriage and Family

Our men were created to provide for the physical needs of the family. Many are so callous that they willingly give their children's inheritance to another woman. In our culture, these women are the ones that benefit and not the child. It is little wonder that these children will become drunk with wine, beer, and liquor. These cold-hearted men will blame the children from the first marriage for any wrongs that they do. They will not lift a finger to help them. All responsibility will be carried by the children and wife of the first family. In actuality, it is this father and his other woman that are at the root of our nation's problems. These two are cursing our families!

> "And I say unto you, That many shall come from the east and west, and shall sit down with Abraham, and Isaac, and Jacob, in the kingdom of heaven. But the children of the kingdom shall be cast out into outer darkness: there shall be weeping and gnashing of teeth." (Matthew 8:11–12)

I think that it is interesting that Jesus used Abraham, Isaac, and Jacob as examples of sons of God and fathers. We should all note that none of these men married and none of them abandoned their first wife or the children of their first wife! All three of these men kept their family unit together.

Abraham did have to deal with Hagar by sending her away because she wanted her son to be first. Abraham would have been like my husband's father if he had let Hagar take over his family. Abraham never let that happen. Jacob, Abraham's grandson, had a very complicated family because of the way that Laban tricked him (I will explain this more fully in the next chapter.) Laban thought that he was so important that he could arrange a marriage for Jacob and get away with it. There are men and women today that think that they can forcibly arrange their children's marriage just as Laban. And so it was that for three generations—Abraham, Isaac, and Jacob—the family tree remained intact. It was within the next generation that things began to unravel. This was when the kingdom of men began to rise, and it has survived to this very day.

The children of the kingdom are the ones that have bought into our laws, the commandments of men. They are the children of men. They have the prefixes of "Mr.," "Mrs.," and "Dr." before their names. In this kingdom, the man IS the family, and wherever his penis faces, that is where his family is. He can legally divorce his wife, go on to another woman, and even give her his last name and his entire family while eliminating his first natural family. This man has the freedom to go from woman to woman prior to "marriage." A marriage is only legal with a piece of paper and a justice of the peace or minister to sanctify it and make it holy. In this kingdom, a woman and child have little legal standing without this piece of paper.

Mr.　　　Mrs.　　　God

The structure of our family encourages irresponsibility on the part of our fathers. It gives them a false sense of autonomy and superiority. All marriages are based on law. We have mothers-in-law, daughters-in-law, fathers-in-law, and sons-in-law. All marriages are based on law and can be destroyed with a writing of divorcement. Young women are referred to as "Miss" prior to marriage and then "Mrs." after marriage. A man always carries the prefix of "Mr.," which does not change before, during, or after marriage. It does not matter if he is a father or not. He is the king in this country, and many think of themselves as god.

> "And greetings in the market, and to be called of men, Rabbi, Rabbi. But be not ye called Rabbi: for one is your Master, even Christ; and all ye are brethren. And call no man your father upon the earth: for one is your Father, which is in heaven. Neither be ye called masters: for one is your master, even Christ. But he that is greatest among you shall be your servant." (Matthew 23:5-11)

This is the reason that titles such as Mr., Dr., Rabbi, Pastor, etc. are not to be used. All of these terms demand respect. A man should not go by Dr. . . . , instead he or she should say, "My name is Luke. I am a medical doctor. I can help you." In this way, this person is introducing themselves as a servant.

"And he said unto him, Why callest thou me good? *there is* none good but one, *that is*, God: but if thou wilt enter into life, keep the commandments."

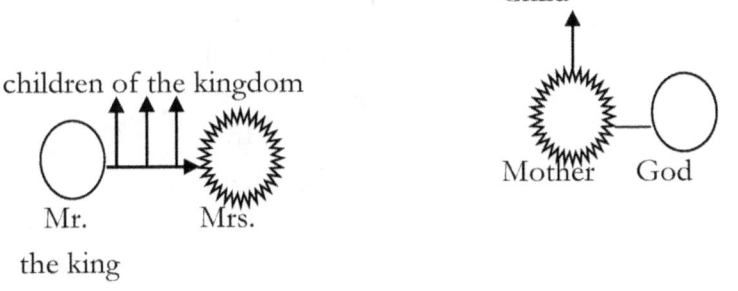

Our men are freely offered the opportunity to go from woman to woman before "marriage" and afterward. This is the cause of child poverty, mental illness, homelessness, and a host of other problems. The tax payers will have to pick up the expense to support these unwanted women and children.

The Step-Father's Step-Son

Jesus was homeless also. We know this because He said in Matthew 8:20, "The foxes have holes, and the birds of the air *have* nests, but the Son of man hath not where to lay *his* head." You might wonder how this could have been the case.

Jesus did not have an earthly father. His family is much like those of today when men leave their wife and their children to move in with another woman. My husband is a good example of this scenario.

Mary was engaged to Joseph when she became pregnant with Jesus. Joseph had planned to put away Mary privately after he found that she was pregnant with "someone else's" (God Himself is the Father of Jesus) child. God intervened because He knew that Mary would need a man to help her to provide for His child. God discourages women from committing adultery by marrying another man, but He knows that we need a man to support our Families and to help us, especially when a child's father has abandoned his own children for another woman. But a woman should never have intercourse with any other man except her first husband.

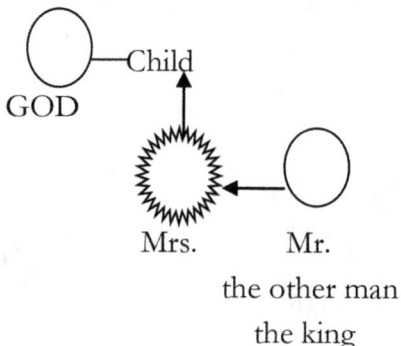

the other man

the king

"But I say unto you, That whosoever shall put away his wife, saving for the cause of fornication, causeth her to commit adultery: and whosoever shall marry her that is divorced committeth adultery" (Matthew 5:32).

Men that marry a divorced woman are committing adultery. The woman that marries for a second time commits adultery. A married man that lusts after another woman commits adultery. A woman that separates a man from his wife commits adultery. A man that separates a woman from her husband commits adultery. Jesus said, "What therefore God joined together, let not man put asunder" (Matthew 19:6).

In the above scripture, it is obvious that God is looking at the root cause of the breakup of the family. If the man puts his wife away for any reason except fornication, he is the one that caused her to marry someone else. In this case, the responsibility rests on him and the other woman, and ultimately, they will be responsible on Judgment Day because they are the cause—he is the "ass" that carries the burden of responsibility. Even still, none of us should commit fornication or adultery. They are both wrong because they distort and disfigure the family tree. The same is true for a woman if she puts her husband away for any reason except fornication. A man is never ever supposed to lust after any other woman. A man must not bring another woman into the family without his wife's permission and approval. He must not cheat on his wife!

Jesus' half-brother James also had something to say about lust and temptation. At first, he did not believe in his half-brother, Jesus, but he later changed his mind. He said,

> Blessed *is* the man that endureth temptation: for when he is tried, he shall receive the crown of life, which the Lord hath promised to them that love him. Let no man say when he is tempted, I am tempted of God: for God cannot be tempted with evil, neither tempteth he any man: But every man is tempted, when he is drawn away of his own lust, and enticed. Then when lust hath conceived, it bringeth forth sin: and sin, when it is finished, bringeth forth death. Do not err, my beloved brethren. Every good gift and every perfect gift is from above, and cometh down from the Father of lights, with whom is no variableness, neither shadow of turning. (James 1:12–17)

The Step-Father's Step-Son

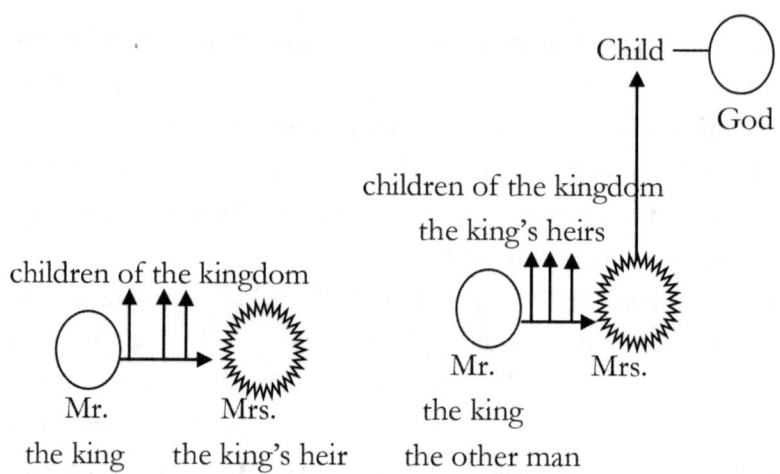

The death that James is referring is not necessarily physical death, but instead, one that is much worse: the death of the soul! Lust is lust, fornication is fornication, and adultery is adultery. There are no variables and no grey areas. This rule is concrete!

Jesus' family

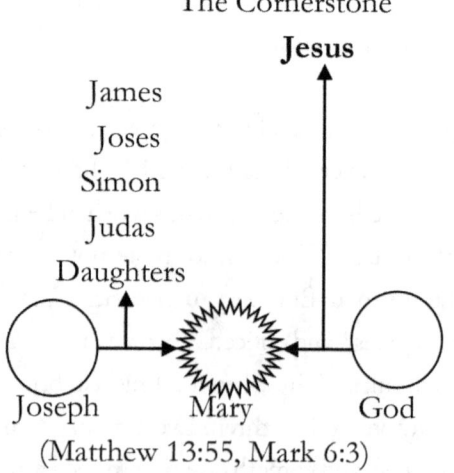

(Matthew 13:55, Mark 6:3)

This family tree is very similar to the family trees of men that have abandoned their first wives and firstborn children for another woman. Jesus was a step-father's step-son just as my husband was. My husband's father was never a part of his life. This man gave everything that belonged to my husband to another woman and her children.

Jesus was the firstborn son of Mary. Jesus identified himself as the "son of man" and the "son of God." Mary was the female that gave him life because no male was involved in His conception. Jesus is the cornerstone between the soul and the body. Jesus was the cornerstone of this family and His half-brothers did not believe in Him.

Jesus said, "I am the way, the truth, and the life: no man cometh unto the Father, but by me" (John 14:6). God made this all happen. Could it be that our fathers also do not enter into Heaven without the wife and children of their first family? I think that this is the case! The first family is so important that Jesus recommended castration for those that could not keep the commandments.

Jesus was born into a society that was very similar to ours today—the family structure was much the same, and He spoke out against it many times. Jesus was an heir because the wise men brought gold as a gift. This helped Joseph to provide for the needs of Jesus and then, ultimately, the needs of his half-brothers and half-sisters as well. The family property most likely went to Joseph's sons—James, Joses, Simon, and Judas—and daughters, who would be considered the children of the second family. This is the way that men handle the situation today.

In my husband's family, both his mother and his father gave everything that they had to their second spouses, who, in turn, gave control of everything that they owned to their own children and not my husband. My husband, like Jesus, was left with no place to lay his head. His half-brothers and half-sisters got control of everything.

In my husband's family, my husband would have been the natural heir within the natural family tree. Of course, all of this depended upon his parents respecting that tree. That did not happen because my husband's father thought that he was the tree and that his family tree was where he was! If it had not been this way, the other woman could never have established her roots as strongly as she did within my husband's family. My husband's step-father thought that he was the family tree, even though he had married another man's wife and committed adultery. All of my husband's natural inheritance was given to this woman and this man. This is what happens in full-blown adultery.

Over lunch one day at work, one of my female coworkers told me a story about her father. Her father had an old saying, and it went something like this: "I grew up in a time where you didn't throw things away—you fixed them." Our families are disposable, much like trading in a used car for a new one, so, too, are our children. People in this country don't like to fix anything, especially problems within their family. They would rather go out and get a new one. We are all disposable, especially the members of the first family.

This man was the exception rather than the rule back in the day. Adultery was commonplace then just as it is today. I know this because my grandfather committed adultery with a married woman, my father was divorced and then married my mother, my husband's father ran around on my husband's mother, and my husband's mother said that her second husband was running around on her, too. Adultery has been built into our family structure since the founding of this country.

Jesus' half-brothers did not believe in Him just as my husband's half-brothers and half-sisters did not believe in my husband. In this way, it made it easier for them all to take everything that was my husband's and Jesus'. Even though both Jesus and my husband, were the oldest in the "family," my husband's half-brothers and half-sisters wanted everything for themselves. They were the oldest children of the second "marriage," and Jesus and my husband were in their way.

The biggest difference between Jesus' family and my husband's family was that Jesus' mother, Mary, never put her children with Joseph first. Jesus was her firstborn son, and she stayed with him until His death on the cross and beyond. And since Mary never broke her covenant with her firstborn child, Jesus gave her to His disciple John to care for her until she died.

> When Jesus therefore saw his mother, and the disciple standing by, whom he loved, he saith unto his mother, Woman, behold thy son! Then saith he to the disciple, Behold thy mother! And from that hour that disciple took her unto his own *home*. After this, Jesus knowing that all things were now accomplished, that the scripture might be fulfilled, saith, I thirst. (John 19:26–28)

Mary did not stay with Joseph's sons and daughters after Jesus died. Joseph's sons acted like the "children of the kingdom" of today. Mary stayed with her firstborn son in the place that He chose. Jesus took care of his mother.

I wish that my husband's mother and father could have loved my husband the way that Mary loved Jesus! Both of my husband's parents made their second spouse the primary person in their lives. My husband became baggage from the past! He was in the way, and he was occupying space in another man's and woman's home—that of his "step-parents." It is little wonder that we have homeless men and women today. Their parents have given everything to their next spouse. Instead of blessing the children of the first marriage, they are cursing them and their offspring! I can understand how our sons would have little respect for women. I can understand how some of our daughters could become lesbians themselves. I can understand how some could become alcoholics. Talk about confusion. Our children should never have to experience this craziness!

This child of the first marriage will be forced to make some serious decisions. Jesus said in John 8:31–38,

> Then said Jesus to those Jews which believed on him, If you continue in my word, *then* are ye my disciples indeed; And ye shall know the truth, and the truth shall make you free.

The Step-Father's Step-Son

> They answered him, We be Abraham's seed, and were never in bondage to any man: how sayest thou, Ye shall be made free? Jesus answered them, Verily, verily, I say unto you, Whosoever committeth sin is the servant of sin. And the servant abideth not in the house for ever: *but* the Son abideth ever. If the Son therefore shall make you free, ye shall be free indeed. I know that ye are Abraham's seed, but ye seek to kill me, because my word hath no place in you. I speak that which I have seen with my Father: and ye do that which ye have seen with your father.

The children of the kingdom will not do as Jesus said of His own Father. They will do what they have seen with their own fathers.

My husband was forced to make a decision to follow after his Father in Heaven, the Father of his soul, or his earthly father, the father of his body. My husband chose God, his Father, because he could not condone what his father had done. His father abandoned him for another woman and her children. He did not follow in his father's footsteps. He had to go his own way, go on his own, and leave his father behind. This has been a very difficult journey for my husband, our children, and me.

My husband's step-mother, if you can call her that because she was never a part of my husband's life, said that my husband's father was alone when they met. This is what she used as justification for starting a relationship with him. This is the perfect time, when a man or a woman is alone, for someone to take advantage of them and their family, especially if they have something to offer.

"The disciple is not above *his* master, nor the servant above his lord" (Matthew 10:24). Jesus is the Son of God. He is the way, the truth, and the life. He is the one that will be coming on the clouds on our last day! Mohammad will not be there. Paul will not be there. Buda will not be there. No other man will be there with Him on the clouds. Just as we can see lightning over the horizon, so, too, will we be able to see Jesus coming with His angels. We had better get ready because He is going to come! (Matthew 24:27-30)

Jesus said,

> Are not two sparrows sold for a farthing? and one of them shall not fall to the ground without your Father. But the very hairs on your head are all numbered. Fear ye not therefore, ye are of more value than many sparrows. Whosoever therefore shall confess me before men, him will I confess also before my Father which is in heaven. But whosoever shall deny me before men, him will I also deny before my Father which is in heaven. Think not that I am come to send peace on earth: I came not to send peace, but a sword." (Matthew 10:29–34)

It is not a physical sword that Jesus is talking about here. It is the act of separating the believers from the unbelievers, the truth from the untruth. The sword of truth separates the children of the kingdom from the children of God. God tore the temple curtain in half following Jesus' death. God supported and backed Jesus in this statement. I wonder if this saying of Jesus doesn't, in some way, imply that if a man denies the existence of his own child that God will deny him also. It does because a man cannot divorce and remarry—it is considered adultery!

> He that loveth father or mother more than me is not worthy of me: and he that loveth son or daughter more than me is not worthy of me. And he that taketh not his cross, and followeth after me, is not worthy of me. He that findeth his life shall lose it, and he that loseth his life for my sake shall find it. (Matthew 10:37–39)

My husband's father's oldest daughter from his second marriage loved her mother more than my husband, her father, my sons, or Jesus.

The Step-Father's Step-Son

My husband's father loved his oldest daughter with his second wife more than he loved his firstborn son, his grandsons, or Jesus.

My husband's father failed to take up his cross and follow Jesus. He made no attempt to apologize or to right his wrongs.

My husband found his life with his father, the man that abandoned him shortly after his birth. But he had to lose his life with his father for Jesus' sake. He had to choose. He had to choose God or his father. My husband chose God, his Heavenly Father.

Abraham, Isaac, Jacob, and Their Families

One of the most important Biblical marriages of all time was that of Abram and Sarai, who later became known as Abraham and Sarah. They made mistakes in their family that caused a great deal of anguish for both of them. God worked with them to clean things up.

Now, let's go back in time to Abraham and Sarah's family for a closer look and see what kind of knowledge can be gained. First of all, we begin with the simple family, the way that all families start out. Instead of their names, you could insert yours.

Abraham and Sarah were a very special couple. Just as Mary was chosen to give birth to Jesus, these two were chosen to be examples of family for all of their future generations. God's plan worked for three generations because we know that Abraham, Abraham's son Isaac, and Isaac's son Jacob all went to Heaven—Jesus told us so (Mark 12:24–27). But something happened with Jacob's children that distorted God's plan. These three sons of God commanded their children and household after them "to keep the way of the Lord, to do justice and judgment" (Genesis 18:19).

Because of Abraham and Sarah's family "shall all the families of the earth be blessed" (Genesis 12:3). This was God's plan. This marriage was not based on a piece of paper or any laws. Abraham never left Sarah nor moved in permanently with Hagar. Abraham was charged with the responsibility of keeping the family unit intact and keeping his generations perfect. He managed to do this despite the family's shift from simple to complex following the couple's decision to bring Hagar into their FAMILY.

In order for God to accomplish his plan, Abram and Sarai had to leave behind their country and their family. God said, "Get thee out of thy country, and from thy kindred, and from thy father's house, unto a land that I will shew thee" (Genesis 12:1). There was something wrong in that land and in his family of which God did not approve.

Abram and Sarai had grown up in a country and a family filled with men. God knew that a plain man and woman would not be able to accomplish what He was planning—it would take a son of God, a daughter of God, and a future mother of God's children. Over time, God was going to work with Abram and Sarai to make them into a son and a daughter of God. In order to do this, God tested Abram and Sarai along the way to ensure that they were making progress.

Abram, who was seventy-five, did as God commanded and left with Sarai (his wife), Lot (his brother's son), all of their possessions, and other souls. When they arrived in Canaan, God appeared to Abram and said, "Unto thy seed will I give this land" (Genesis 12:7). Abram built an altar there "and called upon the name of the Lord" (Genesis 12:8).

There was a severe famine in the land and Abram took his family and animals down to Egypt. As they approached Egypt, Abram became fearful and pleaded with Sarai to tell the Egyptians that she was his sister instead of his wife so that he would not be killed. Men in those days killed a husband so that they could take his wife as their own. Today, all they have to do is divorce and then remarry. (Even King David sent Uriah, the husband of

Bathsheba, to the front lines of the battlefield so that he would be killed. He tried to encourage Uriah to go home to his wife, but instead, loyal Uriah stayed with his troops. If Uriah had gone home, he and Bathsheba could have hidden their adultery. Uriah might not have guessed that Bathsheba's child was with another man. At that time, Bathsheba was pregnant with King David's child (II Samuel 11:1-17).

Sarai did as Abram requested to protect him from death. And just as Abram had predicted, Pharaoh's princes saw beautiful Sarai, told Pharaoh about her, and took her into Pharaoh's house. God plagued Pharaoh's house because of Sarai. Pharaoh anxiously sent all of them away once he found that Sarai was Abram's wife instead of just his half-sister.

Abram's family

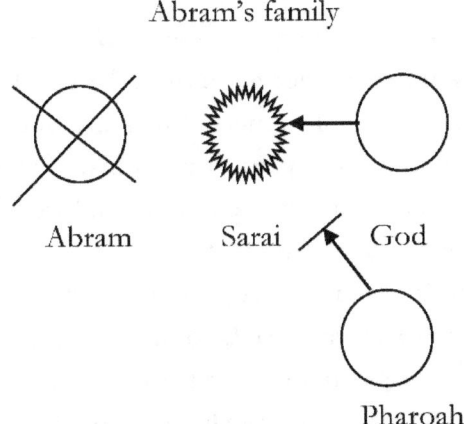

Abram Sarai God

Pharoah

The lesson here is that no man should ever take another man's wife for his own. Even John the Baptist told King Herod that he could not have another man's wife. He said, "It is not lawful for thee to have her" (Matthew 14:4). King Herod wanted his brother's wife, Herodias. For this reason, John the Baptist was sent to prison. While John was in prison, King Herod had a birthday. At his party, Herodias' daughter danced for him, and he was very pleased. He foolishly told this young woman that he would give her anything that she would ask. In order to please her adulterous mother, she asked for John's head. The king sadly fulfilled the request. They brought his head to her on a charger; her daughter then carried his head to her mother.

The first bad decision that Herod made was to get involved with his brother's wife, Herodias. Herod was a step up for Herodias. Herodias most likely felt that her husband was not good enough for her. The next bad decision that Herod made was to marry this woman, his brother's wife. The third one was to promise anything to his adulteress' daughter who had danced for him. Were there other bad decisions to follow? He was living with a woman that did not love his own brother. Surely he must have wondered if she truly loved him. Now, he became responsible for putting away his own brother and killing John the Baptist. Herod became a broken man. This is part of the cost of adultery.

A son of God should never marry the daughter of an adulteress. She is practiced in the art of adultery and the commandments of men. This young woman loved her mother more than she loved Herod, John the Baptist, Jesus, or God. The daughters of men are this way. Herod most likely regretted his decision to marry this woman. He was beginning to experience the consequences of his poor decision. I would also expect that he made other poor decisions after that time.

Abram had a vision, and the Lord told him that He was his shield and his reward. This is when Abram told God that he was childless and had no heirs who could receive any reward that the Lord would give to him. God told him that he would have a son from his own bowels, meaning the bowels of Sarai, who was one flesh with Abram. I think that, at the time, Abram and Sarai both thought that the Lord was referring to Abram's bowels only, because she could not conceive. The Lord told him to look toward heaven and count the stars—this is how large his family would grow (Genesis 15:5).

Then, Sarai came to Abram and beseeched him selfishly to have intercourse with Hagar, her maidservant. In doing so, he took Hagar as his second wife (Genesis 16:3). It appears that Abram and Sarai both loved each other more than they loved God because Sarai called Abram her lord (Genesis 18:12) and Abram did as she requested. This is much like how men and women of today will seek out a surrogate mother, a sperm donor, or a test tube laboratory so that they can have a child. We have many men and women that adopt other people's children so that they can have a child rather than wait.

When Hagar became pregnant, she despised Sarai (Genesis 16:4, 5). Sarai asked Abram to make a decision: she wanted him to choose her or his child with Hagar. Like many women, this second wife wanted to separate the father from his first wife. These women want everything for themselves and for their children. Sarai repented the mistake that she had made in making such a selfish request of Abram. Abram told her to deal with Hagar as she pleased. Sarai dealt with her harshly, and Hagar left to go into the wilderness.

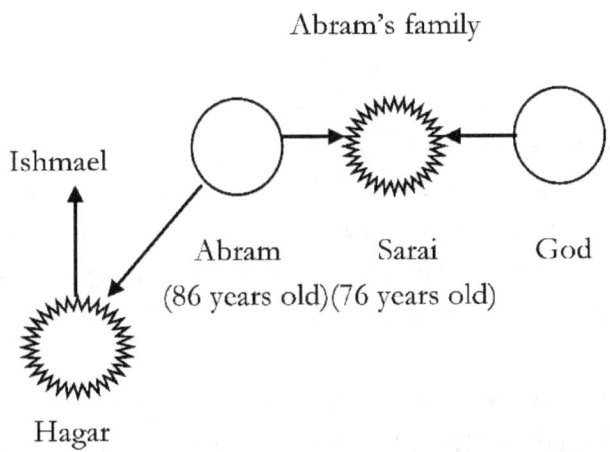

Abram's family

For the benefit of Ishmael, God encouraged Hagar to return to Abram and Sarai. An angel told her that her seed would be multiplied exceedingly and that it would grow so large that it could not be numbered. Ishmael was going to become a wild man. The angel was preparing her for things to come (Genesis 16:6–12). Abram was eighty-six years old when Ishmael was born. When Abram was ninety-nine years old, the Lord appeared to him again. The Lord told him to walk before Him and to be perfect. This is when Abram and Sarai became a son and a daughter of God. Again, He reiterated that nations, kings, and many people would come from him. God said that He would be their God. And He changed his name to Abraham. He also said that the land of Canaan would forever belong to his descendants (Genesis 17:8). The binding covenant would be the circumcision of every male child eight days old and older.

There is significance with the eighth day. Our doctors circumcise small children right after birth. I think that it is important to wait until the eighth day. This gives the small male child an opportunity to adjust to his surroundings in a new and different world. He also told him that Sarai's name would now be Sarah (Genesis 17:8-14). He said that He would bless her, give Abraham a son with her, and make her a mother of nations—kings would come from her.

> "Moses therefore gave unto you circumcision; (not because it is of Moses, but of the fathers;) and ye on the Sabbath day circumcise a man. If a man on the Sabbath day receive circumcision, that the law of Moses should not be broken are you angry at me, because I have made a man every whit whole on the Sabbath day? Judge not according to the appearance, but judge righteous judgment." (John 7:22-23)

Circumcision is not required by God. It was a law created by Moses himself for the fathers. It must have been something that the fathers wanted at that time. This could be very similar to the ritual surgery that is done to young girls in Africa where the clitoris and/or labia are removed causing intercourse to be painful. I don't know exactly what the fathers in that country want or do to the females, but I think that I am close on the assumption that I have made. In this country, our ritual surgery is the circumcision of males. Many men in Moses' time thought of themselves as God just as many of our men do today. The words "lord" and "God" in many scriptures in the Bible are referring to a man of high regard. We must be very careful that we are serving God and not the commandments of men when we read the scriptures written by men. The only way to distinguish between the two is to read thoroughly Matthew, Mark, Luke, and John. These are four men's eyewitness accounts of the life of Jesus, what he said, and what he did. Jesus specifically said that he is the way, the truth, and the life! If we do not study the life of Christ, we most likely will be keeping the commandments of men rather than the commandments of God.

Abraham, who was one hundred years old, and Sarah, who was ninety years old, both laughed at the thought of having a son. Then, the Lord, who knew Sarah and Abraham's thoughts, said, "Is anything too hard for the Lord?" (Genesis 18:14). God told him to name his son Isaac (Genesis 17:19). He said that He would return at the appointed time of their life and that she would have a son (Genesis 18:9–14).

The Lord said, "For I know him, that he will command his children and his household after him, and they shall keep the way of the LORD, to do justice and judgment; that the LORD may bring upon Abraham that which he hath spoken of him" (Genesis 18:19).

Again, another man, Abimelech, King of Gerar, took Sarah, Abraham's wife, to be his own. God told Abimelech in a dream to let Sarah go. Abimelech went to Abraham and asked him why he told him that she was his sister. "And Abraham said, Because I thought, Surely the fear of God *is* not in this place; and they will slay me for my wife's sake. And yet indeed *she is* my sister; she *is* the daughter of my father, but not the daughter of my mother; and she became my wife" (Genesis 20:11, 12). Abimelech gave Abraham sheep, oxen, men servants, women servants, and released Sarah to him.

The Step-Father's Step-Son

Abraham's family

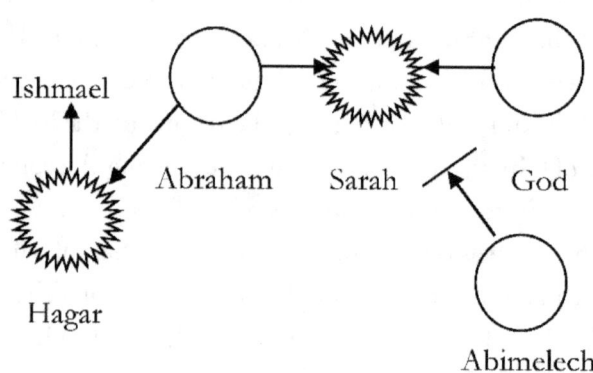

After this experience with Abimelech, Sarah became pregnant with Abraham's son, and when he was born, they named him Isaac.

Abraham's family

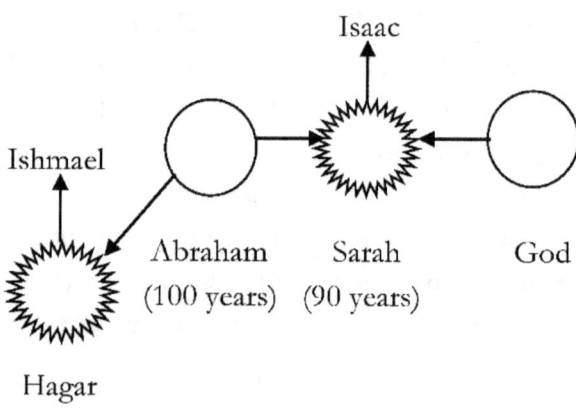

Things had been difficult for this family even before Isaac was born. But after his birth, things became even more complicated. Abraham prepared a great feast to honor his son when he was weaned from his mother's breasts. It was on the day of the feast that Sarah saw Ishmael mocking them. This was when Sarah told Abraham to cast Hagar and Ishmael out. She did not want Ishmael to be an heir with their son, Isaac.

Abraham was heartbroken at the thought of sending away his son Ishmael. Again, God spoke to Abraham and told him that he should not be grieved. He told him to listen to what Sarah had said and to do as she had requested (Genesis 21:11, 12). So, the next day, Abraham rose early from sleep, collected bread and a bottle of water, gave it to Hagar and Ishmael, and sent them away. When the water was consumed, Hagar began to cry and worry that her son would die. God heard Ishmael crying and called upon Hagar. He said, "[F]ear not" (Genesis 21:17). He told her to rise and lift up the child for he would become a great nation. This was when God opened her eyes so that she could see a well of water nearby (she had been focusing on the problem and could not see the water well). She filled the bottle and gave water to her son. God loved Ishmael, and he grew as they lived in the wilderness. He became an archer. Hagar found a wife for Ishmael in Egypt.

Hagar became the head of her household, and God was there to help her take care of her family. This had to be so because we are to let "no one" separate what God has joined together (Matthew 19:4–6). This applies to women as well as men! The man is never supposed to move in and live with the other woman! If a man does move out and moves in with another woman, he has split the family asunder. Our primary family members must remain primary. No one from a secondary position should ever be permitted to move into a primary position and replace that person or child. Yes, a man can stay briefly with another woman, but she has to remain on the side. He must maintain his primary residence with his wife and their children. He must never move in with or marry the other woman! If he should do so, she and her children will become his heirs instead of his children with his first wife. This must never be permitted.

The Step-Father's Step-Son

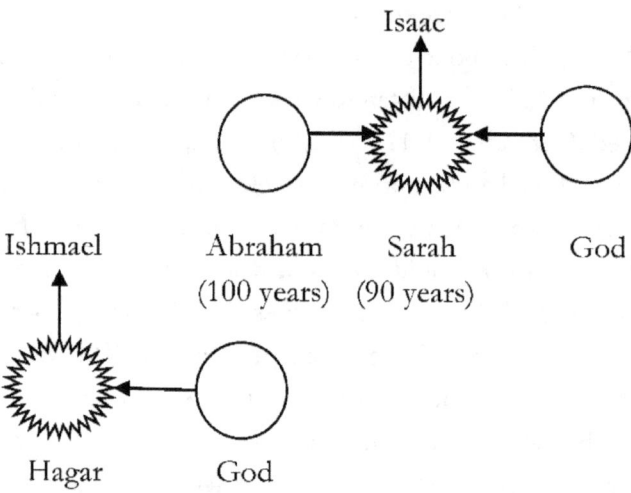

A woman can raise a family without a man if the need should arise. Women have been doing this since the beginning of time, before God separated the genders. God does prefer that we have a helpmeet. Hagar had to be sent away because she wanted to split up the family. She wanted to come between Abraham and Sarah. If Abraham had left Sarah and moved in with Hagar, Sarah would have been replaced and eliminated from the family. Ishmael would have been the replacement for Isaac. Abraham, in this setting, would not have been chosen as an example by God. The first family would have been destroyed just as we do in this country today. It happened this way in my husband's family. The second wife took over the family, and then her daughter replaced my husband. It was a forced separation. My husband once mentioned in the presence of the "step-mother" that someone had come to visit him when he was small that had a small mole like growth on their eyelid. (It was one like the one that my husband had on his eyelid.) My husband's "step-mother" firmly stated that no one ever came to visit my husband.

Abraham, Isaac, Jacob, and Their Families

No man or woman is ever supposed to be permitted to separate what God has joined together (Matthew 19:3–6). The first family must always be the core of all families. This is the only way to keep the family unit intact and to keep our generations perfect.

Furthermore, family members are not expendable; abortions and replacements are never to be permitted. Family members are not to be traded in like we trade in a used car for a new car. The man goes home to his first wife and lives with her and their children. The man and his wife can add another woman to the family unit, but it must be a joint decision. This relationship must always be on the side and not primary or permanent.

The husband and wife can separate if the need should arise. We all need time alone to grow. But a second woman or second man should never be permitted to move in and replace our spouses. But if a man ever beats his wife and/or children, once fear has been instilled in them, it will be unlikely that they will ever want to let this man be a part of their lives again.

Before we reach a judgment about who is actually responsible, I think that we need to look deeper for the root cause. Please understand that I am not defending people that abuse their spouses or their children. But how many of these men and women grew up with a father, mother, step-father, or step-mother that abused them? How many grew up with a mother or father that did not protect them from their second spouses? Where adultery exists, love does not. These abusive adults were most likely raised in a home with adulterers who started abuse within the family. Adulterers do not love someone else's child as they would their own children. They will frequently abuse these children because they are in their way and interfere. In turn, these abused children, the victims of adulterers, will abuse their own children. The grandchildren will pay the price for the grandparent's adultery. Adultery is at the root of our nation's ills.

> Jesus saith unto them, Did ye never read in the scriptures, The stone which the builders rejected, the same is become the head of the corner: this is the Lord's doing, and it is marvelous in our eyes? Therefore say I unto you, The kingdom of God shall be taken from you, and given to a nation bringing forth the fruits thereof. And whosoever shall fall on this stone shall be broken: but on whomsoever it shall fall, it will grind him to powder. (Matthew 21:42–44)

The firstborn child of the first wife is the cornerstone that holds a family together. Jesus Himself was a step-father's step-son in the physical sense because no earthly father was present. Jesus was Joseph's step-son. Most people thought that Joseph was Jesus' father (Luke 3:23, 2:48–49). This is like my husband, whose father abandoned him for another woman. Almost everyone thought that Mr. Cox was my husband's father. Very few knew that Mr. Frizzell was his real father. The step-father gave control of everything to his firstborn son and not to my husband. My husband's father gave everything that he had to his second wife and her children. My husband did not have a father at all with either of the two "families."

The builders are the mother and the father. If the builders remove this child from this choice position as cornerstone, they will fall on the stone just as my husband's father and mother fell from their positions as protector and guardian of the FAMILY. But the ones that kill the child, the cornerstone between a man and a woman, by abortion or other methods will be crushed to powder.

A man should not ever lust after another woman. As most of us know, lust is the precursor to intercourse. Both of these are considered adultery to his wife and to God (Matthew 5:28). This secret liaison destroys trust between the two. It is not permitted for any man to lust after another woman. Troubles, problems, and chaos will be the result. This confusion will cause unnecessary problems for the wife and children to bear.

Abraham, Isaac, Jacob, and Their Families

So, Hagar and her son had to be sent away. This was Abraham and Sarah's way of protecting their firstborn son and heir. If they had not done this, Isaac's life, most likely, would have been in danger. His social position in the family would have been given away to Ishmael. Thirteen-year-old Ishmael was ready and willing to compete with Isaac, who was a small toddler. When Isaac was older, Ishmael returned to be with his half-brother and to bury their father. There are other Biblical examples of situations where the children of the second family did desire to kill the child of the first family.

Parents must be very cautious about leaving their children with a "step-parent," or what they might incorrectly call a "boyfriend" or a "girlfriend." Half-brothers and half-sisters can also endanger the lives of our firstborn children of the first family if they do not respect the entire family unit. My husband's father and his second wife did everything but kill him. By abandoning him completely as they did, it was as though he had died or never existed.

Sarah, Isaac's mother, was one hundred twenty-seven years old when she died. Isaac was thirty-seven years old when this happened. Following her death, Abraham sent his most senior servant back to his homeland and his kin to find a wife for Isaac. Abraham did not want Isaac to go there himself. He must have been afraid that their ways would influence his family.

Abraham's servant met Rebekah, the daughter of Abraham's brother's son at a water well. Abraham's brother was called Nahor, and he had named his son Bethuel. And Rebekah was Bethuel and Milcah's daughter. Rebekah's brother was Laban.

Rebekah's family asked Rebekah if she would go with Abraham's servant, and she said, "I will go" (Genesis 24:58). "And they blessed Rebekah, and said to her, Thou *art* our sister, be thou *the mother* of thousands of millions" (Genesis 24:60). Rebekah's family requested that she have ten days with the family before leaving to go to Abraham's house.

Rebekah traveled with other damsels to Abraham's home. Isaac was in a field meditating in the evening of the day when he saw the camels coming.

The Step-Father's Step-Son

The servant told Rebekah that this man was Isaac. When Rebekah saw Isaac, she got off the camel and covered herself with a veil. The servant told Isaac about everything that had happened. "And Isaac brought her into his mother Sarah's tent, and took Rebekah, and she became his wife; and he loved her: and Isaac was comforted after his mother's *death*" (Genesis 24:67). Isaac was forty years old when he took Rebekah as his wife.

Abraham took another wife after Sarah died, and her name was Keturah.

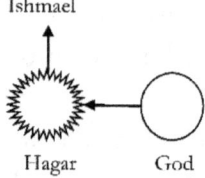

Abraham and Keturah's children's names are Zimran, Jokshan, Medan, Midian, Ishbak, and Shuah.

But "Abraham gave all that he had unto Isaac. But unto the sons of the concubines, which Abraham had, Abraham gave gifts, and sent them away from Isaac his son, while he yet lived, eastward, unto the east country" (Genesis 25:5, 6). Abraham lived to be one hundred seventy-five years and died. His sons Isaac and Ishmael buried him in a cave. Abraham was buried with Sarah in the field which Abraham purchased from the sons of Heth (Genesis 25:10).

Abraham, Isaac, Jacob, and Their Families

Isaac was placed in charge of the family property and possessions. It was Isaac's responsibility to share with Ishmael and his other half-brothers and half-sisters that which he had received from Abraham, his father. Isaac was not responsible for the children of Abraham's concubines.

Next, God transferred his covenant to Isaac, Abraham's son: his next generation. God said to Isaac, "And I will make thy seed to multiply as the stars of heaven, and will give unto thy seed all of these countries; and in thy seed all the nations of the earth be blessed; Because that Abraham obeyed my voice, and kept my charge, my commandments, my statutes, and my laws" (Genesis 26:4, 5). God trusted Isaac to carry on His plan.

My mother, like Hagar, was the head of her household. She never divorced my father because she knew that he would do the same thing with another woman. My mother freed him so that he could go back to the children of his first marriage and to save her life. She worked hard to raise, clothe, shelter, and feed five small children. Despite the fact that my mother never divorced my father, my father did marry again and then got divorced three years later.

My mother saw a vision after she left my father and she was alone with us. In her vision, she saw a golden throne with stairs leading up to it. The throne was empty. I firmly believe that this is the throne that the Lord has prepared for her. Perhaps she will be judging the decisions that some women in adulterous situations have made. I do not know for sure, but I do know that my mother walked with God. I know that a great disciple and friend of Christ is with her heavenly Father. I grew up in a healthier home than my husband did because my mother loved us and she loved God. She will forever be my hero.

My husband's father's second wife was also the head of the household, like Hagar and my mother, even though my husband's father was present. She ruled the household and made decisions that profoundly affected my husband and his father. Her children are the children of man. If my husband's father had sent her and her three children on their way, this woman

The Step-Father's Step-Son

would have grown to rely on and trust in God. My husband's father may have become a son of God himself for doing such a brave thing.

My husband's father never took a stand for the son of his first marriage. This enabled the step-mother to separate father and son. She successfully replaced my husband, and everything that ever could have been my husband's and my sons' she took and gave to her children and grandchildren. In this way, she successfully separated my husband from his father and my sons from their grandfather. She wanted everything for herself. She took everything that she could from my husband and our children's children. My husband's father gave him a pair of house shoes that he wore.

Each year, approximately 104 boy babies are born for every 100 girl babies. There is one male for every female. This woman did not have to take my husband's father and my sons' grandfather away. There were plenty of other men out there that would have been more than willing to be her husband.

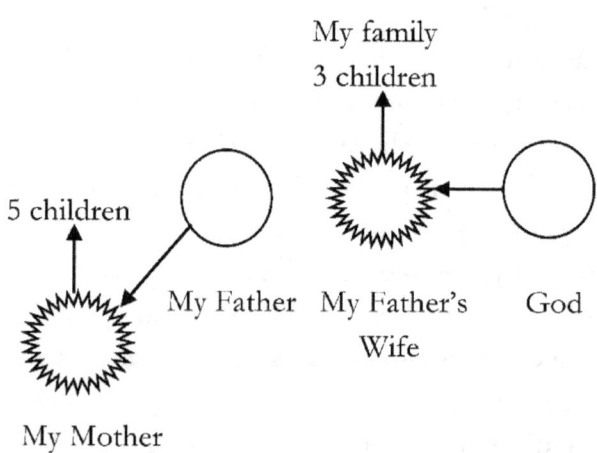

My father was my mother's second husband. My mother's first husband used her like a hired hand. She worked the cows down on the coast of Texas. A hurricane hit the coast of Texas, and she was out there trying to round up the herd. She roped a cow and was drug among tree stumps and other debris. Her hip was broken, and no doctors were available because they had gone to care for the troops fighting the war. Instead of a cast, she used a burlap feed sack to hold her broken bones together until they could heal.

When she became pregnant, her husband set up an appointment with a doctor. The doctor gave her a shot, and she quickly aborted the child that she was carrying. The one thing that my mother wanted more than anything else was children. My father gave her five children to love. She loved us despite our poverty and the hardships that she endured for us. My father, her second husband, told her that we were not his children. Well, it is true that the children of the second family will look different from the children of the first family because they have a different mother. But we were definitely his children.

My father did realize, after she left him, what he had lost. He returned to beat the windshield out of her car and to damage other things. This is ironic because my husband's father did the same thing to their family car. My mother had property and money when she married my father, but it soon evaporated. She bought a business for him, but he let it go to ruin. (My father's mother died when he was very young, and his father had given him away to family members. It is very likely that his father abandoned him for another woman.) My mother lived in fear that he would return until he died of complications associated with prolonged alcoholism. My father did not pay child support, and my mother did not go on welfare. My mother did accept rice, milk, cheese, and other food items from the U.S. Department of Agriculture. Until her death, she remained faithful to our family, our future generations, and to God.

Now, let's examine Isaac's life a little more closely to see if we can learn something.

Isaac took Rebekah for his wife when he was forty years old (Genesis 25:20). She was barren and could not bear a child, so Isaac asked God to help them. She conceived and gave birth to twins. God told her that two nations were inside her womb and that the older son's children would serve the younger son's children. Esau was born first and was very hairy.

The second twin was Jacob, who would become a plain, ordinary man that dwelled in tents. Esau became a cunning hunter. Isaac loved Esau; Rebekah loved Jacob.

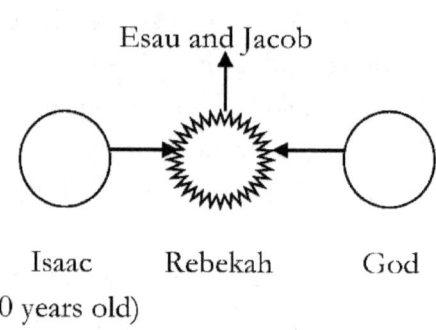

Isaac's family

Esau and Jacob

Isaac   Rebekah   God
(60 years old)

After the boys grew up, Esau had been in the wilderness hunting and was very hungry. Jacob offered him some of the food that he was cooking—for a price. He wanted Esau's birthright. Esau thought that he was so hungry he would die, so he agreed to let Jacob have his birthright. He simply could not wait a little longer without food. He sold his birthright for a meal! He ate bread and lentil soup. Esau regretted his decision later, but he had given Jacob his word.

Isaac faced a situation similar to that of his father. Rebekah was very pretty. There was a famine, and Isaac took his family to the land of Gerar ruled by King Abimelech. The men noticed Rebekah's beauty, and when they asked Isaac about her, he told them that she was his sister so that they would not kill him. They had been in the land of Gerar for quite some time when King Abimelech looked out his window and saw Isaac playing with his wife. Abimelech called Isaac to him, and Isaac explained that he had to do this "lest he die for her." Abimelech expressed concern that one of his men might have gone in to have intercourse with her (Genesis 26:10). Then, the king told all of the men that if they touched her, they would be

Abraham, Isaac, Jacob, and Their Families

killed. Isaac's flocks and herds multiplied, and it came time to leave the land because men dumped earth into the wells that his father's men had dug. Esau and Jacob matured. Esau became a cunning hunter, and Jacob was a plain man that dwelt in tents.

Rebekah expressly told Isaac that she did not want Jacob to take a wife of the daughters of Heth. She said in Genesis 27:46, "I am weary of my life because of the daughters of Heth: if Jacob take a wife of the daughters of Heth, such as these *which are* of the daughters of the land, what good shall my life do me?" Then, Isaac blessed Jacob and told him not to take a wife of the daughters of Canaan. He asked him to take a wife of the daughters of Rebekah's brother, Laban.

Jacob left his land and his family in order to escape the wrath of Esau over the birthright issue. He came to a well of water and Rachel, the daughter of Laban, his mother's brother, appeared with sheep. She kept her father's sheep, so she was a shepherd. Jacob rolled the stone from the top of the well and watered Laban's sheep for her (Genesis 29). Rachel hurried home to tell her father that Jacob had come. Laban ran to Jacob, hugged him, and kissed him. Jacob had lived with Laban and his family for one month when Laban suggested that Jacob work for him. Jacob loved Rachel, his youngest daughter, and told Laban that he would serve him for seven years for Rachel. He loved Rachel so much that seven years of work seemed to be only a few days (Genesis 29:20).

Laban had two daughters. The older was Leah, and she was tender eyed, but Rachel was beautiful. Jacob came to Laban and told him that his seven years of labor were completed and said unto Laban, "Give *me* my wife" (Genesis 29:21). Laban hosted a great feast, and that night he took Leah, his oldest daughter, and brought her to Jacob. Jacob went to her, believing that she was Rachel. Laban also gave Leah a handmaid whose name was Zilpah. In the morning, Jacob awoke and found Leah in bed with him. He went to Laban and asked him how he could have done this to him since he had made it clear that he had been working all of these years for Rachel. Laban explained, "It must not be so done in our country, to give the younger before the firstborn" (Genesis 29:26). Laban asked him to give Leah one week, and then he could have Rachel if he worked for him for another seven years.

He waited one week, and then Laban gave Rachel to Jacob. Jacob loved Rachel more than Leah, and he worked another seven years. Laban also gave Bilhah to Rachel as a handmaid.

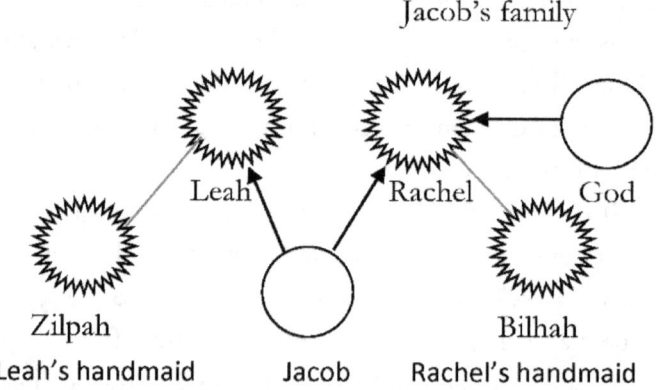

Jacob's family

Leah conceived a son and named him Reuben. She was hoping that finally Jacob would love her and leave Rachel since she bore him a son. Then, she bore another son and named him Simeon. She had a third son and named him Levi. Now, she was hoping, finally, that Jacob would move in with her and be joined with her. Jacob did not live with her and did not leave Rachel (Genesis 29:34). Leah bore another son and named him Judah. Then, she decided that she did not want to give birth to more children.

Abraham, Isaac, Jacob, and Their Families

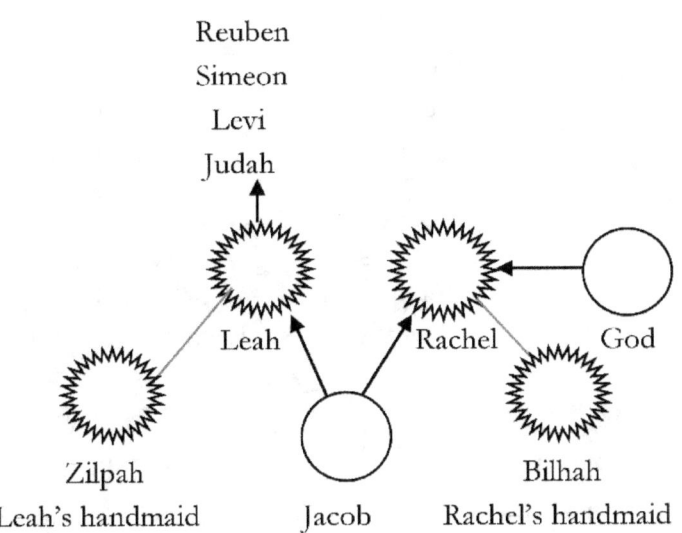

Rachel saw that she bore Jacob no children. She became jealous of Leah, her older sister. She told Jacob that she had to have a child or else she would die. Jacob was angry because he knew that he could not be the one that was keeping her from getting pregnant. Then, she asked Jacob to go to her handmaid, Bilhah, and take her as a wife. When it was time for her to give birth, Bilhah sat upon Rachel's knees so that she could have a child by her. Rachel named the child Dan. Then, Rachel's handmaid bore another child, and Rachel named him Naphtali. Rachel's envy toward her sister was minimized now that her handmaid had given birth to two children for her.

The Step-Father's Step-Son

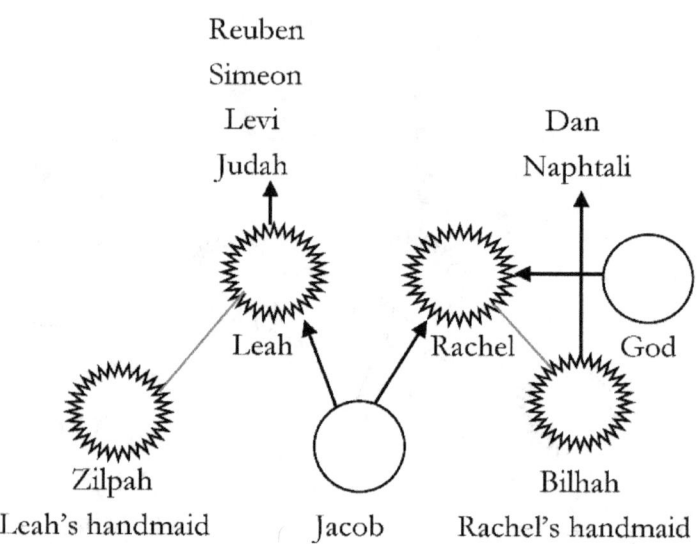

Jacob's family

Now, Leah decided to bring Zilpah into the picture and gave her handmaid to Jacob to wife. Zilpah gave birth to a son, and Leah named him Gad. Then, she gave birth to another son, and Leah named him Asher.

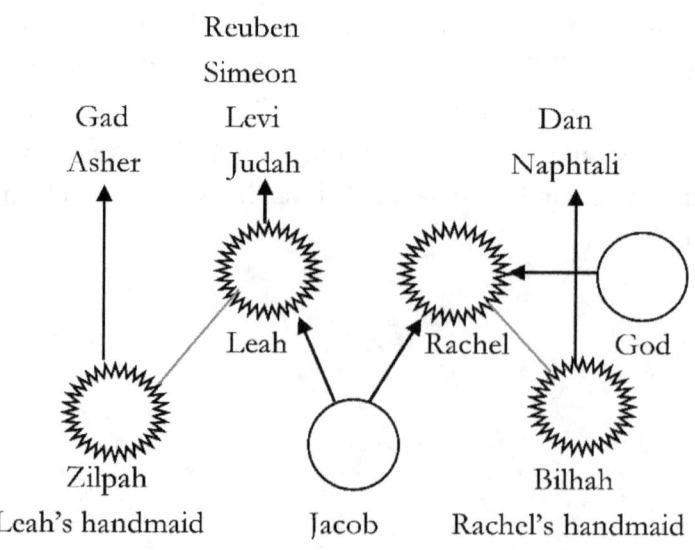

Abraham, Isaac, Jacob, and Their Families

Reuben, Leah's firstborn son, went out into the wheat field at the time of harvest and found some mandrakes growing. These plants were known as "love plants" because they were believed to have fertility powers, especially for those that were having trouble conceiving. When Rachel found out that Leah's son had found mandrakes, she asked Leah to give her some.

> And she said unto her, *Is it* a small matter that thou hast taken my husband? and wouldest thou take away my son's mandrakes also? And Rachel said, Therefore he shall lie with thee to night for thy son's mandrakes. And Jacob came out of the field in the evening, and Leah went out to meet him and said, Thou must come in unto me; for surely I have hired thee with my son's mandrakes. And he lay with her that night. (Genesis 30:15, 16)

She conceived another son and named him Issachar. Then, she conceived again, gave birth to another son, and named him Zebulun. For the last time, she conceived and gave birth to a daughter, and her name was Dinah. Can you imagine what it would have been like if Jacob had married this woman and abandoned Rachel? He would have been her servant for sure.

Now, Leah said, "God hath endued *with* me a good dowry, now will my husband dwell with me, because I have born him six sons" (Genesis 30:20). Jacob still did not live with her. He stayed with the woman that he loved from the first, and her name was Rachel! He never moved out and lived with Leah, his second wife. He kept his family intact.

There are women that will cheat a man when he is alone or when he is drunk. These women will think only of themselves and what they hope to gain by jumping in bed with this man. In Jacob's situation, it was Laban and Leah that both tried to cheat him and Rachel. But being a son of God, Jacob also accepted responsibility for Rachel's sister, Leah, but he never ever put her first in his family! He never let Leah separate his family. He kept his family intact. For this and other reasons, God

The Step-Father's Step-Son

changed his name to Israel. He proved himself over time to be a son of God. He kept his promise to Rachel. Rachel, his first love, would never have stayed with him if he had moved in with Leah permanently. She would have been heartbroken!

Jacob's family

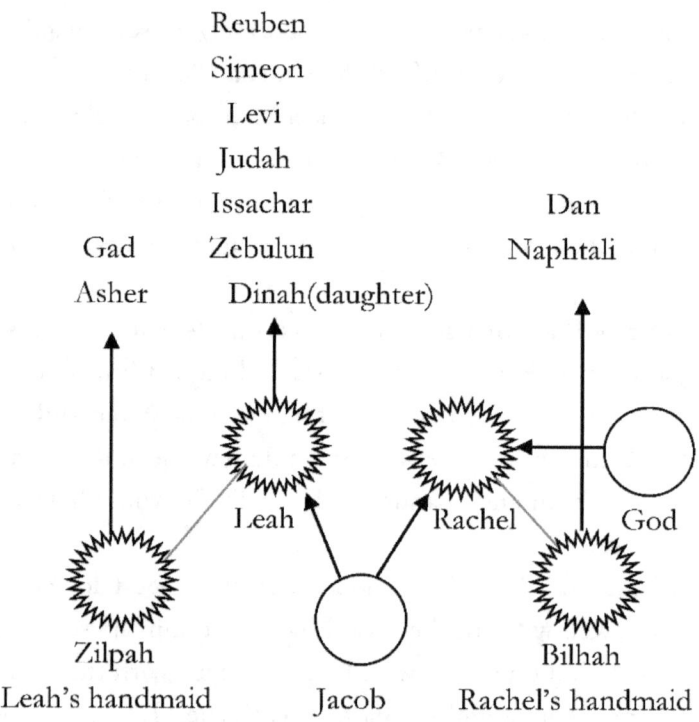

Abraham, Isaac, Jacob, and Their Families

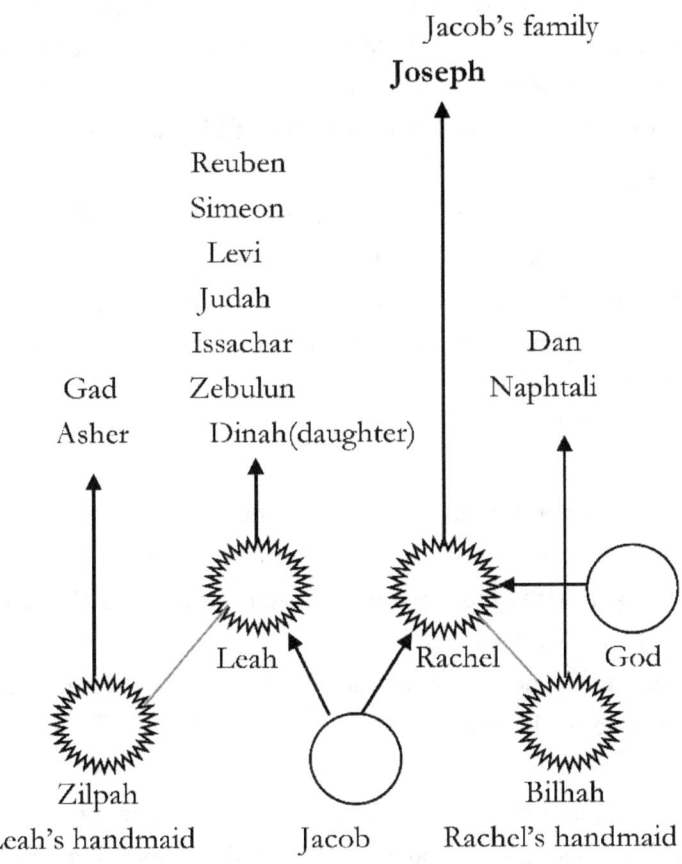

Then, Rachel became pregnant for the first time, gave birth to a son, and named him Joseph.

Now, Jacob went in to Laban and asked him to give him his wives and his children and let him go for his service was done. Jacob told him that when he came to work for him that Laban had little, but now Laban had a multitude of herds. Jacob told him that he needed something to provide for his family. Jacob told him that he would separate and keep the speckled and spotted cows, goats, and sheep, and they would be his. Any animal that had white mixed in with color was his. His herd and flock increased exceedingly compared to Laban's.

The Step-Father's Step-Son

Jacob heard Laban's sons talking. They were unhappy because Jacob was taking everything that belonged to their father. It was true that Jacob was taking some of the herd, but he was not taking everything. Jacob had managed the herd himself, and because of his management, the herds grew in size.

He called Rachel and Leah into the field to look at his flock. He told them about their father's anger toward him. Jacob said, "[Y]e know that with all my power I have served your father. And your father hath deceived me, and changed my wages ten times; but God suffered him not to hurt me" (Genesis 31:6, 7).

Then, Rachel and Leah said,

> *Is there* yet any portion or inheritance for us in our father's house? Are we not counted of him strangers? for he hath sold us, and hath quite devoured also our money. For all the riches which God hath taken from our father, that *is* ours, and our children's; now then, whatsoever God hath said unto thee, do. (Genesis 31:14–16)

Women were heirs in those days, too. It was the firstborn son that was given the responsibility of managing the family property for the benefit of all. Laban's sons must not have seen the opportunity at their father's house or their father was too possessive of the little that he had to involve his owns sons in his occupation. Either way, Jacob worked as a hired hand. But Jacob was more than a hired hand because he had two of Laban's daughters as his wives. When Jacob and his family left Laban, no one said goodbye. They mounted camels and headed to the land of Canaan, his father's homeland, with all of his cattle and sheep.

Just as Laban had had a problem with Jacob taking cattle and sheep, so, too, did Laban have difficulty in letting his daughters leave. Genesis 31:26 says, "And Laban said to Jacob, What hast thou done, that thou hast stolen away unawares to me, and carried away my daughters, as captives *taken* with the sword?"

Jacob answered him and said,

> Thus have I been twenty years in thy house; I served thee fourteen years for thy two daughters, and six years for thy cattle: and thou hast changed my wages ten times. Except the God of my father, the God of Abraham, and the fear of Isaac, had been with me, surely thou hadst sent me away now empty. (Genesis 31:41, 42)

Based on the things that Laban said, I get the feeling that he grew up in a home where things were taken from him as a child. This reminds me of my husband's family that took everything that was his and gave to it his step-parents and their children. This unfortunate situation leaves long-lasting scars that will last into adulthood and even to the grave. This will affect this man's children and also his wife. It is something that should never be permitted, but it is common practice in this country, just as it was thousands of years ago. Our sons and daughters are a threat to the other woman and the other man. When a man leaves his wife for another woman, he divorces his children also, especially his son.

And Laban said to Jacob,

> If thou shalt afflict my daughters, or if thou shalt take *other* wives beside my daughters, no man *is* with us; see, God *is* witness betwixt me and thee. . . . And early in the morning Laban rose up, and kissed his sons and his daughters, and blessed them: and Laban departed, and returned unto his place. (Genesis 31:50, 55)

Laban was afraid that Jacob would take other wives, most likely as his father had taken other wives. Laban knew how damaging this could be to a family because he most likely experienced it as a child. He did not want Jacob to do what his father or other men that he had known had done.

In Canaan, Jacob's children grew up. Dinah, Jacob and Leah's daughter, went out to see the daughters of the land. And when Shechem the son of Hamor the Hivite, prince of the country, saw her, he took her, and lay with her, and defiled her. And his soul clave unto Dinah, the daughter of Jacob, and he loved the damsel, and spake kindly unto the damsel. And Shechem spake unto his father Hamor, saying, Get me this damsel to wife. And Jacob heard that he had defiled Dinah his daughter: now his sons were with his cattle in the field: and Jacob held his peace until they were come. And Hamor the father of Shechem went out to Jacob to talk with him. The sons of Jacob came out of the field when they heard *it*: and the men were grieved." (Genesis 34:1–7)

Shechem had done something that he should not have done. Hamor told them, "The soul of my son Shechem longeth for your daughter. I pray you give her him to wife." He suggested that they marry into each other's family. "[G]ive your daughters unto us, and take our daughters unto you. And ye shall dwell with us," trade with us, and get your possessions from us (Genesis 34:9, 10).

He told them if they wanted a dowry, he would give it.

> And the sons of Jacob answered Shechem and Hamor his father deceitfully, and said, because he had defiled Dinah their sister: And they said unto them, We cannot do this thing, to give our sister to one that is uncircumcised; for that *were* a reproach unto us: But in this will we consent unto you: If ye will be as we *be*, that every male of you be circumcised; Then we will give our daughters unto you, and we will take your daughters to us, and we will dwell with you, and we will become one people. But if ye will not hearken unto us, to be circumcised; then we will take our daughter, and we will be gone. And their words pleased Hamor, and Shechem Hamor's son. And the young

man deferred not to do the thing, because he had delight in Jacob's daughter: and he was more honorable than all the house of his father. (Genesis 34:13–19)

When Hamor and Shechem went out to meet Jacob, they came upon Jacob's sons first. These sons, Dinah's brothers, spoke to Hamor and Shechem. They spoke for their father in their father's absence. They lied to these men. They should have consulted their father and Dinah first, but instead, they took matters into their own hands. These sons were Jacob's children with his second wife, Leah, and Dinah was their sister. They were taking a stand for their family! These sons seemed to feel as though Jacob did not love them because Jacob lived with Rachel and not Leah, their mother. They did not respect Jacob, Jacob's family, or their position within the family. These sons wanted everything for themselves.

This is a very good example of why a man should have only one wife. With closer examination of Abraham, Isaac, and Jacob's families, it is clear that there is conflict when a man takes more than one wife. It complicates family matters. But there are times when situations arise where another woman does become involved with the family. When this happens, decisions must be made that protect the whole family and not the part. Like Leah, these women will want to move in and take over the family for themselves and for their children. This is what my husband's step-mother did. This must never ever be permitted to happen. And when it does happen, a man is involved with this woman and not a son of God.

And so, based upon the deceitful words of Jacob's sons with Leah, "Hamor and Shechem his son came unto the gate of their city," and said to the people,

> These men *are* peaceable with us; therefore let them dwell in the land, and trade therein; for the land, behold, *it is* large enough for them; let us take their daughters to us for wives, and let us give them our daughters. Only herein will the men consent unto . . .

them, and they will dwell with us. And unto Hamor and unto Shechem his son hearkened all that went out of the gate of his city; and every male was circumcised. (Genesis 34:21–24)

On the third day, when all of the men were sore from pain, Simeon and Levi, Dinah's brothers, came into the city and killed all of the males, including Hamor and Shechem, with a sword. Finally, after Hamor and Shechem were dead, they took their sister and left. They took the sheep, oxen, asses, and grain from their fields. Also, they took the wives of the dead men captive.

And Jacob said to Simeon and Levi, Ye have troubled me to make me to stink among the inhabitants of the land, among the Canaanites and the Perizzites: and I *being* few in number, they shall gather themselves together against me, and slay me; and I shall be destroyed, I and my house. And they said, Should we deal with our sister as with an harlot? (Genesis 34:30, 31)

Jacob's sons chose to kill Shechem. If they had treated Dinah as a harlot, they most likely would have burned her at the stake. It would not have mattered to them if she was pregnant or not. Either Shechem or Dinah had to die according to the laws of their lords—they chose to kill Shechem. This scenario is much like the one we have in this country today. A true marriage is not respected or recognized without a ceremony, a ring, a marriage license, and a minister. Shechem and Dinah both bypassed the traditions of the day. They skipped the pomp and circumstance and became man and wife by themselves with God.

Jacob's sons took matters into their own hands and did not consult their father. They followed the laws of the land. It may have been that Dinah loved Shechem as much as Shechem loved her. We will never know how Dinah felt because no one recorded anything concerning her side of the story. We do know that she stayed with Shechem instead of returning home to her father and her brothers. Jacob did talk about how his sons Simeon

Abraham, Isaac, Jacob, and Their Families

and Levi had made him to "stink," and then later, upon his death bed, he gave more revealing information.

Shechem accepted responsibility for what he had done and tried to make it right with Jacob's sons. They all were circumcised so that they could be like Dinah's family. This is love at its best. Jacob's sons obviously thought of women as property, much as Laban considered his daughters and their children property. Jacob acted more as a guardian of the family rather than as a dictator. His sons were deceitful and murdered these men, and Jacob was not pleased. These same brothers that wanted to kill Joseph killed Shechem. They also killed the other men along with him.

There was no adultery in Jacob's family. He never abandoned Rachel to move in with Leah or any of the handmaids. He did not cheat on Rachel. Had it not been for Laban, he most likely only would have had one wife—Rachel—like his father Isaac. But his sons with Leah became the victims of confusion. Their father did not live with their mother, Leah. Leah expressed her desire for Jacob to come and live with her many times, but he never did. Laban caused a lot of problems for Jacob, Shechem, Hamor, and many others. These sons of Leah wanted to be first in the family. Shechem, Dinah, Hamor, and others paid the price.

Following this event, at God's request, Jacob moved his family and all that he had to Bethel. But before they left, he asked them to get rid of their strange gods, bathe, and change their clothes. "And they gave unto Jacob all the strange gods which *were* in their hand, and *all their* earrings which *were* in their ears; and Jacob hid them under the oak which *was* by Shechem" (Genesis 35:4).

As they traveled, no one challenged them because they were afraid of the sons of Jacob.

> And God appeared to Jacob again . . . and said unto him, Thy name *is* Jacob: thy name shall not be called any more Jacob, but Israel shall be thy name: and he called his name Israel. And God said unto him, I *am* God Almighty: be fruitful and

The Step-Father's Step-Son

multiply; a nation and a company of nations shall be of thee, and kings shall come out of thy loins; And the land which I gave Abraham and Isaac, to thee I will give it, and to thy seed after thee will I give the land. (Genesis 35:9–12)

As they left Bethel and were headed for Ephrath (Bethlehem), Rachel was in hard labor. She died during this journey. Before Rachel died, she named her second son Benoni, "but his father called him Benjamin" (Genesis 35:18).

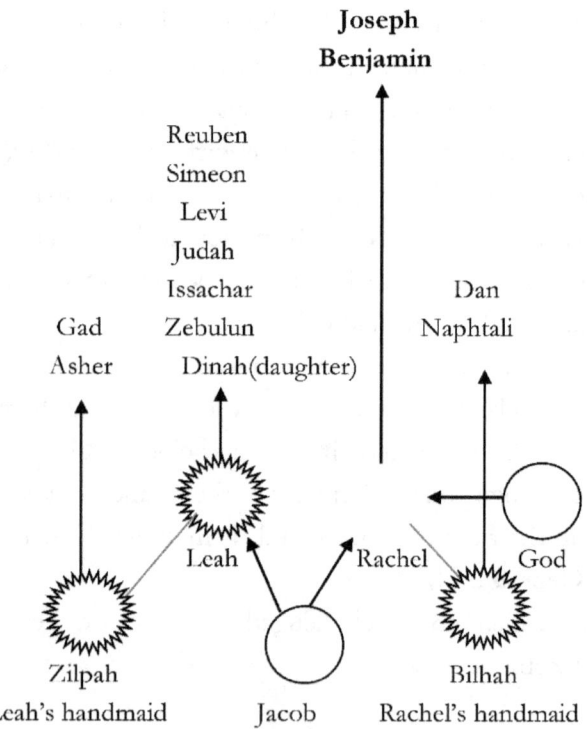

Israel journeyed with his family to Edar and erected his tent there. Reuben, Israel's oldest son with Leah, went and lay with Bilhah, one of his father's concubines, and Israel found out about it. It is obvious that the children of the second family did not love or respect their father. Their father refused to move in with their mother. Then, Isaac, Jacob's father, died at the age of one hundred eighty years, and Esau and Jacob buried him in Mamre.

> And Jacob dwelt in the land wherein his father was a stranger, in the land of Canaan. These *are* the generations of Jacob. Joseph, *being* seventeen years old, was feeding the flock with his brothers; and the lad *was* with the sons of Bilhah, and with the sons of Zilpah, his father's wives; and Joseph brought unto his father their evil report. (Genesis 37:1, 2)

My husband's father would not have been receptive to any complaints that my husband would have had regarding his half-brothers and half-sisters. My husband's father was busy trying to protect what he thought of as "his family." My husband was not a concern of his. Jacob did care about what Joseph said, though. I feel certain that someone would have wanted to kill my husband, too. He was hated so much that they took almost everything. The only thing that stopped them from getting it all was a piece of paper. On my husband's father's side, it was because of a piece of paper that my husband's half-sisters and half-brother got it all. If my husband had been the heir, as he should have been, they most likely would have fought him. Without his father and mother's support, they would most likely have killed him in some way. Since the family was split as it was, there was no one that could have protected my husband from the greed and selfishness.

> Now Israel loved Joseph more than all his children . . . and he made him a coat of *many* colours. And when his brethren saw that their father loved him more than all his brethren, they hated him, and could not speak peaceably unto him." Joseph dreamed a dream, and his brothers hated him for that too. In that dream, "We *were* binding sheaves in the field, and, lo, my

sheaf arose, and also stood upright; and, behold, your sheaves stood round about, and made obeisance to my sheaf. And his brethren said to him, Shalt thou indeed . . . have dominion over us? And they hated him yet the more for his dreams, and for his words." Then he dreamed another dream. His father's response was to ask, "What *is* this dream that thou hast dreamed? Shall I and thy mother and thy brothers indeed come to bow down ourselves to thee to the earth?" His brothers were jealous. They left to feed their father's flock in Shechem. . . . Later Jacob said to him, "Go, I pray thee, see whether it be well with thy brethren, and well with the flocks; and bring me word again." (Genesis 37:3–14)

Joseph, who was seventeen years old, went out and was wandering in a field when a man found him. Joseph told him that he was looking for his brothers that were shepherding the sheep. The man told him that they had gone to Dothan. As Joseph approached the flock, his brothers came up with a plan to kill him. They joked and said, "Behold, this dreamer cometh" (Genesis 37:19). They were planning to kill him and cast his body into a pit. Reuben, Leah's firstborn son, heard about their plans to kill Joseph. "Let us not kill him. And Reuben said unto them, Shed no blood, *but* cast him into this pit that *is* in the wilderness, and lay no hand upon him; that he might rid him out of their hands to deliver him to his father again" (Genesis 37:21, 22).

When Joseph arrived, they took his coat of many colors and cast him into a pit that had no water. As Joseph stood in the pit, they "sat down to eat bread" (Genesis 37:25). While they were eating, they saw from afar a company of men coming their way with camels. These men were hauling spice, balm, and myrrh to Egypt. Judah, one of Leah's sons, said, "What profit *is it* if we slay our brother, and conceal his blood? Come, and let us sell him to the Ishmeelites, and let not our hand be upon him; for he *is* our brother *and* our flesh" (Genesis 37:26, 27).

Abraham, Isaac, Jacob, and Their Families

The Midianites arrived first and "lifted up Joseph out of the pit, and sold him to the Ishmeelites for twenty *pieces* of silver" (Genesis 37:28). The Ishmeelites are the ones that took Joseph to Egypt.

Reuben returned to the pit, but Joseph was gone. They took Joseph's coat of many colors and dipped it in the blood of a kid goat that they had killed. They took the coat and showed it to their father.

Joseph's half-brothers hated him. Joseph was outnumbered much like my husband was outnumbered on his mother's side and his father's side. The one thing that Jacob did that my husband's father did not do is that he did not abandon Joseph for Reuben, Leah's firstborn son. My husband's father abandoned him for the firstborn daughter of his second wife.

Israel cried out for his son and mourned his death. It was later that he found that his firstborn son with Rachel was alive. The rest of Joseph's story can be found in the book of Genesis. His brothers did indeed bow down to him in Egypt!

As the story progresses, Judah left his brothers to look for a wife. He took Shuah and went in unto her, and she conceived and later delivered a child. Judah called him Er. Onan was born into Judah and Shuah's family next, then Shelah. When Er was mature, Judah brought Tamar to be his wife. The Bible tells us that Er was wicked and that "the Lord slew him" (Genesis 38:7). Judah then told his second son, Onan, to go to Er's wife, marry her, and give her a child for Er, his deceased brother. Onan went in and lay with her, but he ejaculated onto the ground because he did not want to give away his child as his brother's. We are told that God also slew Onan.

Then, Judah came up with a plan so that Tamar's wish could be fulfilled. He told his daughter-in-law, "Remain a widow at thy father's house, till Shelah my son be grown: for he said, Lest peradventure he die also, as his brethren did" (Genesis 38:11). So, Tamar went and lived at her father's house. While she lived there, Judah's daughter died. It does not say how she died; all we know is that she also died. Judah left his house to comfort himself and went out alone to his sheepshearers. He most likely left his wife, Shuah, to mourn for her daughter alone. (It is written that God

The Step-Father's Step-Son

killed all of them. We do not know how they died.) We will never know the whole story. And as many men do today, they will secretly take another woman when they are alone. Judah was no exception. He took advantage of a prostitute, or so he thought.

Tamar, his daughter-in-law, heard that her father-in-law was going to Timnath to shear sheep. She took off her widow's mourning clothes, secured her clothing tightly so that her female figure was more prominent, put on a veil as harlots did in those days, and sat out in the open. She knew that Judah, her father-in-law, had not kept his promise to give her to his youngest son, Shelah, who was grown-up now. She was going to find her own way to get pregnant. Shelah most likely did not want to risk a relationship with her because he just might die also, like his brothers and sister did.

Judah saw her and asked to have intercourse with her. She inquired about how she would be paid for her services. He told her that he would give her a young kid goat from his flock. She asked for proof that he would indeed send the kid goat. She asked for his signet (It most likely was a finger ring with a seal that was used as a signature stamp.), his bracelets and his staff. Judah agreed and gave her all of those things so that he could sleep with her. So Judah had intercourse with her and she became pregnant that day. She put on the clothes of widowhood that she had been wearing and went on her way. As payment, Judah sent the kid goat, but the men could not find the harlot.

Three months later, it was heard around town that Tamar was pregnant. through whoredom. Judah's response was, "Bring her forth, and let her be burnt." When she was brought for burning, she explained that she was pregnant by the man to whom the signet, bracelets, and staff belong.

And Judah acknowledged *them*, and said, She hath been more righteous than I; because that I gave her not to Shelah my son. And he knew her again no more. (Genesis 38:16–26)Jesus said in Matthew 21:31, "Verily I say unto you, That the publicans and the harlots go into the kingdom of God before you." This scripture puts a greater burden of responsibility on the man that cheats a woman and her children by paying for intercourse.

Abraham, Isaac, Jacob, and Their Families

In this country, we put the woman that is involved with prostitution into jail, but the man seldom or never goes to jail. The man is the one that gets to decide where he puts his penis. The woman that he cheats with very well may end up in heaven before he does!

As we can see from the scripture, Judah's family structure was exactly as ours is today. They had daughter-in-laws and father-in-laws. Marriage and family were based upon laws—laws that made it possible to dissolve relationships and eliminate family members. God's laws never mention remarriage after divorce. We also know that the woman and child were held responsible if conception occurred outside of "marriage" because Judah suggested that Tamar be burned at the stake.

Obviously, the man was innocent because there was no mention of punishment for Judah for impregnating his daughter-in-law. Laws are similar in this country today. We do not burn women at the stake, but we do hold them accountable for the decisions that a man makes. We have abortion, adoption, and abandonment to eliminate the child, especially since "marriage" never occurred. The man has little or no responsibility for the woman that he impregnated outside of "marriage." He can just ejaculate and move on. This man thinks that he is god.

As we can see from the family stories of Abraham, Isaac, and Jacob, a simple family is much easier to manage than a complex family. Isaac was the only one of the three that had just one wife. There were disagreements between Jacob and Esau, his twin sons, but in the end, they grew very close. Abraham had to eliminate Hagar, his second wife, from the family because she wanted to split his family up. Fortunately, he never permitted this to happen. Jacob was the one with the most complex family of all, but he did a very good job of managing his family until his sons with Leah grew up and were outside of his control. His family would have been much simpler if Laban had not done what he did; unfortunately, that can never be undone. It was his children, though, that grew up in confusion. Leah never came to respect her sister's primary position within the family, and her children gave no respect to Rachel's first born son, Joseph. Even worse, these sons did not respect their own father, Jacob.

As we can see, there are many problems that come out of these complex relationships. The most important lesson of all is that the primary members of the family cannot and must not be eliminated. If this happens, chaos will ensue.

The Lost Children of the House of Israel

Jesus sent His twelve disciples forth, "and commanded them saying, Go not into the way of the Gentiles, and into *any* city of the Samaritans enter ye not: But go rather to the lost sheep of the house of Israel" (Matthew 10:5, 6).

"I am not sent but unto the lost sheep of the house of Israel" (Matthew 15:24).

Jesus was referring to Israel's (Jacob's) children as the lost sheep. He called them "lost sheep" because they had abandoned the covenant that God had made with Abraham, Isaac, and Jacob. The Lord said, "For I know him, that he will command his children and his household after him, and they shall keep the way of the LORD, to do justice and judgment, that the Lord may bring upon Abraham that which he hath spoken of him" (Genesis 18:19).

In order to better understand the laws about family that we have today, we need to go back in time to look more closely at the history of those laws and why the laws were written by men. In the beginning, divorce was not so—Jesus said so Himself. No laws governed "the family" in the beginning. Sons of God respected their family members.

In the beginning, God noticed that "Adam" was alone and did not have a helpmeet. If we reproduced during that time, which most likely we did, there was no one there to help us with the children. We would have been breastfeeding and caring for a child all by ourselves. But at that time, God provided everything that we needed, but we were still alone because we did not have a physical partner.

Then, there was Noah, his wife, their three sons, and their wives. Each of Noah's three sons only had one wife each. "Noah was a just man *and* perfect in his generations, *and* Noah walked with God (Genesis 6:9). We know that God was very pleased with Noah, his three sons, and the way they respected God's family. This family example that God chose illustrates just how much a man is forgiven by God if he stays with his first wife and first children. Through Noah and his wife, we know that God considered the man and his first wife as the nucleus of the family (Genesis 6:8, 9).

Noah's youngest son came into his father's tent and found him naked on the floor. Noah cursed his youngest son for seeing him naked and not keeping it a secret. One of Noah's commandments was that no one was supposed to see their father naked. Noah did not accept responsibility for his own nakedness. He blamed his own son for seeing him naked and telling his brothers instead of keeping it a secret.

Noah must have been born into a family where there was a lot of adultery. He drank like many of our sons that have fathers that abandoned them for another woman. But despite his drunkenness, God still chose him and his sons as examples for all of us. He stayed with his first wife and kept his family intact.

Noah's FAMILY

Ham
Shem
Japheth

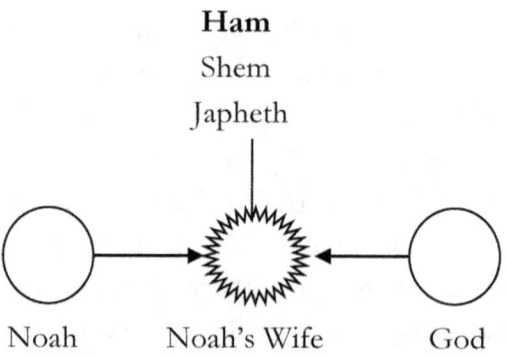

Noah   Noah's Wife   God

Then later, Moses had to permit divorce or separation in order to protect the lives of battered and abused family members because of the hardness of man's heart (Matthew 19:8). Our sons' hearts are hardened when their fathers abandon them for another woman. It is because of adultery that this happens.

Our next example of family is Abraham (Abram) and Sarah (Sarai). There are two specific scriptures that give us valuable information about how their father's family was structured at this time:

> And Terah took Abram his son, and Lot the son of Haran his son's son, and <u>Sarai, his daughter in law,</u> his son Abram's wife, and they went forth with them from Ur of the Chaldees, to go into the land of Canaan; and they came unto Haran, and dwelt there. (Genesis 11:31)

> And Abimelech said unto Abraham, What sawest thou, that thou hast done this thing? And Abraham said, Because I thought, Surely the fear of God *is* not in this place; and they will slay me for my wife's sake. And yet indeed <u>*she is* my sister; she *is* the daughter of my father, but not the daughter of my mother;</u> and she became my wife. (Genesis 20:10–12)

God took Abraham from the land of his father's family for a reason. This is the first time that it is recorded that family positions were based upon a law. But the unique thing here is that Sarai was Terah's daughter, but he still referred to her as his daughter-in-law. His second wife was most likely referred to as his wife-in-law.

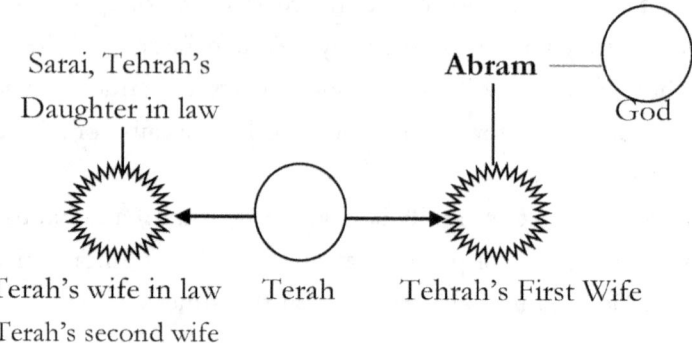

Tehrah's marriage to his second wife was based upon a law, a man's law. Also, Terah's first wife might have been considered a central figure in the family. The "in-law" terminology most likely indicated that, through a law, the wife-in-law (the second wife) and her children could be divorced and forced to leave the family if her presence caused too many problems for the nuclear family to bear. Hagar would be a good example of this scenario.

The wife-in-law legal terminology could also have meant that the man had divorced his first wife and married for a second time. It was now that the second wife would have been referred to as wife-in-law to distinguish between his first marriage and his second marriage and his children with his first wife and the children of his second wife. In our country today, there is no way of knowing how many times that someone has been married or whether the man is living with his first wife, second wife, or third wife.

Once again, we can see the significance of the firstborn children of the first wife. Abraham, his son Isaac, and Isaac's son Jacob (Jacob and Esau were twins, but Esau gave up his birthright for a meal) are further examples of family that God has given to us. It is not considered incest for a child to marry his or her half-brother or half-sister on his or her father's side. If God had objected, He would never have used Abram and Sarai as examples. But we must remember that it was his father's daughter with his second wife that he took for his own wife. If a woman has children with more than one man—which should never happen but does—these children cannot ever marry. This would be "true incest" because the same mother gave them life and raised them. Abram and Sarai were born into two separate families within one family but with the same father. Furthermore, Terah's marriage to his second wife was a marriage based upon adultery because we are not supposed to marry for a second time.

When Sarah died, Abraham took Keturah as his wife, and she obviously could not fill Abraham's empty heart for Sarah because Abraham had many concubines. Abraham never abandoned Isaac for Keturah. Keturah was secondary to the main family nucleus, which remained in place even after Sarah died.

Never did Abraham refer to Rebekah, his son Isaac's wife, as daughter-in-law. None of Jacob's sons' wives were ever referred to as daughters-in-law. They were referred to as Jacob's sons' wives. A true marriage is not and never can be based upon a man's law and a piece of paper as it is today (Genesis 46:26).

Here are some family rules that can be learned from these stories:

- A man is never supposed to put his penis into the vagina of another man's wife. That includes the vagina of a divorced woman.
- Another woman, such as Hagar, is never ever to be permitted to separate the members of the nuclear family, the first wife and first husband! If this woman ever tries to do this, she is supposed to be sent away with nothing but bread and water. Her child and/or children can come back to the nuclear family, but she cannot. And when the children do come back, they come back second under the children of the first wife/family.
- A man is never supposed to secretly cheat on his wife by lusting after or having intercourse with someone else. New members can only be added to the family with the wife's consent and approval. Both the man and the woman may later regret their decision just as Abraham and Sarah did.

Jacob's family would never have been so complicated had it not been for Laban, the father of Rachel and Leah. He was also the brother of Rebekah, Isaac's wife. Jacob worked seven whole years for Rachel, but Laban gave him Leah first. Then, he worked seven more years for Rachel who was at his side. She was indeed his first wife, and Joseph is Jacob's firstborn son with his first wife.

It is the firstborn son of the first wife that has great significance in God's plan. This child is the cornerstone that holds the entire family together. This child will be the one to carry the family into the next generation in this physical world. A daughter is also a cornerstone, but her role within the family is different. Her job is not to provide for the physical needs of the family to the same degree as a man. She is the one that will give birth to our grandchildren. She is the vine, and children come from her.

Jacob's family is an excellent example of the confusion that is created for our children when we have relationships with multiple people within a family. A simple family structure is a lot easier to manage than a complex family structure with multiple families within the one family.

It is important to note in Jacob's family that all four of these families stayed intact and went together through time. This was only possible because Jacob kept his first wife and children primary. If he had replaced Rachel with Leah, he would have split his family asunder.

Before Jacob died, he had some important messages for all twelve of his sons. Here is what he said. Pay close attention to what he told Judah.

> And Jacob called unto his sons, and said, Gather yourselves together, that I may tell you *that* which shall befall you in the last days. Gather yourselves together, and hear, ye sons of Jacob; and hearken unto Israel your father. Reuben, thou *art* my firstborn, my might, and the beginning of my strength, the excellency of dignity, and the excellency of power: Unstable as water, thou shalt not excel; because thou wentest up to thy father's bed; then defiledst thou *it*: he went up to my couch. Simeon and Levi

are brethren; instruments of cruelty *are in* their habitations. O my soul, come not thou into their secret; unto their assembly, mine honour, be not thou united: for in their anger they slew a man, and in their selfwill they digged down a wall. Cursed *be* their anger, for *it was* fierce; and their wrath, for it was cruel: I will divide them in Jacob, and scatter them in Israel. Judah, thou *art he* whom thy brethren shall praise: thy hand *shall be* in the neck of thine enemies; thy father's children shall bow down before thee. Judah *is* a lion's whelp: from the prey, my son, thou art gone up: he stooped down, he couched as a lion, and as an old lion; who shall rouse him up? The sceptre shall not depart from Judah, nor a lawgiver from between his feet, until Shiloh come; and unto him *shall* the gathering of people *be*. Binding his foal unto the vine, and his ass's colt unto the choice vine; he washed his garments in wine, and his clothes in the blood of grapes. His eyes *shall be* red with wine, and his teeth white with milk. Zebulun shall dwell at the haven of the sea; and he *shall be* for an haven of ships; and his border *shall be* unto Zidon. Issachar *is* a strong ass couching down between two burdens: And he saw that rest *was* good, and the land that *it was* pleasant; and bowed his shoulder to bear, and became a servant unto tribute. Dan shall judge his people, as one of the tribes of Israel. Dan shall be a serpent by the way, an adder in the path, that biteth the horse heels, so that his rider shall fall backward. I have waited for thy salvation, O Lord. Gad, a troop shall overcome him: but he shall overcome at the last. Out of Asher his bread *shall be* fat, and he shall yield royal dainties. Naphtali *is* a hind let loose: he giveth goodly words. Joseph *is* a fruitful bough, *even* a fruitful bough by a well; *whose* branches run over the wall: The archers have sorely grieved him, and shot *at him*, and hated him: But his bow abode in strength, and the arms of his hands were made strong by the hands of the mighty

God of Jacob; (from thence *is* the shepherd, the stone of Israel:) *Even* by the God of thy father, who shall help thee; and by the Almighty, who shall bless thee with blessings of heaven above, blessings of the deep that lieth under, blessings of the breasts, and of the womb: The blessings of thy father have prevailed above the blessings of my progenitors unto the utmost bound of the everlasting hills: they shall be on the head of Joseph, and on the crown of the head of him that was separate from his brethren. Benjamin shall ravin *as* a wolf: in the morning he shall devour the prey, and at night he shall divide the spoil. (Genesis 49:1–27)

I think that Simeon and Levi are the ones that killed Dinah's love, an innocent man.

Judah is the one that started referring to his son's wife as daughter-in-law and her father as father-in-law, just as we do today. It was in Judah's family where we see it recorded for the first time. None of this is possible without lawyers and "law enforcement" officials. This is the only way that a man can build a kingdom like this one. Jacob said that Judah would have a lawgiver between his feet. For every step that a man takes in this type of kingdom there must be the protection of a lawyer and law enforcement officers to defend and protect his "laws." Many of our medical doctors, politicians, and others have lawyers on retainers.

In Judah's family, no longer were the ways of the Lord obeyed—men had taken over the family using laws. Judah and his brothers despised Joseph, Rachel and Jacob's son. Leah was very troubled that Jacob never left Rachel and lived with her. Worse still, Jacob loved Joseph more than he loved his other older sons that he had with Leah. Judah came up with a way to take the laws for family one step further. Judah found a way to eliminate the first wife and the children of the first wife in such a way that they could be replaced by the second wife and her children. He found a way to eliminate them without killing them in order to make room for the second wife and her children.

He tweaked the existing laws regarding family structure in such a way that the second woman got her man. Leah would have gotten Jacob if he had followed this standard, just as my husband's "step-mother" got her man. With laws such as this, he would have to abandon his first wife in order to marry another. He introduced the "one man and one woman" concept. In this type of kingdom, a man can only have one woman at a time. He has to choose.

These laws are not written out of love for the man that commits adultery, as most would think. These laws are written for the other woman. Leah was the other woman that never got her man! Leah's sons fixed the laws so that other women could get what their mother did not. These laws are for the benefit of the other woman so that these other women do not have to endure what Leah had to endure alone. Remember that Leah's sons did not love Jacob, their father. We can know this because one of them even slept with one of his wives/concubines.

Jesus tried during His life to warn our fathers about the consequences of adultery and remarriage. He tried to explain to them that castration was better than committing adultery. He tried to stop what Leah's sons started, but few of our fathers have listened. Even fewer are listening today. Adultery is everywhere we look.

The family unit was being disfigured and distorted. Women were no longer respected. Judah cheated on his wife and had intercourse with a woman that he abandoned after ejaculation—one that was pregnant with his own child. This type of behavior is common place today. Men and women both frequently cheat on their spouses. Few accept responsibility for children that were conceived during their secret liaisons. Other men abandon their first wife and children by divorce and "marriage" to the other woman.

There is no other way that a kingdom such as this could exist for any period of time because it is contrary to God's laws. Lawyers and "law enforcement" officials make it possible. In our country we have a police force and armed forces. All of these force the laws of lawyers upon the citizens of this country and around the world. We are like a crouched lion, and our hand is constantly in the neck of our enemies worldwide.

Judah's kingdom was ruled by the commandments of men. It was defended with weapons just as we have guns and war machines today. When you have a society that eliminates members of the family with laws, you will find a lot of men that drink a lot of wine, beer, and other alcoholic beverages. It helps to dull the senses and the nagging sense of being rejected, eliminated, and separated from the family to which they belong. These men end up with no family at all because of a foolish father that was stupid enough to give it all to another woman and her children rather than to his firstborn child.

This is just the way that Leah's sons would have wanted it. It is because of them that we have the family laws that we have today. They could not change it for their mother or for themselves, but they were able to change it for all of the other children of the second family. And just as Judah tweaked the laws in his family's favor, I hope to help put the laws back the way that God intended them to be. I want to reverse what Judah did so that this will be a better world for our firstborn sons and for the children of the first wife. This is what Jesus wanted for God's children!

During this time, it was obvious that intercourse was considered a casual thing, and an unmarried woman that conceived a child through whoredom could be burned and killed. Judah was the one that suggested that his own daughter-in-law be burned. Just as in this country, the responsibility is placed upon the woman and the child. The man bears little responsibility for his actions or his ejaculation. This kingdom benefits the second wife, not the first wife or the child! In this kingdom, the man is the king! It encourages a man to be unfaithful. This is the reason that we have Mr. and Mrs., one man and one woman. It doesn't matter if it is the man's thirteenth wife, he will still be Mr. and she will be Mrs. . . . All of the others have been eliminated.

Anytime that someone's position in the family is based upon a law, it means that they are expendable and replaceable. All it takes is a divorce decree and then remarriage, and the spouse is considered permanently separated from the family. This is how men of the kingdom keep their generations perfect: they eliminate family members. They make themselves the central figure and think of themselves as the "family." In doing so, the direction the penis faces truly is where they consider their family.

Almost everyone wants to come to America. They praise this country, the freedom to do as they choose within the scope of our "laws," and our accomplishments. Our children worship this country as they would worship God. We claim that it is one nation under God with liberty and justice for all. They volunteer in our armed forces to defend the laws of this land worldwide. They bow down to "heroes" from the past—inventors, creators, mathematicians, doctors, architects, generals, soldiers, presidents, etc. These sons and daughters bow down to their fathers and forefathers. And yes, there is liberty for adulterers, and there is justice for the unwanted spouses and children of the first family when they fail to respect their replacements. This country would never be able to stand without our armed forces and our lawyers. These two must be present until the end of this world when Jesus comes on the clouds.

There are many that falsely believe that the gathering spoken of here by Jacob is the gathering of Jews to Israel the land. The real gathering is the gathering of families into the whole family unit, a time when the parts of the family realize their position on the family tree and accept their actual natural position within the family.

Instead of each individual family thinking themselves as the family, they will be brought to the Family vine and assume their proper place. The foal will be brought to the vine, the man's first wife. This foal is the young child of the second wife or the second husband if the woman abandoned her husband, married for a second time, and moved in with this other man. This child will be brought to the Family vine—the first wife. It must be done this way because the man has left the Family vine to live with another woman or the woman has left the Family to move in with another man. The man is charged to cleave to his wife. His first wife and her children are the core. He comes to her and her children even if she has children with

The Step-Father's Step-Son

another man. Both spouses together lift the children of the first family into their primary position within the family. This must be done early when the children are small because foals and colts are young animals. The man must not wait until his own firstborn son is 60 plus years old like my husband's father and even then he never placed his firstborn son into the primary position within "the Family." My husband's father and his second wife wanted my husband to come to their "family." This is the reverse of God's plan for a united family.

The man that married the child's mother and committed adultery with her is responsible for the children that he had with her. A mother must never abandon her small children no matter who their father is. This child is a part of her—more so than the man that decided to play a builder within another man's family and with the child's mother. We must remember that we are the mother of God's children, the soul family. Our role is greater. The man is only the father of the body. We are the mother of both the soul and the body. This is how God made us. When our children are old enough we can leave them to focus on uplifting our firstborn children into their rightful God given position within the family. In this way, these children of the first family do not have to suffer through the things that my husband and sons did for his mother, father, step-mother, and step-father—and most especially, their children. He and our family gave up everything so that two families, separate from the whole, could pretend that they each are a Family. It was all smoke and mirrors.

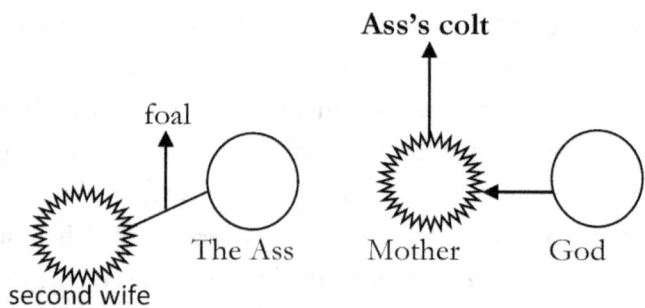

The Lost Children of the House of Israel

The ass's colt is the abandoned child of the first wife, the one that he left for the other woman. The ass is the father that abandoned his children of the first family. The man and this child, the ass and his colt, are the ones that are carrying the burden so that the second woman and her children can have everything—that is why the word "ass" is used. When the gathering occurs, this child, the ass's colt, will be given the choice position within the family vine as the cornerstone. My husband's family tree is the perfect illustration of what Jacob was talking about. The only problem is that his father is deceased and will never perform the act of bringing his children to the family vine, his first wife or uplifting his firstborn son, my husband, into his rightful position within the family. He wanted my husband to come to "his" family vine instead of him coming to the FAMILY vine. The man is never the vine unless you think of his last name as a "vine"! A last name does not endure, but a family of souls does. These children mistakenly think that they are the family, but that is not true—they are only part of the FAMILY.

The one that leaves the children of the first family is no longer considered a central figure. My husband's mother never abandoned my husband, but she never left her second husband's children for her firstborn child, my husband. This would have been a requirement for her firstborn son to assume the choice position when his father has totally abandoned him as my husband's father did. It is very difficult for a woman to place her oldest son as the cornerstone by herself. The father must do his part also to lift his child up. Both of my husband's parents died before the step-parents died. For this reason both of the step-parents became the primary heirs and my husband was on the sidelines for them both.

Jesus said, "And many of the children of Israel shall he turn to the Lord their God. And he shall go before him in the spirit and power of Elias, to turn the hearts of the fathers to the children, and the disobedient to the wisdom of the just; to make ready a people prepared for the Lord" (Luke 1:16, 17).

The Step-Father's Step-Son

My husband's mother never left her firstborn. She did marry another man and have children with him, which complicated the family tree significantly. But just as in Jesus' family, the mother will eventually have to leave her second husband's children to ensure that her firstborn child can assume the proper position within the family tree. Her second husband committed adultery by marrying a woman that another man had put away. Her second husband's children can never be placed in the choice position either. This position is reserved for the child of her first marriage.

In our culture, it is acceptable for both a mother and a father to abandon their children by putting them up for adoption. It is not uncommon for a father to abandon his children for another woman. Women abandon their living children less frequently than men do, but unfortunately, that happens. With the advent of contraception and legalized abortion, I think that the numbers might be even on the number of men and women that abandon their children.

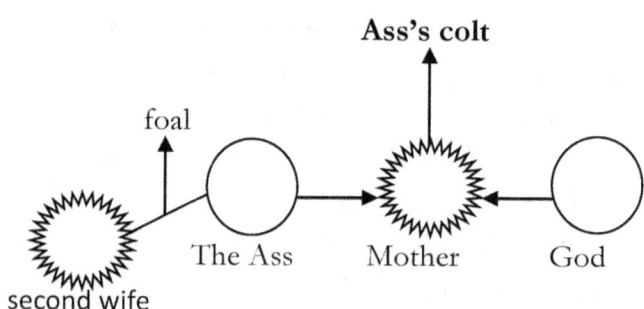

The urine that is produced from the consumption of wine and other spirits has become a part of the water in our rivers, streams, and aquifers. We are washing our clothes in the urine excreted from the breakdown of wine and alcoholic beverages. These adulterous men will blame their victimized sons for drinking too much when fathers, step-mothers, and adultery are the root problems. Our clothes are laundered in the blood of violence that has been washed into our water supply. This blood is shed by the people that paid the price so that this man could live with another woman instead of his first family.

Our men consume much wine and liquor, and their eyes are bloodshot from drunkenness and overconsumption to numb the pain and hurt of fathers that have abandoned them.

This describes our nation today! Drunkenness is normal. Our men drink and drive. Our sons kill each other with guns and any other way that is conceivably possible. A knife can be a weapon, a broomstick can be a weapon, a rock can be a weapon—the possibilities are endless. They can all be lethal weapons. Our sons are hurting because their fathers have left them for other women. The only way to drown out the emptiness and loneliness is for them to get drunk! Only with lawyers is it possible to break up the family in such an unnatural and unhealthy way!

These fathers that abandon their sons must think that they are the family. Furthermore, this is exactly what the other woman will want him to think. This is his reward for making the second wife his heir. She gets everything, and he gets to think of himself as a god. In this way, the abandoned son will have to come to his father and his "father's family." The father will not go to his son. This is the reason that the daughters of men should never become the wives of the sons of God. They will twist the truth just as their mothers did and help to propagate false teachings that will propel this society into another generation without coming to Christ and His teachings. The man is not "the family"; he is supposed to be the guardian and protector of the family!

Once, for my husband's father's birthday, I went to a well-stocked card shop to get a birthday card for him. I never thought that there would be any problem in finding a card for this man. But when I arrived, there were no cards for this man at all, and I spent a considerable amount of time searching. Finally, I gave up the search there and went to another store. There I found a card that said something like this, "It's all in the jeans." Inside an open pair of jeans were three little kittens looking out. I bought this card and mailed it to him.

The Step-Father's Step-Son

While I was there, I also bought another card. On the cover of the card was a large older model fancy car with fins on the back. In the front seat were a man and woman smiling. In the back seat was a boy with a purple mohawk and wearing purple eye shadow sitting between two girls. My oldest son mailed this card for me one day. Inside I had inscribed the following words, "Adultery does not erase or separate what God has joined together with the creation of a little child—the one that you omitted from your entire life. We will miss you forever. The Cox Family." In this message, I was making a statement. My husband's father had smiled when I had suggested at our second meeting that we "change our name to Frizzell." After looking at the situation, I took that option off of the table. There was no need to take this man's last name as our last name. He did absolutely nothing for my husband or our children. We would have taken the last name of his second wife, the head of his household, because he gave her everything. The only thing that did anything for my husband and my sons was this man's penis.

My husband's father later had the opportunity to bring his own firstborn son, my husband, to the family vine. I had carried this man's phone number in my pocket for quite some time. There was a day that came when I knew that I had to make that call. I did not rehearse anything, and I did not know what I would say when I called. This man's second wife answered the phone. (During all other times that my husband had called, she had always been on the phone. According to family members, she had done this for a number of years. She had been screening all of his calls.) This time, I knew that I needed to talk to him, so I demanded that she put him on the phone. When he took the phone, the first thing that he said was "Who is zish?" in a very angry and gruff way. My answer was "This is Barbara." Then, he repeated his first statement in exactly the same way, "Who is zish?" After a brief hesitation, I said, "I am your oldest son's wife." I quickly added, "Let us know if you need anything." Then, I hung up the phone because I knew that someone would take the phone away from him.

The next thing that happened was that I got a phone call on our other number from that same area code. The female caller, that I did not recognize, said that it was a wrong number. They called our land line most likely to see if I was at home or on my cell phone and possibly in their area. I think that there was a family get-together when I called. They would not have wanted us there. His second wife's family may have been there and I doubt that they had ever been told that my husband ever existed. This would have been my husband's father's last opportunity to acknowledge his firstborn son with his family members present. He could have finally introduced my husband as his oldest son and given him his proper position within the family vine. Instead, he denied any connection. I doubt that he ever told anyone other than his second wife and their children that my husband was his own son. My husband did not see his father for the first time until he was in his twenties. His father totally abandoned him. My husband had to give up everything so that his father could give everything to another woman.

Later, when my husband's father's oldest daughter with his second wife called to tell us that he had died (I had suspected something previously because I had smelled an unusual fragrance in our house), I answered the phone and said, "This is Barbara." She said, "Who is this?" just like her father had answered during my phone call with him. I identified myself again. Again she said, "Who is this?" ("I speak that which I have seen with my Father: and ye do that which ye have seen with your father." John 8:31-38) Then, she told me that her father had died. I told her that I had smelled something that reminded me of him (the smell of Tide detergent, which we do not use). I told her that I was sorry to hear that he had died. I said something like, "His penis was the only thing that did anything for my husband. I wish that we could have known the man." I told her that I would not be coming to the funeral. I also told her that I had not attended the funerals of my husband's mother or his step-father. Then, I told her that I would tell my husband and that he would call her.

The Step-Father's Step-Son

Sometime after the funeral that my husband attended alone, something unusual happened. I was sitting on our sofa watching TV with our little Cairn Terrier, Muffin. We have sliding wood doors on the closet in that room, and something hit the sliding doors to the closet so hard that it startled me and Muffin barked. Then, it happened again. I did not look in the direction of the sound but, instead, said, "Get your ass out!"

This was the last time that this happened. My husband did not have a soul connection with his father because his father abandoned him for another woman and her children. I firmly believe that this soul connection is important for our passage to Heaven. I think that he was trying to visit his "oldest" son's house for the first time but without acknowledging my husband in his proper position. I don't think that my husband sensed his presence even once. I think that my husband's father left behind something that was very important. He never took a stand for his oldest son!

Women that have had two husbands and have children with both men will have to choose between the two families themselves. There are two separate vines coming from one woman. This is never supposed to happen. The man is not and never can be the vine. The man that committed adultery by marrying a man's wife and a child's mother will have to assume all financial responsibility for his children produced with this woman.

Firstborn

Child

○————→●←————○
first   Mother   second

husband   husband

(child/children arrows pointing up from both sides)

My husband's father chose his second wife and her children over my husband.

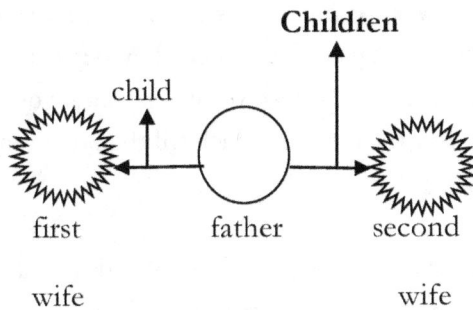

Mary, Jesus' mother, is an example for all women to follow. She did not stay with the children that she conceived with Joseph after Joseph died. She stayed with Jesus, her firstborn Son! Just before Jesus died, He gave her to the disciple that He loved, and this disciple took care of her. Mary kept her first born child first.

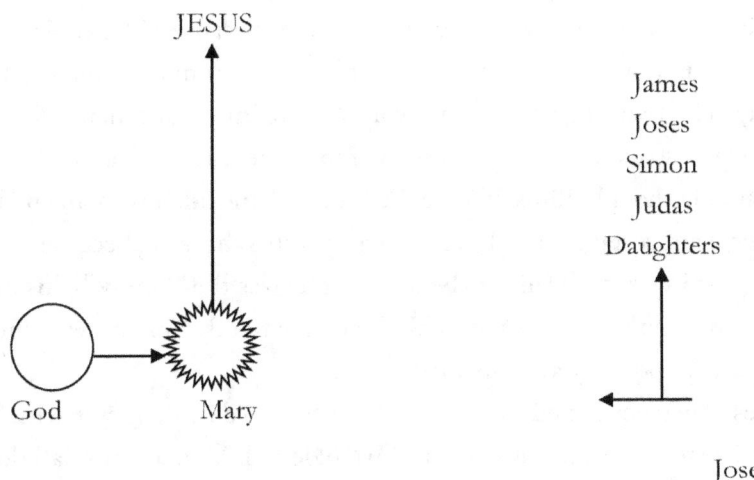

The Step-Father's Step-Son

> And the brother shall deliver up the brother to death, and the father the child: and the child shall rise up against *their* parents, and cause them to be put to death. And ye shall be hated of all *men* for my name's sake: but he that endureth to the end shall be saved. But when they persecute you in this city, flee ye into another: for verily I say unto you, Ye shall not have gone over the cities of Israel, till the Son of man be come. (Matthew 10:21–23)

My husband's father was the perfect "law-abiding" citizen. He honored every single legal piece of paper that was written by a lawyer. He kept every single law that has been written by a man. He divorced his first wife and married his second wife. He gave everything that he had to his second wife and their three children by a will. He honored the adoption agreement whereby the step-father became the father of his son. He severed all ties with his child and never saw the child again until the child had grown up. He most likely never paid any child support because another man and the child's mother had accepted responsibility for his firstborn son.

This man ceased to be a father and a parent because of legal pieces of paper written by a lawyer. Jesus said, "But let your communication be, Yea, yea; Nay, nay" (Matthew 5:37). Our word is more important than a piece of paper. My husband's father was a man among men. He was a man of the kingdom. He thought himself to be the "family." The other woman and her daughter, I am certain, must have encouraged this thinking because it was in their best interests for him to believe that he was the "family." This man expected his adult son to come to him and "his family." He never went to his son except possibly after he died.

These laws permitted my husband's father's oldest daughter with his second wife to replace my husband as "his" oldest child. Because of all these "laws," few knew that this man had abandoned his wife. Few knew that this man had abandoned his child. Few knew that this man had children with any other woman except the one that he had lived with for most of his life.

These laws enabled my husband's father's second wife to take advantage of my husband's father and his firstborn son. The laws of this land enabled a woman and a man, a step-mother and a step-father, to take over the family of my husband's father and mother. The laws of this land are hostile to families and create an environment that is conducive to stressful relationships especially for our husbands, sons, and grandsons.[9] My husband's mother and father both became broken people. The laws of this land made it possible for the children of the kingdom to dominate the family unit.

Today, our laws about family are changing again. Homosexuals desire to marry and live as a family.[10] These homosexuals are the children of confusion because of all of the adultery in their own families. This is all possible with "laws" that encourage adultery. These "laws" are on the verge of failing our entire nation.

Men think that they can determine what a family is and adjust the laws to make their fantasy a reality. This is why Jesus called these men "god" because they have the power to do all of these things and more with "laws." We are indeed "the lost children of the house of Israel!" (John 10:34) We are part of Judah's family tree.

Our Founding Fathers

In our society, the wife and child or children of the first marriage are cast away with the bottled water and bread. We do have laws in this country that divide property fifty-fifty, but there are ways that men can escape. Some are young and just starting out, so there will be no assets to divide. Some hide their assets. Also, men are valued for their work more than women, so their income is higher. When he is no longer there to provide financial support for the family, the wife and children suffer. Many will be forced to go on welfare, and tax payers will have to foot the bill. The man will desire to use his income to support his second wife and "their children." These men cannot afford both women and both families. They will have to choose one or the other. Second wives would be less willing to join the holy union if they received little or nothing. They would have to have intercourse with this man for love and not money. But in our country, they marry for the money and/or status and are rewarded accordingly.

When a man abandons his family for another woman, he is putting the burden of responsibility on his first wife and children. This is totally contrary to what God has intended for His children born of the holy union when man and woman become one flesh.

We start with a family that looks much like this. This is the core of our families. This is where it all begins.

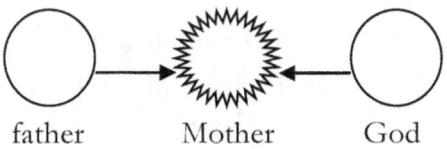

The Step-Father's Step-Son

Then, at the appointed time, a child is born.

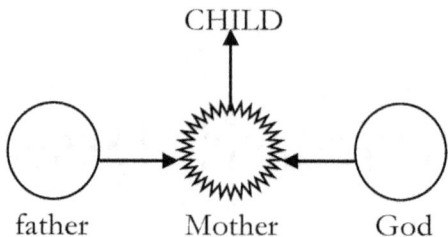

We complicate this structure by adding other relationships to the union. Combining families creates a very difficult environment for the child and the future children to bear because of the confusion. We put unnecessary burdens on our children when we bring strangers into the family home.

The Child's FAMILY

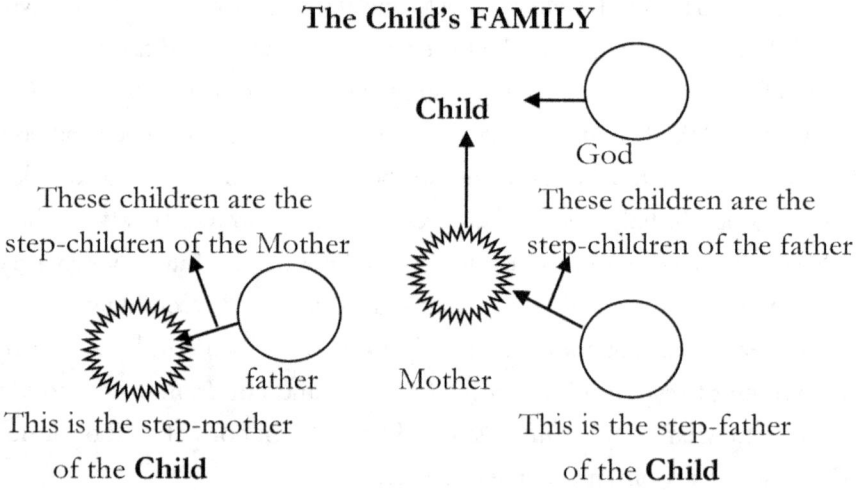

Dysfunction is everywhere!

In this diagram, the child will be stripped of his social position in both families. He is the oldest child of nothing that neither the father nor mother values. If they valued it, they would not have married for the second time.

They are cursing their own child by remarrying, by committing adultery. The dysfunction that the child experiences as a result of the confusion created by the adultery will cause many problems when the child becomes an adult. The child may act out and cause "problems," which are indicators that something is wrong. The "parents'" reaction may be to ignore the child, neglect the child, force the child into servant hood, and/or abuse the child.

We have three separate and distinct families. The only problem is that there is only one person left of the most important part of the family. This child, soon to be an adult, will have to bear the load alone. There is no one fully devoted to that family anymore; both adults have abandoned the family for someone else.

Also, using Abraham and Sarah as an example, this child could marry offspring from the other family that his father created by marrying another woman. If Abraham's mother had had two men in her life and children with both, these children could not have intermarried between the two families. The children of the mother with two men are more closely related than the children of the father with two women. (An egg is enormous when compared to a tiny sperm.) They all will be raised by the same mother like brothers and sisters. But the man that she is living with will want his children to be first before her firstborn child. This child is the natural heir, but this man is responsible for the physical needs of her two families, even though he committed adultery by marrying another man's wife. Her property will become his property in the end. This is another reason why women should not have children with two men or even marry for a second time. It is unhealthy for our firstborn children and then their firstborn children. She is actually cursing her future generations of the firstborn child because this other man is separating the child's family.

The split within the family widens when this happens. A woman will find it very difficult to honor her firstborn child in situations like this. She will be torn between blessing her second husband or her firstborn child. It is best to bless the firstborn child over the second husband, but it is extremely difficult. A child should never be put into a situation where there is competition for property of which they are the natural heir. This is the reason that adultery is so very damaging to our children and to our families. These issues do not arise in a normal family unless adultery happened in the previous generation.

Adultery is very damaging to the children of this child, especially his firstborn child. This abandoned heir will take from his own family in order to compensate for his losses much like Laban. He was passed over as heir and will still have the strong need to be an heir. He will take from his own children in a very unnatural way. It is not the child's fault; rather, it is a problem with the system of adultery that was established long ago and is highly encouraged in this country. Indirectly and without any understanding of the history of their father, our children are exposed to situations that should never happen because they are unnatural. Because they are unnatural, they are harmful. Step-mothers and step-fathers must never be allowed to compete with our children for what is not theirs to take.

No child should ever be denied their natural position within a family.

> "For neither did his brethren believe in him. Then Jesus said unto them, "My time is not yet come: but your time is always ready. The world cannot hate you; but me it hateth, because I testify of it, that the works thereof are evil." (John 7:7)

No adult should ever be permitted to take a child's natural position within the family and give it to their own child or children. It is in situations such as this that Munchhausen by proxy and other behavioral issues start. The root cause is adultery by our grandparents, step-grandparents, parents, and step-parents, and then the curse is passed on to the children of this abandoned child. Adultery is a crime against our children and grandchildren. It is too confusing for our children to understand. I am an adult, and it has taken me almost forty years to understand the damaging effects. It is a subtle sin on the surface, but the consequences to our families are long-lasting.

God never intended for a woman to be saddled with the responsibility for providing for the physical needs of two families should one or both men abandon her and the children. Furthermore, it is extremely confusing for our children when there are questions about "who is their father." Parenthood is obvious with one man and one woman. It gets complicated when two men's sperm enter into one woman's vagina. Without DNA testing, it could be almost impossible to know the child's father. This is confusion that a child does not need. This is a sin against children who have a right to know who their true mothers and fathers are.

It is very confusing for a woman to give life to one child and then have a second child with another man. These children are not true brothers and sisters, even though they will be raised side by side as though they were. The children with the first man are at a greater disadvantage and at greater risk than the children that she will have with the other man that stays with her. This second man will be much more likely to mistreat, abuse, or kill the child from the first marriage because this child has no father and he knows that he is not the father of this child. In the end, this man will most likely take everything from this child and this child's future generations.[11]

But it is usually a man that abandons his wife for another woman which causes her to go to another man. This is why the man's responsibility is greater. But there are some women that will abandon their husband and even children for another man, thereby causing him to commit adultery himself by marrying another woman. In this case, the woman that abandoned her husband has the greater responsibility because she opened the door to the destruction and breakup of the family.

This lone child will have to break the yoke of this dysfunctional family tree and develop his own independence. This is a difficult process because there will be little to no family support—emotional or financial. Most of the resources will stay with the second wife and the second husband. Esau had to break the yoke of his brother, Jacob; so, too, will this son have to break the yoke of the other two families (Genesis 27:37–40). It takes time, but it must be done. This child must not assume a secondary role in a family where he is a primary member. This child will have to choose God, his father, or his mother.

Let's look at the distribution of property when we devote our inheritances to our children.

The father's and Mother's FAMILY

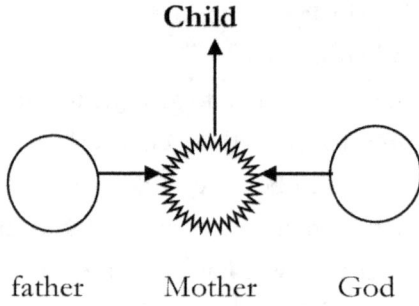

father   Mother   God

100 % stays with the Family

Now, let's take it one step further and look at the distribution of property when the mother and father divorce.

The Mother's family

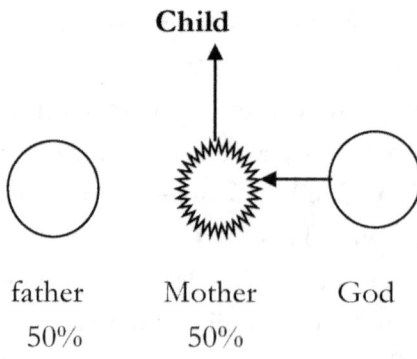

father   Mother   God
50%   50%

If neither parent commits adultery by remarrying, the child could still inherit 100 percent of the property and would still retain his position as the oldest child in the family.

Now, let's complicate things tremendously by adding children-in-law to the picture.

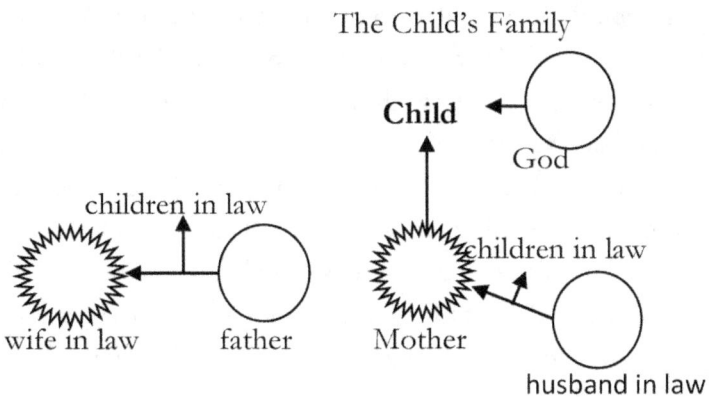

The second man or woman has little legal standing in our society unless there is a valid marriage license. Her marriage to the child's father is based on a piece of paper, on man's laws. His marriage to the child's mother is based on a piece of paper, on man's laws. Furthermore, both marriages are based on adultery.

Both parents will most likely treat the second marriage as their primary marriage and will give their property through a will to their second spouse. The second woman will want the child's father to give everything to her and their children. She will want the child of the father's first marriage to receive nothing. The second man will want the child's mother to give and will everything to him, and then he may include the child of his wife's first marriage in his will. However, he will not want this child to be in a controlling position. He will want his oldest child to have this position.

The property will be controlled in whole or in part by the oldest child of each new family that is created through the process of adultery. In the step-mother's family, the man will become property like all of the other physical assets. This man will be dominated by an adulterous woman. (Abram never allowed this to happen in his family.)

One of the main reasons that this will happen is because of the dysfunction created by the confusion caused by the adultery. The child will be rendered defeated—he is neither the oldest child, nor an only child, nor anything that anyone values—in his ability to lead in managing any assets because of the burden of responsibility placed upon him from an early age. Another reason will be the step-father's desire to enrich his prodigy. The child will have no social standing except possibly with the mother, but that will be limited by her second husband ruling over her. The ones that control the property will use it for their own purposes and enrichment. The only heirs that matter are the half-brothers and half-sisters, and they will put themselves first.

The father and his second wife will most likely ignore the child completely. It will be as though the child did not exist or were dead. In this scenario, the father will most likely be ruled by his second wife. The woman will most likely despise the first wife and, especially, the child, just as Hagar despised Sarah, so it is in her best interests to pull the man as far away from the child or children of the first marriage as she can. She will want everything—the father's family (aunts, uncles, nieces, nephews, and grandparents) and property—for her children.

My best guess is that the child will most likely receive nothing on his father's side because he was never permitted to be a part of the family in whole or in part. (I wrote this before my husband's father died, and this is exactly what happened. He did not mention his firstborn son in the will that he signed twenty-five years earlier at all. He gave everything to his second wife and "their" children.) Now, let's think one generation ahead. And when the child grows up and has children, what will his children receive since the child has no social standing? Each of these grandchildren will be given a stone because the child of the first parents was cursed by both parents and their adulterous spouses. It will be most damaging for the firstborn son of this abandoned son. My oldest son paid the price for what his grandfather and his adulteress did. He had dreams of doing great things for the whole family. He was a leader, as you would expect firstborn sons to be. The only problem was that there were no men from the family to support him and his goals—men that you would find in a normal family where grandparents actually bless their grandchildren. My husband's father was busy blessing his children with his second wife while abandoning his firstborn son and firstborn grandson for this woman and her children. The roots have been chopped off by a man and a woman, not by God.

A man cannot walk away and abandon his children! Let's look at what Jacob (Israel) said. I think that this will give us a better understanding of "family." Joseph, his firstborn son with his first wife (Rachel, the one that he loved), heard that his father was sick so he took his two sons, Manasseh and Ephraim to visit his father. When Israel heard that Joseph was coming he mustered the strength to sit up in bed. He said,

> "And now thy two sons, Ephraim and Manasseh, which were born unto thee in the land of Egypt before I came unto thee into Egypt, are mine' as Reuben and Simeon, they shall be mine. And thy issue, which thou beggettest after them, shall be thine, and shall be called after the name of their brethren in their inheritance." (Genesis 48:5–6)

He immediately accepted Joseph's two sons as "family." This was very much unlike my husband's father who thought that only his two girls and one boy with his second wife and their children were his family. Despite the terrible things that his children from his second family, Reuben and Simeon, had done, he still acknowledged that they were his children and a part of the family. And he also said that Joseph's "issue" or children born from his children will "be called in the name of their brethren in their inheritance." This meant that the family property was to be handed down to all of the generations of this family and not Reuben and Simeon's family only. Property goes from parent to children, parent to children, parent to children. Again, this is totally contrary to the way that my husband's father, step-mother, and their oldest daughter handled the situation. They set up everything so that my husband, his children, and their children could never be heirs to any of the "Frizzell" property. On my husband's mother's side, things are almost as bad. My husband's mother did not let the children with her second husband get everything, but through my husband's step-father they got control of almost everything.

Israel did not eliminate any of his children from an inheritance despite the things that they had done. He favored Joseph, his firstborn son with his first wife, the one that he loved, above all of his brethren, but all of the other children he treated equally in the distribution of assets. He counted them all his heirs. Based upon what I saw with my husband's father's family, they only considered heirs to be family members. Because my husband received nothing he was not a family member—the second wife was not his mother. But Israel said, "Moreover I have given to thee one portion above thy brethren, which I took out of the hand of the Amorite with my sword and with my bow." (Genesis 48: 22) Israel treated all of his other children equally. He never said, "Because you did this . . . , your portion will be given to someone else." He counted each and every one of his children as his heirs. He never denied being the father of any of them because they all were his children! All of Israel's children were his heirs.

My husband's family was so confusing that it took me almost forty years of marriage to begin to understand just how damaging adultery is to children. If it was this complicated for me, it was even more complicated for my oldest son and his brothers. My sons grew up in confusion. My husband grew up with four adulterers that were just starting out on their "new" lives. My sons grew up with full-blown adultery around them. There is so much that cannot be challenged because of existing laws, tradition, and an ancient system that still exists today in this country. We have all grown up in this system and most (especially those that are from the second family) think that it is perfectly normal because they are the ones that should benefit the most. They are the ones that do like their fathers did. But I am going to tell you that it is the reverse of God's plan. We should never put the children of the second marriage first! What we do in this country and around the world should never ever be allowed anywhere.

Our Founding Fathers

Before Jacob died, he blessed Joseph, his firstborn son with his first wife, by giving him twice the inheritance of all of his other children (Genesis 48:21, 22). On his deathbed, he asked Joseph not to bury him in Egypt (Genesis 47:29). He did not give these instructions to Reuben, his oldest son with Leah. He gave these instructions to the first born son of his first wife, Rachel! My husband's father left no burial instructions because his second wife's oldest daughter was in charge of everything. They cremated him, as other family members had done with one of his brothers who had preceded him in death. He left no burial instructions with his wife's oldest daughter.

Jacob did not abandon his firstborn child with his first wife for any other woman.

Israel's Family

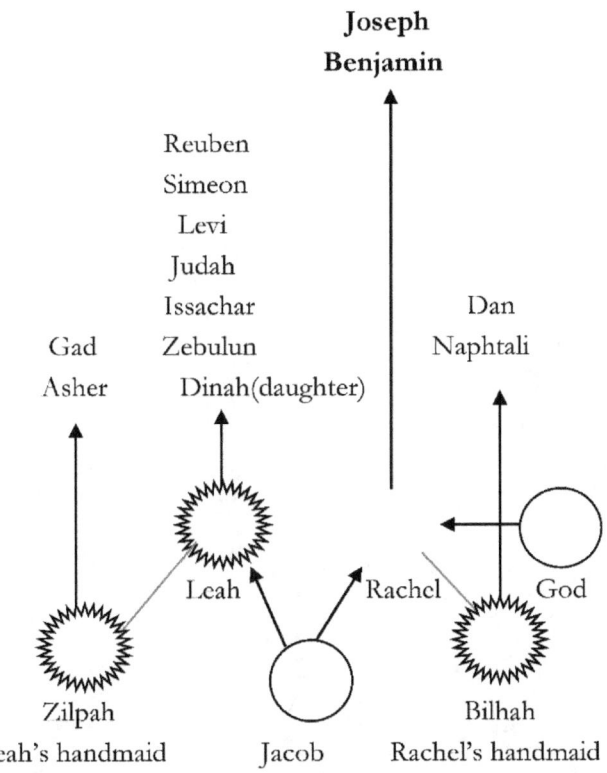

Who is the Greatest?

He saith unto them, Moses because of the hardness of your hearts suffered you to put away your wives: but from the beginning it was not so. And I say unto you, whosoever shall put away his wife, except *it be* for fornication, and shall marry another, committeth adultery: and whoso marrieth her which is put away doth commit adultery. His disciples say unto him, If the case of the man be so with *his* wife, it is not good to marry. But he said unto them, All *men* cannot receive this saying, save *they* to whom it is given. For there are some eunuchs, which were so born from *their* mother's womb: and there are some eunuchs, which were made eunuchs of men: and there be eunuchs, which have made themselves eunuchs for the kingdom of heaven's sake. He that is able to receive *it*, let him receive *it*. (Matthew 19:8–12)

A man's devotion to his "first" wife and children is so important that castration was recommended by Christ. If a man cannot govern his sexual organ, then castration is in his best interests. This one organ could affect a man's salvation forever. Our families are that important to God! He loves His children very much. Our child sex offenders and rapists do not need to experience a life in prison because all that is needed is castration. But I would like to say one thing and make it perfectly clear. I do not believe that these men would commit these crimes if their fathers, mothers, step-fathers, step-mothers, grandfathers, grandmothers, step-grandfathers, and step-grandmothers had not committed adultery. Where you find adultery, you also find homosexuality and these similar patterns of behavior. Adults send confusing messages to their children when they bring strangers into the family, most especially when they marry them and move in with them. Grandfathers and fathers freely go from woman to woman. Our fathers expect a child to respect the woman with whom he has committed adultery. Many of our sons, as a result, will grow up and have little respect for their wives and other women. These early childhood memories leave life-long scars.

The amygdala in our brain stores these confusing memories for later processing. A betrayal may be the precursor that causes these stored memories to be released in the form of a temptation. If the adult child is not strong enough to overcome the temptation, they will act it out and find themselves in a very unforgiving world. Few have any compassion for homosexuals, child molesters, or rapists. No one looks deeper to look at the father, grandfather, mother, grandmother, and, most especially, "step-parents and step-grandparents." They only blame the child.

Adultery looks perfectly normal on the outside and even more so with the passage of time. You have to look deeper to see the damage that it causes. Adultery has the potential to separate a man or woman from God for an eternity because of the impact that it has on God's children and the Family.

Even Christ experienced similar temptations early in His life. He was tempted to rule over all of the kingdoms of the earth, to turn rocks into bread, to fall and let the angels catch Him, and other things. Christ's faith was strong enough to overcome these temptations (Matthew 4:1–10, Luke 4:3–13). These temptations are similar to the ones that our children can experience early in their adult life. If their faith is not strong enough to overcome the temptation, they may fall for it.

Christ came calling for men. The call is for men to become servants of God, just as women have been for thousands of years. Christ came as the ultimate example of the type of service that He expects of men.

Servants and slaves give without expecting anything in return. And the recipients of their service often do not feel compelled to give anything

Who is the Greatest?

or to say "thanks," for their service is expected. Women have become the property of hard-hearted husbands in the past and even still today. We slave and serve our husbands, while they live the life of a god in the home. They have the best seat in the house. The family is named after them. Some think that they have the freedom to cheat on their wives. Some even like to name their firstborn male son after themselves (Luke 1:57–63).

Many worship actors, monarchs, and presidents as though they were God. (Look at the followers that Adolf Hitler had and what he was able to accomplish with the help of his followers.) All of these individuals want us to follow their "laws" and because many worship them like "God," they will follow their commandments without question. Many become so trusting in the leadership of the day, that they don't question their judgment—they become followers. Even Sarai called Abram her Lord.

Perhaps this is the reason that Judah said that the Lord killed his sons (Genesis 38:7–10). It very well could have been a man that condemned their behavior based on the law of the Lord (the law of the fathers), which resulted in their death. Judah even described them as wicked. What I gathered when I read the story is that they did not do what their father wanted them to do and they had good reasons for not doing it. These young men had to choose between God and their fathers. It was most likely because of the law of their fathers that they were considered wicked and killed.

In Luke it says the following: "As it is written in the law of the Lord, Every male that openeth the womb shall be called holy to the Lord." This verse is very specific because it refers to males ONLY. Then in Luke 2:27 we are told, ". . . and when the parents brought in the child Jesus, to do for him after the custom of the law . . ." Then, "when they had performed all things according to the law of the Lord, they returned into Galilee, to their own city Nazareth" (Luke 2:39). The word "Lord" in this context means a man of high standing.

Jesus said, "Get thee behind me, Satan: for it is written, Thou shalt worship the Lord thy God, and him only shalt thou serve." (Luke 4:8)

The Step-Father's Step-Son

We must be careful about who we worship. Our Lords' laws permit the killing of unborn children, the separation of the first family from the father, and the remarriage of the parents of the first family. We had better make sure that we are worshiping the real God and not a man, a Lord! This is the reason that Jesus told us not to be called Rabbi! In this same context, we should not go by Deacon Cox, Pastor Cox, Father Cox, President Cox, Rabbi Cox, Dr. Cox, Mr. Cox or Mrs. Cox. All of these prefixes demand respect even before these individuals have earned our respect by proving themselves to be faithful servants.

A Doctor of History knows who, what, why, when, and where about thousands of different historical events. But don't think for a minute that knowing the exact year, month, day, hour, minute, and second that the Civil War started is going to help any man get to Heaven. None of these facts are requirements for going to Heaven. As the matter of fact, they are not essential to going to Heaven at all. Our poor have a better idea of what it means to go to Heaven than most of our doctors and lawyers do—they Love! Most of our poor are still with their first wife and first husband and are mothers and fathers to the children of the first wife!

We should be known just as Jesus was, by our first names. Jesus never said, "I am God's son, Jesus, he never said that he was Dr. Jesus, he never said that he was Father Jesus, he never said that he was President Jesus." Instead he said, I am "the son of God"; I am "the son of man." He is the example that we all should be following. Titles go last, not first. In the law of the Lord, men are exalted as though they are God himself.

Men have time to watch sporting events on television, time just for themselves, their interests, and their friends. Many enjoy spending their weekend away from work, naked on the floor, sofa, or bed, drunk following an unloving and selfish romp with their beloved spouse, just as Noah did. Noah even blamed his youngest son when he accidently saw him naked on the floor of his tent. It is interesting to observe how men use their children and even pass the blame to them.

Who is the Greatest?

I once saw my father drunk on the floor with an arc of urine coursing through the air. God did not curse me. It was a "commandment of men" that the children could not see their father naked. I did not deliberately go into the room just to see him. I had no idea that he was in there or that he was on the floor naked. Noah should have accepted responsibility for his foolishness instead of cursing his youngest son. How irresponsible our men can be! I am thankful that my father did not see me. But Noah was the husbandman that did his Master's will. He had only one wife, just as his three sons had only one wife each. The Lord made him ruler over all that he had.

The woman is the only one responsible enough to respond to any emergency or problem that may arise during his period of utter stupidity. This is not to anyone's benefit, materially or spiritually. Even in the home, a man should be humble and serve as an example to his wife and children. He can help with meal preparation, the dishes, homework, and housework. The children need to see him making contributions to the family. And above all, he needs to be involved with the family.

In the present age, we find men in direct competition with women. Men are behaving as though they are losing something—their masculinity, for one thing. We hear men frequently declare that the women's liberation movement is taking something away from them. Men think that they are literally becoming the victims of women who are stealing their masculinity and their self-respect. As we see this shift toward fear among men, it seems that our men respond by becoming more and more self-centered. As victims, they have become irrational. They abuse their wives and children because they believe that they are not being respected as they deserve. Sadly, the further men fall into self-centeredness, the further they will push women and children from them and the more isolated they will become. As a result, women will continue to become more independent of them. The only way out of this cycle is for men to cleave to their wives as God commanded.

Our young men are truly being victimized by their fathers. But our young men need to realize that not all women are taking advantage of them. Their first wives will, in most cases, be devoted to her husband and family. Only when we get involved with adultery do we see this shift among women whereby they become the unnatural legal heir within families. In many cases, it is a woman that will inherit everything that his father has. If I were a young man, I would be disturbed at this fact also. A man cannot correct this problem, only women can fix this one. It is something that only daughters of God and mothers of God's children can stop! These adulterous women must be stopped. Unfortunately, this has been going on for thousands of years and our fathers don't seem to mind one bit. If the other woman did not benefit in this way, it would be unlikely that the child's father would be able to find another "wife" so easily.

We refer to all men as "Mr.," unmarried women as "Miss," and married women as "Mrs." All of these titles are based on the physical and not the spiritual. Why don't we refer to each other as sons of God, daughters of God, and mothers of God's children? If our focus were on God, we would do just that. But in a man's world, our focus is on the physical, the body, and not the spiritual, the soul. This may be because, in the spiritual realm, they are only "sons of God" and not "fathers"—God is our Father, the Father of our souls. In the physical realm, a man's role is to care for the physical needs of God's family. God gave them facial hair to keep them warm while working outdoors and to protect their skin from the sun's damaging rays. If they can rule and call themselves "fathers" in the physical and spiritual realm, they can expect their wives and children to serve them and can be as god on earth.

A son of God can be a father when he does his Master's will—God's will—cleaves to his wife, and serves. But in the physical realm, a man is nothing more than a "man." Christ even said that *"there is* none good but one, *that is,* God" the Father (Mark 10:18). The word "men" is like a dirty word in the book of Genesis. In our country, all men are treated like sons of God even before they have proven themselves to be sons of God.

Not all men get to be heads of households—only the ones that are "faithful and wise stewards" (Luke 12:42–44). For those men that beat their wives and children and eat and get drunk, this man will be appointed his portion with the unbelievers and will not go to heaven (Luke 12:45–46). Then there is the servant that knew what God expected of him, but failed to do so. This man will be severely punished (Luke 12:47). Last of all, we have the man that did not know what he was doing even though he did things that were worthy of severe punishment, he will be punished but not as harshly (Luke 12:48). All of our husbands fit into one of the categories. Which one describes your husband? Noah was a husband that did not know what he was doing.

Men's self-centeredness, which is often disguised as jealousy, fuels their violence against their spouses. Anger seems to be their primary emotion. When confronted about their primary emotion, many will deny feeling angry. They don't seem to understand their emotional side and seem to be totally unaware of feelings of sadness, jealousy, failure, shame, or guilt. Some men experience jealousy if their wives interact with other men at work. Some will be resentful and even try to limit visitation by family or her female friends after marriage. Some will control access to information concerning income and expenditures. Some will come and go as they please but expect to have constant updates on where she has been and where she is going. Some may even refer to their wives as "bitch" in order to put her in "her proper place." He may override her decisions.[12] Control mechanisms are used to denigrate what God has created and make it into property. In a society that discourages repentance without punishment, this is the product. No wonder our men have problems in this non-Christian society. Repentance is the only way to get in touch with the emotional side within us: our souls.

Christ said in Matthew 12:7, "But if ye had known what *this* meaneth, I will have mercy, and not sacrifice, ye would not have condemned the guiltless." The guiltless are the ones that have repented. They experience no guilt because they have confessed their sins openly and accepted responsibility. In this country, repentance and accepting responsibility for what we have done is discouraged. Those that do repent risk a harsher punishment.

The Step-Father's Step-Son

Even our Miranda rights warn us that anything that we say can be used against us. Second wives do not want their husbands to repent and accept responsibility for what they have done – our lawyers don't want them to know either.

I have witnessed, on several occasions, men exercising authority over their spouses and claiming superiority. In most cases, I found the wife's recommendation and suggestion to be in the best interests of the family and their neighbors. However, these self-centered, insecure men still ruled against their wives in a selfish way. They put their desire for greatness and importance before God's will.

Here is an example of what can happen. Homes built fifty years ago had a gas mounted heating unit on the wall that did not have adequate guards. Now, picture a small child with a bib tied in a knot around his neck sitting in a high chair (this was before the days of break-away bibs like the ones that we have today). We have a woman and a man sitting near the child at the dinner table while the child is being fed by the mother. The child asks to go to the bathroom, so the mother gently lowers him from the high chair onto the floor. The mother starts to remove the bib by untying the knot. The step-father intervenes and tells her to just turn it to his back. She submits to his "authority over her" and turns it to the child's back. The child then goes to use the restroom. As the child backs away from the toilet, the bib that is tied around and hanging from his back comes in contact with the flames of the gas furnace. The cloth catches fire, and the child runs screaming from the bathroom. The mother rushes to find a way to extinguish the flames that are eating at her child's flesh. Unfortunately, the child is needlessly burned.

This child was my husband. His mother knew what was best, but his "step-father" ruled over her. How sad that such a thing could happen, but similar events are happening every day in our homes with fathers, mothers, step-fathers, and step-mothers present. Adulterers do not cleave to anything. They don't want to humble themselves and do the job according to God's will!

Who is the Greatest?

Here is another example. When my oldest son was a very small infant, my male doctor told me that it was too restrictive on the mother to breastfeed over three months. Foolishly, I listened to him and stopped breastfeeding at three months. How ridiculous for any man to make such a ridiculous recommendation to a woman. We are the ones doing the work of the Lord, caring for God's children. We have a man that thinks that he is so important that he can create his own commandments—commandments which are in the best interests of the man and not the child. We must beware of the commandments of men! I often wonder if the physician benefitted from the sale of the injected drug that caused my milk production to cease.

Today, many children are born through induced labor. The child no longer gets to choose his or her birth date. This is something that should be decided between God, the child, and the mother. Complications can arise creating a situation where, after many hours of hard, difficult, induced labor, the child is still unable to come. At that point, the only option that is left is a surgical C-section.

Women need to be just as independent as men are, but we need to remember that we are all equally dependent upon each other. There must be a balance between independence and dependency. Both partners must be able to care for the family if something should happen to either one of them. In some cases, it is the woman that can get a job while the man cannot.

The parents' second spouses find it very difficult to care for another person's child and some will actually compete with and despise the child. These grown-ups want everything for themselves. This is why so many children of the first family are killed, and many that are not killed are abused both physically and emotionally. Some step-parents find the capacity within themselves to love step-children, but they are very rare. Our children do not need to grow up in a household with unrelated strangers!

Women can do just about any job that men can do. My mother built her own garage, dog houses, barn, sheds, and corral. Women may be limited by physical strength, but if the need arises, we can still get almost any job done. A man must be able to provide care to the children should the wife become ill or die. How many men do you know, in the present or in the past that have helplessly given their children to other family members or offered them out for adoption when their wife became seriously ill or suddenly passed away? How many of these men went on to another woman while their wife was still alive? With flexibility, we can all adapt to difficult circumstances. It is about maintaining and protecting our families and future generations. We each need to learn from the other.

In our barnyard, we have no roosters because they all died, but we have one hen that crows for the flock. We have a lot of tom turkeys, but the females still strut like the toms. Our female dogs kick their hind legs after going to the bathroom like the male dogs. Males and females in the animal world are very similar.

What men fail to realize is the dire fact that they are the ones responsible for pushing the very women and children that love them even further away from their grasps. No woman will stay with a dominating and abusive man unless she gives up the very essence of her life in order to serve an irrational dictator. For a woman in that situation, the only option is to fight back and risk the loss of life, limb, or sanity should she lose or give up.[13] She can leave him. Without a clear understanding of our roles as God created us, it will be easy for women and children to be dominated by sinful men.

Man's fear of loss is causing this shift. God never intended for women to be dominated since "we"—men and women alike—were created by God to be equal. It takes both to tend the garden and the family. And if man would fulfill his role as husband and father in a loving way, their problems would vanish. Man's cup would literally be overflowing. Instead, men have created their own rules separate from God. They have literally given themselves entitlements to sin. They take in order to receive rather than serve. Drunkenness, fornication, adultery, ruling over women and children, cursing, and lusting are considered to be normal, acceptable male activities. Such activities might be frowned upon by some, but they are expected because it is understood that men cannot rise above certain standards. Intercourse is not an entitlement. By contrast, men expect women to be perfect examples of godliness. Expecting more of women and less of men is hypocritical and puts a terrible burden upon women and children. Men of this type will not lift a finger to lift that burden either. They are hypocrites, just as Christ described them!

The more men focus on their sexuality and the sexuality of others, especially that of women, the less spiritual and loving they will be. But could it be that they are imitating their earthly fathers who have abandoned them for another woman. In most cases, when a man leaves his wife, he will be looking for a better body than the one that his first wife had. Our sons are growing up in an adulterous world where the physical is more important than their families. Our fathers and grandfathers are the ones directly responsible for our sons' inability to love their wives and children as God intended. Adultery is at the root of the breakdown of our families.

FOCUS ON BODY – NOT ON SPIRIT

Extreme masculinity	Extreme femininity
Steroids	Breast implants
Alcoholism	Sexy clothing
Tobacco	Flashy jewelry
Football pads	High heels

Men with this set of expectations assume that women will unconditionally submit to them just because they are male. Such an approach is totally backward and omits the requirement that they must serve in order to be great. They are to come and cleave to their wives. When they do this as God intended, their lives will be overflowing with love, and their happiness will be beyond measure. Instead, too many men enter into marriage expecting to receive. They want the woman to come to them, dish out sex when they want it, follow three steps behind, provide a clean house, clean clothes, prepare tasty meals, earn a full day's pay, and be the wife that lets them do as they please without questioning. These are what they consider their "entitlements."

The Step-Father's Step-Son

This is what Christ meant when he said our men are "whited sepulchres . . . full of dead *men's* bones" (Matthew 23:27). They are alive on the outside but spiritually dead on the inside. If they don't feel like talking to their wives, they can simply avoid conversation or change the subject if they find the topic unpleasant. If they watch television, they don't want to be bothered. In other words, they want to be king or god on earth. This is not what God intended. God is the only king on this earth, and no man can take His place nor should he ever try. Instead of receiving, these "men" should be giving of themselves. The more they give in the home, the more they will receive, but conversely, the less they give, the less they should receive.

Women everywhere must remember that they serve God and not an earthly man. Many have chosen to follow Pharisee teachings in resolving the conflict between expectations and reality. Christ told the disciples, "Wherefore I say unto thee, Her sins, which are many, are forgiven; for she loved much: but to whom little is forgiven, *the same* loveth little" (Luke 7:47). Men are counseled to cleave to the woman – the vine, just as Christ came and cleaved to His church, a church which has no walls and is built upon the rock of faith. Many men think that intercourse is the only way to cleave to a woman!

As an example to men, Christ repeatedly gave of Himself. He took the time to talk to the little children, to heal the sick, and to talk to men and women. In response, He was adored, especially by women. On occasion, He did leave the masses of His followers to go pray and talk to His Heavenly Father. It was a woman that gave birth to Christ, a woman that perfumed His head in preparation for His burial, a woman that washed His feet with her tears and dried them with her hair, and a woman that went to the tomb. Following His death and resurrection, Christ chose to appear to women—Mary Magdalene and others. When Mary Magdalene went and told Jesus' male disciples that she had seen Him, they failed to listen to her. Christ was testing men, and He rebuked them for not listening to the women. Women have so much to offer! Men could do it, too, if they would only come to Christ. Christ's love is unconditional. He forgives but expects man to repent and sin no more.

Who is the Greatest?

By creating dependency and attempting to be the perfect wife and perfect mother, we are encouraging men to move into the realm of kingship to the point of making themselves into gods on earth. It is the man's responsibility to reciprocate and give as his wife gives to him. This would reduce the burden that many women have been forced to assume in providing for the care of the home, family, job, and husband. Ultimately, men's energy becomes focused on ensuring that they continue to receive the attention and care that we have led them to believe is their entitlement. They must be encouraged to become a fully functional participant in the life of the family. Furthermore, we weaken ourselves by devoting all of our energy and strength toward trying to be the perfect lover, caregiver, parent, and homemaker. This creates a huge distraction and diversion from God and our ultimate purpose on Earth. We actually accomplish little because we are working against God and ourselves.

Eventually, we are all to leave our homes, families, husbands, and wives and go outdoors, stepping aside from those duties in order to meet others and help them in their journey to Heaven. We don't have to be a missionary overseas. We have plenty of people that need our presence in our own neighborhood, city, county, state, and nation. If we remain at home serving our husbands within the confines of four walls, we can make little difference except possibly with our own families. We need to teach our children how to serve. They need to see us in action.

We are expected to go beyond the home as well and connect spiritually with others. Sometimes, our husband may be left at home with the responsibility of preparing the family meal and doing the dishes so that the wife can go and help someone in need. Conversely, the husband may need to leave the comforts of home to help someone that is in need. And our children may be called to provide service to the Lord, so the parent may have to take up some slack and do the child's chores that day.

The Step-Father's Step-Son

Two Different Ways to Rule

Rule of Law – Separated Looks good on the outside, But dead on the inside Two key elements: One partner takes and the other one submits	Rule of Spirit – Connected Life, Vitality, Purpose Two key elements: Giving and loving by both partners

punishes   controls   dependent
lies   blames
fears →   SELF-   ← rigid
              CENTERED
takes →   ← rules
commands   anxious   dominates
	accepts responsibility flexible
	independent forgives
	trusts ← OTHER → truth
	              CENTERED
	loves serves
	shares patient tends

John 10:34 Jesus answered them, "Is it not in your law, I said, Ye are gods?"	Matthew 19:17 And he (Jesus) said unto him, "Why callest thou me good? There is none good but one, that is God. But if thou wilt enter into life: keep the commandments."

We are not the property of man. We are the property of God! Husbands and wives are partners! Our children are God's children. God has loaned them to us temporarily (Matthew 22:23–32).

Many of our men living today are "dead" spiritually. There is no substance on the inside, no oil in their lamps. Yet Christ told us that Abraham, Isaac, and Jacob are alive today (Mark 12:24–27). Why is it that our men are dead even before they die? Why is it so difficult for our men to make the distinction between the physical and the spiritual? I think that we already know the answer. They want to rule over God's kingdom. And if they can raise their sons and daughters the way they were raised, the cycle will never end.

It is obvious that women were, indeed, considered property in the day and age of Christ. It is also obvious that men then, as well as today, do not understand the scriptures. To this day, women are treated as property, even as slaves, for they have been raped, dominated, stoned, beaten, and murdered at the hands of men worldwide. Christ made another profound statement that has been overlooked and seldom mentioned by men. He said that we are like "the angels of God in heaven" (Matthew 22:30). We are many! We are numerous! Mothers that stay with their first family—do go to Heaven! If necessary, she can leave him, but not for another man. We all need some time alone. Christ came as a man not to raise them up and set them on a pedestal but rather to humble them and call them into service as women have been since the beginning of time.

If women do not belong to men after they die and go to Heaven, neither do God's children. We are all children of God, even while living. Marriage is a physical thing whereby we become one flesh through intercourse and our children. Women are not married to nor do they belong to any man in Heaven. Men are not married to nor do they belong to any woman in Heaven. On Earth, the man belongs to the woman and the woman belongs to the man. Neither husband nor wife is property but, instead, are devoted partners in raising God's family and keeping their generations perfect for the Lord. We are all children of God, but we must obey God's commandments in order to demonstrate our love.

The following verses give us some very important insight into what Jesus had to say about God's family.

> Then came to him *his* mother and his brethren, and could not come at him for the press. And it was told him *by certain* which said, Thy mother and thy brethren stand without, desiring to

see thee. And he answered and said unto them, My mother and my brethren are these which hear the word of God, and do it. (Luke 8:19–21)

There came then his brethren and his mother, and, standing without, sent unto him, calling him. And the multitude sat about him, and they said unto him, Behold, thy mother and thy brethren without seek for thee. And he answered them, saying, Who is my mother, or my brethren? And he looked round about on them which sat about him, and said, Behold my mother and my brethren! For whosoever shall do the will of God, the same is my brother, and my sister, and mother. (Mark 3:31–35)

While he yet talked to the people, behold, *his* mother and his brethren stood without, desiring to speak with him. Then one said unto him, Behold, thy mother and thy brethren stand without, desiring to speak with thee. But he answered and said unto him that told him, Who is my mother? And who are my brethren? And he stretched forth his hand toward his disciples, and said, Behold my mother and my brethren! For whosoever shall do the will of my father which is in heaven, the same is my brother, and sister, and mother. (Matthew 12:46–49)

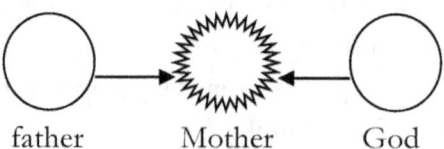

father   Mother   God

the father of the body   the Father of the soul

Who is the Greatest?

The man is the father of our body. God is the Father of our soul. The woman is the mother of the body and the mother of the "living soul." In the physical world, we are members of one family. In the spiritual world, we are all brothers, sisters, and mothers. The man is never a father of our souls.

Men have established their own kingdoms on Earth. The man wants to rule on Earth. Through the "church," man can propagate his teachings from generation to generation, framing them as commandments of God when, in actuality, they are "commandments of men." He wants to establish his own unique rules and exercise his authority over others, especially his wife and children. There is strong evidence of this in scripture since many earthly men rebuked Christ for such things as healing on the Sabbath, not seeing that His disciples prayed and fasted sufficiently, plucking grain on the Sabbath, eating and drinking with tax collectors, and not washing hands before eating. All of these complaints were based on rules established by men within the home and synagogues and not God. In His teachings, Jesus interfered with man's established kingdom, and it made many men very unhappy. We still have many men today who choose to do their own will instead of the Lord's will within God's kingdom.

The most intimate moments between a man and a woman are of the greatest interest to God. It is in this privacy between a man and a woman that intercourse occurs. Some men trivialize the importance of women and use them in ways that God never intended. Intercourse is of the highest priority to many of our men today. In most cases, no other man knows what happens between a man and a woman in private unless he brags about his prowess. These men are literally taking women and using them for their own purposes, just like the time written about in Genesis. They have little desire for any type of commitment with any of them. They are interested only in what they receive.

Women and children are left with the terrible burden of trying to please an oversized and immature adult who will not lift a finger to help with anything that he doesn't have to do. The honey-do lists are looked upon as something his wife is telling him to do. He actually believes that he has no responsibility for completing any of the tasks. A simple announcement that the food is served might be perceived as the wife telling him what to do. Some will sit on the sidelines waiting for the meal to be prepared, never lifting a finger to provide any assistance to his spouse. Some will be careful not to come to dinner too soon for fear of being called into service by their wives.

The home is where the true heart of the man is revealed. This is the reason why Moses had to permit separation between two spouses: divorce. Had he not permitted such a thing, more women and children would have been killed or abused. Moses permitted divorce, but there is no record where he allowed remarriage, at least not among the sons, daughters, and mothers of God's children. Men and women can divorce and remarry any time they so choose because Heaven is not a part of their plan.

The home has been man's kingdom on Earth. He can rule, abuse, get drunk, curse, lie, steal, and do pretty much as he pleases, and so this would be the place where a man's heart is tested the most. No one else knows what goes on behind closed doors except the wife and children. Men show little concern for God and His commandments when it comes to women and children. In most religions, it doesn't matter what the wife and children think or feel. It is demanded they be submissive in all things.

To make matters worse, Paul suggested that women not speak in church. If she had a question about the scriptures, she was instructed to ask her husband at home (1 Corinthians 14:34, 35). His interpretation of the scripture becomes the rule of law in the home because he cares little about what the woman believes. His primary objective is to rule and get what he wants. He has the freedom to distort the truth to his own advantage.

I once bypassed the congregation to talk directly with a minister concerning a commandment of my husband. The priest said nothing. It was as though he thought that I had no right to question my husband's commandments. This man and any other man that thinks this way is wrong! Women and children both have the right to ask questions. Women are very important. We are the ones that give life to God's children. We had better be ready and able to speak up! If we serve God, we will speak up!

Woe on us! Our men are no better today than they were in years past. Paul's purpose was to spread the name of Jesus Christ. God would not have been successful in spreading the name of Jesus Christ unless He had permitted men to maintain their kingdoms in the home and on Earth. It is through Paul and his churches that we know about Jesus today. If it were not for Paul, I doubt that many of us would know Jesus. Christ even said that men preferred the old wine more than the new. As a result, Paul, a strict Pharisee himself, was chosen to spread the name of Jesus while permitting men to keep their old wine, the Pharisaical teachings. However, Christ said that once they knew of Him, they had no excuse but to follow him.

Here we are, over two thousand years after the death of Christ, and most men still prefer the Pharisaical teachings more than Christ's. Now is the time, since most men have accepted the existence of Jesus Christ, for them to compare the teachings of Paul with the teachings of Christ. Perhaps the Spirit of truth can help them to give up their earthly kingdoms at last and serve the Lord in Spirit and genuine truth (Mark 12:24–27).

Ironically, one of the easiest places for men to establish a kingdom is within the physical church itself. Christ declared Himself to be the one shepherd of His church. (John 10:14-16) Jesus said in Matthew 12:6, "But I say unto you, That in this place is *one* greater than the temple." Most of our churches are established based on the rules of men, who take the old covenant and use it to their advantage. Notice how many denominations and religions that we have. It is through these "churches" that men can establish their power within the home using the "commandments of men." If Christ were, indeed, our shepherd, we would only have one church. Jesus said that He is "the way, the truth, and the life" (John 14:6).

Christ spoke of men that would cross the seas to bring a new convert home, only to make him worse than he was before they converted him to their "religion." Wouldn't it be absolutely amazing if our best men were those that did not attend church on Sunday but, instead, served the Lord on the sidewalk, in the business, in the post office, at home, and anywhere else that there was someone in need?

We don't have to be in one of those churches to be with the Lord. Our churches are bridges to Christ. The only problem is that few ever graduate from our physical churches. Most stay for the spiritual milk for their entire lives. Most attend church for a short time once a week. What if these men outside the church spent their entire waking hours serving the Lord? What a great and wonderful difference that they could make! Our God is everywhere. Jesus said in Matthew 18:20, "For where two or more are gathered together in my name, there am I in the midst of them."

Jesus said in Matthew 12:3–8,

> Have ye not read what David did, when he was an hungred, and they that were with him; How he entered into the house of God, and did eat the shewbread, which was not lawful for him to eat, neither for them which were with him, but only for the priests? Or have ye not read in the law, how that on the sabbath day the priests in the temple profane the sabbath, and are blameless? But I say unto you, That in this place is one greater than the temple, But if ye had known what *this* meaneth, I will have mercy, and not sacrifice, ye would not have condemned the guiltless. For the Son of man is Lord even on the Sabbath day.

The Catholic Church still has "showbread" today. They even lock this bread up so that no one can eat it except the priests. Our ministers encourage everyone to keep the Sabbath day holy by not working and going to church, and yet they profane the Sabbath as Christ said by working on the Sabbath themselves.

Every religion around the world builds churches so that their special teachings can be taught. The commandments of men are the rule. Virtually every major religion has a "man" that they prefer to follow instead of Christ.

Who is the Greatest?

Most of our churches are based on the teachings of Paul. The Islamic religion is based on the teachings of Mohammad. Others follow Buda. None of these men are the end; they are merely bridges to Christ—the shift from the physical to the spiritual. But unfortunately, few of our men ever make the transition from the physical to the spiritual realm. These "religions" enable men to retain their kingdoms on this earth. Few of our men are willing or ready to give the kingdom back to God and to follow Christ and His teachings.

We honor our father and mother by not permitting a step-parent to replace them. We call our father our "father" and our mother our "mother." We reserve the title for our genetic parents even though they may have been absent in our lives. In spite of the fact that many fathers are never there for their children, the children must eventually let go and love their absent father enough to give him to the family or woman that he chose. What an unfortunate choice we force our children to make in the name of adultery! We honor our father and mother despite the fact that they may not have been there for us during our childhood by saving the "place" for them. But we must not love what they have done. Sin is an ugly beast, and we must not imitate their poor example.

My father was an abusive alcoholic, and my mother left him when I was about five years of age. I missed my father's presence, and I still honor him in the position that will always be empty but is still reserved only for him and no one else. I am so thankful that I never had to deal with a step-father. My mother was a great woman, and she kept our best interests at heart. My father did one very important thing right, too. He went home to the children of his first family. He told my mother that we were not his children. All five of us were my mother's family. My mother was and still is the head of my family. She had been married previously to a very mean and hard-hearted man. This man may have had a father that went on to another woman rather than love his son. Obviously, he had no respect for women because of the way that he treated my mother.

The Step-Father's Step-Son

I remember going to a father/daughter banquet. I brought a sack lunch, and across the table sat a man that I did not know. I was very embarrassed and uncomfortable doing this, eating a meal with a strange man. I still remember it to this day. No one, especially no man, can replace a child's father nor should anyone try to force it. This experience was not beneficial for me at all except to emphasize to me just how important to me that my father actually was.

I just wish that I could have had a father. Neither my husband nor I had a "father." Both of our fathers were somewhere else. No wonder life has been so difficult for my family and my children. Some children only lose one father to another woman, but my husband and I both lost our fathers to other women. My father, though, did the best thing, even though it was not perfect. He could have still included us in his life but did not. He should never have instilled fear in my mother by beating her. He made a giant mistake!

We might have been hungry and even homeless at times, but we had her love and devotion. I honored my mother by helping her when she was in need. I was there by her side during some very difficult times. My mother left an adulterous situation and sinned no more.

If our men would only become more involved with their families, our divorce rates would decrease substantially. Instead, most of our men choose sin over family. They move from a monogamous relationship to polygamy. There is little difference between men in this country and those in Arab countries. Here in America, our men take one wife at a time, but in other countries, many have multiple wives at the same time. Both practice polygamy and adultery. When our men take multiple sex partners during their lives, they are also practicing polygamy. The men that practice polygamy are more likely to be involved in male social groups and competitive adult sports, like football, baseball, basketball, and soccer. These polygamous men may also compete against their own sons for material things.

These men will congregate in groups, and all manner of evil will flow from their hearts. We find wild male animals doing the same thing. But

Who is the Greatest?

you will never see one of them lift a hoof to help the mother with the offspring of their unions. How many of our sports-worshipping men will lift a finger to help a woman with child? How many lust and have adulterous relationships while married and even after divorce or separation?

Sons of God cleave to their wives. They do not have a need to compete against other men or worry about being the greatest among men. They are focused on the wife and the family. They are very involved in family life and are an integral part of the family. Notice how little is said about a man that is devoted to his family. He will not go around bragging about his accomplishments. He will not seek out recognition. He will humbly serve God by cleaving to his wife.

When the disciples asked Christ about divorce, Christ told them that it was not so in the beginning—a man did not divorce his wife. As we have continued through time, our men have become closer to resembling many of our wild animals that compete for mating rights without having any involvement in the care of their future offspring. Instead of using their strength to serve their family, they use their muscles to fight other males on the football field, basketball court, in the Olympics, at work . . .

Christ never raised His fists to another man, and He even commanded that we turn the other cheek. Even on the morning of Christ's betrayal by Judas, some of His disciples carried swords just as other men did for their defense. It must have been commonplace among men, much like the visible gun in the Old West and the concealed guns of today. Only Peter used his weapon as a defense, and Christ restored the man's severed ear. We live in Wild West days today that are similar to those from the past. A Civil War occurred prior to the Wild West days. Many sons had fathers that died in that war. Today, some of our fathers have died in wars, but most have committed adultery by moving in with another woman. Our sons are again fatherless even though their fathers are alive.

Christ said, "Put up again thy sword into his place: for all they that take the sword shall perish with the sword" (Matthew 26:52).

Men often don't appreciate the contributions of women until women leave them. Frustrated and angry, some will seek out their spouse and kill or abuse her when she leaves. Obviously, after she has left, he finally realizes how great her contribution was. If only he could have increased his contribution to the family instead of taking from his wife and children! Men put a terrible burden on their wives and children by being irresponsible "couch potatoes" at home.

Football is a "tournament" sport. For that matter, all professional sports are "tournament" sports. Adult men compete to be the greatest and for the most beautiful young women. These women pursue these men because of their wealth, power, and "status." What about men that sing love songs over the airwaves, stages, and televisions in our homes and cars? Who are they singing to? Maybe their spouses at first thought, but later, they are singing these love songs to women across the land. Think about the fan mail and pictures that they receive from adoring fans that virtually worship them as a god. The more our men are involved in "tournament" activities, the more separate and distant they will be from us. Some men waste many hours of their lives watching and participating in football games nationwide. It is not the family that matters to them; instead, it is their addiction to the adrenaline rush and aggression against others. Many men worldwide believe that it is acceptable for a man to use his strength to battle other men.[14] When he does so, he is working against God's kingdom on Earth and using it in his feeble attempt to establish his own kingdom on Earth.

We have many kingdoms in our society today. Men will decide what you eat, what you drink, what you wear, what you buy. They will use mass marketing to fish for followers from all economic levels. Our franchises today are a legal way of building an earthly kingdom. On top of the regular cost of operating the business, a customer will pay a franchise fee to the "creator." This creator will do little to earn the money that you give for the "privilege" of utilizing one of his chain businesses. This creator will work to dominate the market and get as much of your income as possible while doing very little for the customer. In most cases, you will never know who this "creator" is. But you can guarantee that "he" will benefit from your business.

How many of us know the grocery store owners? Or the farmers that grow the vegetables that are sold there? Where does the milk come from that you drink? Who built the furniture that is in your home? Big businesses and big kingdoms are the rule of law in this land. Our cities are starting to look alike. We have many people with good ideas and talents that have gone to waste because of men that want to be god on earth and take more than their allotted portion. These men are selfish. Instead of having a balance between urban and rural, these men build their kingdoms in large cities and poverty overruns the city. Many of our parents and children go unemployed because of them.

We are dependent victims of their self-centeredness, much like Eve became dependent upon Adam. What would we ever do if we did not have a large chain grocery store or a large chain shopping center? What would happen if there were no alcohol or tobacco tomorrow? Most would be absolutely helpless without them. Furthermore, we have many small businesses that have gone under because of their market dominance. If many of us could not survive without them, then it is obvious to me that they have become our provider, our god. Most have learned to trust in a god that is not real. We must not let ourselves become dependent upon them. We must use our talents to serve the Lord, our families, and our neighbors. A good start is to grow your own garden.

How important in our journey is it to exaggerate our femininity and masculinity? Who benefits? Answer: the one doing the exaggeration because it makes them the center of attention. They become larger than life and stand out before men and women. We need to ask ourselves this one question: When I go before judgment, will my behavior or activity be acceptable before the Lord? If the answer is no, then you shouldn't be doing it or encouraging others to do it! Our Lord never went around flaunting His masculinity or his body. He humbled Himself as a servant for us all—not only before men, but also women and children. To love is the greatest masculinity boost a man can get. This is how our men can acquire the greatness that they so blindly seek. Most do not know how to begin and rely on their penises to make an empty type of love.

Masculinity is something that comes naturally by submitting to God and serving God the way men are supposed to serve Him. Our children need to see their fathers cleaving to their mothers. Men are to humble themselves and serve, not flaunt their muscles, size, or aggressive tendencies.

Sons of men

Men ← **Husband** ← wife ← children

It is easy for this man to commit adultery, become a workaholic, an alcoholic, addicted to pornography, or a drug user. He is not concerned about his family but about himself. He desires to be reverent before other men and thinks of himself as the head of the wife. He is focused on the physical. His eyes are turned away from the family. The woman will be torn between following the man and caring for their children. If she doesn't follow him and please him, he will leave her. We can't serve two masters—God and man. We will have to make a choice.

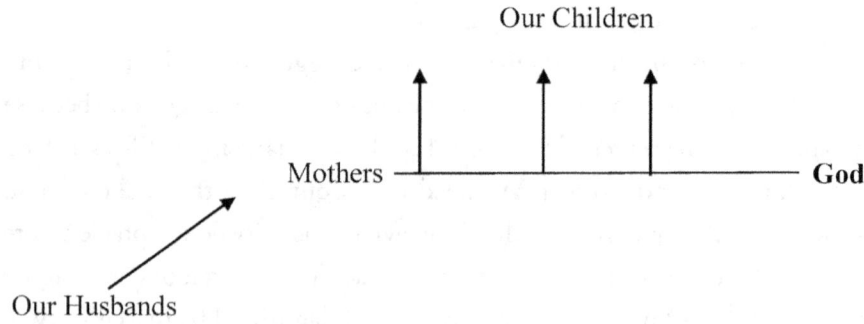

Who is the Greatest?

This man will cleave to his wife and be devoted to his family. This man is the least likely to divorce his wife and commit adultery. He is involved and connected. His eyes are turned toward the family. This relationship between man and wife will be long lasting and fulfilling for both spouses.

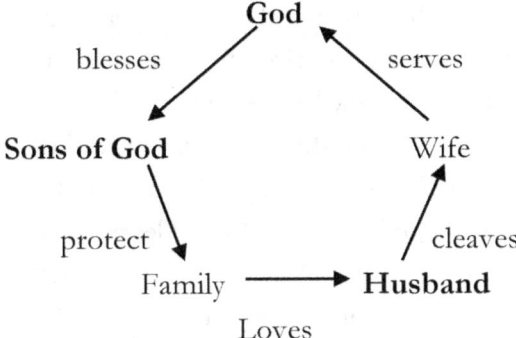

If Christ had come to this earth and demanded that men submit to His authority, He would have been a dictator on Earth. Instead, He humbled Himself and became a servant for all. The people, as a result, came to Him in multitudes—even 5,000 at a time. If men are to follow Christ's example, they must humble themselves as Christ did before men, women, and children. Our men of today want to be served instead of serving. They want to look good before other men, but they do it at the expense of their wives and children. In actuality, the wife is the one that is serving the Lord. The husband is the one that wants to be a god and expects his wife to serve him, too! Woe to our men!

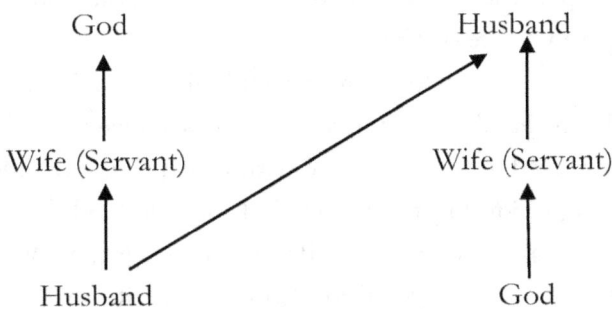

This type of servanthood (the one on the right) is against God's plan, for we are enabling another human being to replace God on Earth. The easiest way to identify a relationship of this type is to stop serving the man in a few ways to test him. If you don't have all of the ingredients to prepare a dish, don't make a special trip to the store. Use a suitable substitute ingredient in the dish. Don't get the mail and the newspaper from the mail box—let him. Tell him that you are too tired to have intercourse when you are really too tired. Don't mow the lawn—let him. If you have an idea of how something can be done better, do it your way instead of his way. In other words, express your independence in the Lord. And if you should make a mistake while learning, it is all right. We all learn by doing!

If his response is anger when he doesn't receive exactly what he expects to receive, then you know that he loves what you give him. He takes more than he needs, more than his apportioned amount. In this case, he doesn't actually love you or God, but he, instead, loves the things that he receives if he finds that they are pleasing to him. You don't have to feel hurt here, although it may come as a shock that he doesn't love you the way that he should. Just know that if he doesn't love you, then he doesn't love God either. Your job as a servant of God is to help him to see the error of his ways. This may take time, because many men of today are accustomed to having the perfect wife who does everything exactly as he wants it done. He may reject your comments on the subject and prefer that you be silent. Many wives do this to keep their husbands happy so that there will be money for the necessities of life. However, we must maintain a careful balance between the love of God and the love of money. God must be first in our lives, even before our husbands.

A man is not supposed to go around reminding his wife and children of the things that he has done for them. A gift does not have strings attached. We are all supposed to serve the Lord without expecting thanks in return or seeking recognition for it is expected of us to do God's will upon this earth. When we give gifts to our children or to others, we should not sit around waiting for a thank you from them. A gift with strings attached is not a gift at all. Some people will give a gift and wait around for a thank you card. Some will even get angry if they don't receive a card or a call. Christ did not wait to receive thanks when He healed the sick, lame, etc. He humbled Himself and served His Heavenly Father (Matthew 3:17, 17:5; Mark 1:11, 9:7; Luke 3:22, 9:35; 2 Peter 1:17). He did not wait for His Father to tell Him thanks for what He did on this earth. Jesus did say, "Well done, good and faithful servant; thou hast been faithful over a few things, I will make thee ruler over many things: enter thou into the joy of thy lord" (Matthew 25:23).

Jesus also said,

> Take heed that ye do not your alms before men, to be seen of them: otherwise ye have no reward of your Father which is in heaven. Therefore, when thou doest *thine* alms, do not sound a trumpet before thee, as the hypocrites do in the synagogues and in the streets, that they may have glory of men. Verily I say unto you, They have their reward. But when thou doest alms, let not thy left hand know what thy right hand doeth: That thine alms may be in secret: and thy Father which seeth in secret himself shall reward thee openly. (Matthew 6:1–4)

Jesus said, "Let not thy left hand know what thy right hand doeth." Jesus is talking about the different sides of the brain. He is telling us not to let our ego that seeks recognition know what we have done. We have a choice between two perceptions.

Women serve in this manner every day. Most go to work for eight hours, care for the children when they get home, prepare the meal, and clean the house. Still, the husband will sit down and wait to be served by his weary wife after working a mere eight-hour shift himself. Men receive elaborate titles for their working positions. They falsely believe that the title will elevate them to a level higher than others. So, instead of serving the people under them, they expect to be served by those under them as though they were a god.

> Then spake Jesus to the multitude, and to his disciples, Saying, The scribes and Pharisees sit in Moses' seat: All therefore whatsoever they bid you observe, *that* observe and do, but do not ye after their works: for they say, and do not. For they bind heavy burdens and grievous to be borne, and lay *them* on men's shoulders; but they *themselves* will not move them with one of their fingers. But all their works they do for to be seen of men: they make broad their phylacteries, and enlarge the borders of their garments, And love the uppermost rooms at feasts, and the chief seats in the synagogues, And greetings in the markets, and to be called of men, Rabbi. But be not ye called Rabbi: for one is your Master, *even* Christ; and all ye are brethren. And call no *man* your father upon the earth: for one is your Father, which is in heaven. Neither be ye called masters: for one is your Master, even Christ. But he that is greatest among you shall be your servant. And whosoever shall exalt himself shall be abased; and he that shall humble himself shall be exalted. . . . Woe unto you, scribes and Pharisees, hypocrites! for ye pay tithe of mint and anise and cumin, and have omitted the weightier *matters* of the law, judgment, mercy, and faith: these ought ye to have done, and not to leave the other undone. *Ye* blind guides, which strain at a gnat, and swallow a camel. Woe to you, scribes and Pharisees, hypocrites! for ye make clean the outside of the cup and of the platter, but within they are full of extortion and excess. *Thou* blind Pharisee, cleanse first that *which* is within the cup and platter, that the outside of them may be clean also. Woe unto you, scribes and Pharisees, hypocrites! for ye are like unto whited sepulchres, which indeed appear beautiful outward, but are within full of dead *men's* bones, and

Who is the Greatest?

of all uncleanness. Even so ye also outwardly appear righteous
unto men, but within ye are full of hypocrisy and iniquity.
(Matthew 23:1–14, 23–28)

The measure of a man is not and should not be based on the goodness of his wife and children. Nor should a wife or a child be dishonest and cover up the man's sinful nature in the home. If he can silence his wife and children, he can build an earthly kingdom within the home.

When we have problems with others, Christ told us to talk to the person first. If he fails to listen, then we bring in one or two more to talk to him. Finally, we are to go to the church—people outside the home—and tell them what is happening (Matthew 18:15–20). The truth is what sets us free. Light must be shed on the problem. This is how we eliminate it. We have to do this if we love others. I have talked to my husband's family, I have talked to some of their friends, and I have talked to some of their lawyers. I have done my best, but now it is time to talk to the church. I am taking this message to each and every one of you that will listen to my plea.

Not once did Christ utter the word "submit" to any man or woman or child. Yet men in religions everywhere expect women and children to submit to them. Could this be one of the reasons that so few of our teenage daughters are virgins? Our young men are imitating their fathers' disrespectful behavior toward their own mothers. Most have carried this notion beyond the household and into the workplace and everywhere that males congregate. At every opportunity, they attempt to exert their perceived "authority" over women both young and old.

Instead of doing things to be seen by men, they should be concerned about doing things for the Lord and that are in the best interests of the family, God's children. Those things done that are seen by men are rewards that are received on Earth. Most of our men seek recognition from men just as the disciples argued about who was the greatest among them. Things have changed very little with men since the time of Christ. They have remained much the same. There are sons of God that have humbled themselves to serve as Christ intended, but they are the exception rather than the rule.

Many men want the best of everything this earth has to give. We have movies with violence and pornography just for them. We have X-rated strip clubs just for them. We have bars. We have alcohol and drugs that are a vain attempt to make them feel good. They have many established ways of separating themselves from women while practicing the usage of women to satisfy their lusts. Foul language is another example.

Jesus said, "A good man out of the good treasure of his heart bringeth forth that which is good; and an evil man out of the evil treasure of his heart bringeth that which is evil: for of the abundance of the heart his mouth speaketh" (Luke 6:45).

Heaven forbid if a woman with a career in a male-dominated field takes a seat at the table. Many will or already have treated her disrespectfully, made sexual advances toward her, told sexually oriented jokes, and left her out of crucial business meetings. These are all things that the Lord is looking for when establishing criteria for our selection as worthy of His heavenly kingdom. He is judging men everywhere, every day, by the words that they utter and the deeds that they perform. Women and children are the greatest test for revealing a man's true heart.

> And he came to Nazareth, where he had been brought up: and, as his custom was, he went into the synagogue on the sabbath day, and stood up for to read. And there was delivered unto him the book of the prophet Esaias. And when he had opened the book, he found the place where it was written, The Spirit of the Lord *is* upon me, because he hath anointed me to preach the gospel to the poor; he hath sent me to heal the brokenhearted, to preach deliverance to the captives, and recovering of sight to the blind, to set at liberty them that are bruised, To preach the acceptable year of the Lord. (Luke 4:16–19)

Who is the Greatest?

As the man rules on Earth, he will want his wife and children to serve him. Part of that service will require that she silence herself and put him on a pedestal everywhere she can. With a servant wife, he becomes god on Earth and does as he pleases whenever and wherever he pleases. He will set a very high standard for his wife and children; when things go wrong, he will blame them, for he will never be at fault nor will he accept responsibility for anything that really matters.

The ego is like a tight skin. It keeps us from growing. The more we shed our ego, the bigger we become.

Sin dulls the senses. The more we sin without repentance, the less common sense we will have and the more mistakes we will make. Sinners are followers. They are the blind leading the blind. They do as others do and seldom consider the needs of others. This is the way that our sons are raised by their fathers, step-fathers, and step-mothers.

In the following scripture, I have inserted in parenthesis what I believe Jesus was talking about in his parable.

> Hear another parable: There was a certain householder (God), which planted a vineyard (our family), and hedged it round about (in order to keep out other men and women), and digged a winepress in it, and built a tower (to heaven), and let it out to husbandmen (our husbands), and went into a far country: And when the time of the fruit drew near, he sent his servants (wives) to the husbandmen, that they might receive the fruits of it (the husband's service to God). And the husbandmen took his servants, and beat one, and killed another, and stoned another. Again, he sent other servants (our children) more than the first: and they did unto them likewise. But last of all he sent unto them his son (Jesus), saying, They will reverence my son (Jesus). But when the husbandmen (our husbands) saw the son (Jesus), they said among themselves, This is the heir: come, let us kill him, and let us seize on his inheritance (wives and children

will serve the husbands instead of God). And they caught him, and cast *him* out of the vineyard, and slew *him*. When the lord therefore of the vineyard (the family) cometh, what will he do unto those husbandmen (our husbands)? They say unto him, He will miserably destroy those wicked men, and will let out *his* vineyard unto other husbandmen, which shall render him the fruits in their seasons. Jesus saith unto them, Did ye never read in the scriptures, The stone which the builders rejected, the same is become the head of the corner: this is the Lord's doing, and it is marvellous in our eyes? Therefore say I unto you, The kingdom of God shall be taken from you, and given to a nation bearing forth the fruits thereof. And whosoever shall fall on this stone shall be broken: but on whomsoever it shall fall, it will grind him to powder. And when the chief priests and Pharisees had heard his parables, they perceived that he spake of them. But when they sought to lay hands on him, they feared the multitude, because they took him for a prophet. Matthew 21:33–46

This country is on the verge of being taken over by Mexico. In San Antonio, Texas, Hispanics are the majority of the population and not the minority. Despite this discrepancy, they still receive minority status, even though they are not. (In many cases, the best jobs are reserved for people that are bilingual—those that can speak Spanish and English.) They seem to value their families more than blacks and whites. Black men have been notorious for going from woman to woman. White men and women are doing the same thing, the only difference is that they marry and then divorce one at a time. Few are loyal to their first spouse, the children of their first spouse, and their entire family. Perhaps God is giving this nation to another nation that is bearing the fruits that He expects of us.

Women and children are the servants that God has sent into His kingdom on Earth. Just as God brought Eve to Adam, He still brings

Who is the Greatest?

His servants to men. Our men are the separated ones. Many women and children have been and are beaten, stoned, and martyred so that men can maintain control of God's kingdom. Whatsoever men do to the least of our brothers—the poor, homeless, widows, women, children, and other men—they do unto the Lord. Women, children, the homeless, the imprisoned, the sick, and the poor are the test of real men's hearts. This is where their true hearts are revealed. Our children are branches that sprout off of our family vine. The harvest that He is talking about refers to our souls going to Heaven. We were created living souls.

Our men want women and children to serve them instead of the Lord! The home is God's kingdom, not man's! It is sacred and is the vineyard that the Lord was speaking about in the verses above. Our men are to be helpmeets. In the end, each one of us individually will be accountable before the Lord. We are God's children, and we have each been entrusted to a mother and a father to raise us according to God's commandments and not the commandments of men.

What About the Step-child?

"Jesus answered them, Is it not in your law, I said, Ye are gods?" (John 10:34)

"And he said unto him, Why callest thou me good? *there is* none good but one, *that is*, God: but if thou wilt enter into life: keep the commandments." (Matthew 19:17)

The aborted or abandoned
Cornerstone of the FAMILY

The Child — GOD

Children of the Kingdom   **Children of the Kingdom**

child   child   child   child   child   child

husband   2ⁿᵈ wife   2ⁿᵈ husband   wife

father Mother God

The Separated Family Tree

The Step-Father's Step-Son

There are two gods in this FAMILY – the father and the step-father. Both have committed adultery.

My husband's father was the king on this side of the family tree.	My husband's step-father was the king on this side of the family.
*He committed adultery by abandoning his first wife and son for another woman and then marrying her.	*He committed adultery by marrying a divorced woman.
*He gave away things that were not his to give away.	*He took things that were not his to take.
*He is the one that gave his son's position, the family name, his family, and his property to another woman.	*He became the heir of everything that was my husband's.
*He became property to his second wife and their children.	*He took over the position as head of my husband's family.
*He became a broken man.	*He used my husband to get the work done.
*His children are the children of the kingdom.	*He gave my husband's mother's property to his children.
	*His wife became a broken woman.
	*His children are the children of the kingdom.

Most of us know from experience that the ones that will care the least about the children of the first family are the child's father and his other woman. But there is competition in the child's mother's home also because the step-father will expect to inherit everything that originally belonged to the child. The child is wedged between two adults competing for something that does not belong to them. We have two adults separating something that God created.

Jesus said,

> And I say unto you, That many shall come from the east and west, and shall sit down with Abraham, and Isaac, and Jacob, in the kingdom of heaven. But the children of the kingdom shall be cast out into outer darkness: there shall be weeping and gnashing of teeth. (Matthew 8:11, 12)

> Take heed that ye despise not one of these little ones; for I say unto you, That in heaven their angels do always behold the face of my Father which is in heaven. (Matthew 18:10)

> But from the beginning of the creation God made them male and female. For this cause shall a man leave his father and

mother, and cleave to his wife; And they twain shall be one flesh: so then they are not more twain, but one flesh. What therefore God hath joined together, let no man put asunder. (Mark 10:6)

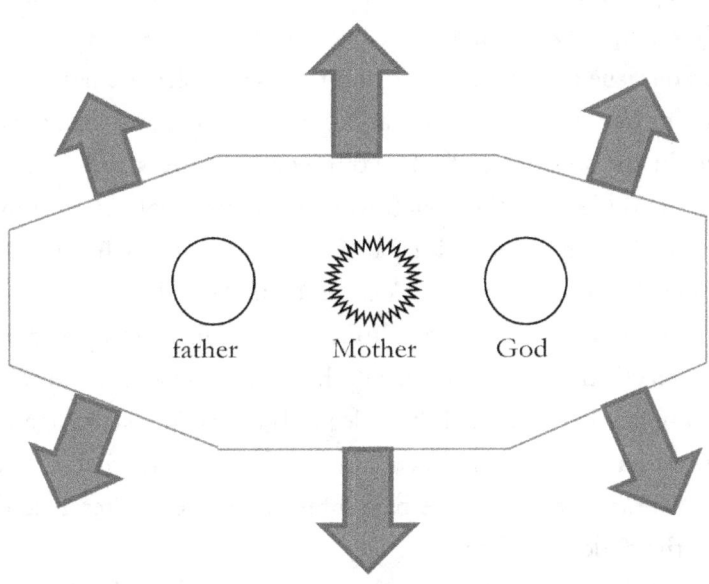

The statistics are astounding about the likelihood that a step-parent will abuse or even kill a step-child. If you want to read about the depressing data, you can easily find it in the newspaper every day. Another great reference would be the "Cinderella Effect" on Wikipedia, the free encyclopedia online. Step-children are neglected with even more frequency. In most cases, the step-child will be the oldest child in the home. In my husband's case, he was the oldest child in the homes of both his mother and his father, even though his father excluded him. My husband's father was the son of a medical doctor. He would have been a great catch for any woman. He married a very beautiful, intelligent, and talented woman who was the daughter of a district judge. My husband's mother quit college to marry this man and have his child. Both had a lot to offer to someone else.

The only problem was that they had a child, my husband. This complicated things when they made the decision to divorce and then remarry.

I have been a witness to things that should never be, things that make me want to cry. Listening to the evening news on the radio or television is depressing. Reading the newspaper or news over the internet is equally depressing. Every day someone has been hurt. The ones that are hurting others are our true victims. They are the victims of broken homes and broken families. The ones that our victims are hurting, are the ones that are paying the price for the sins committed by our legal adulterers and adulteresses. There are no outlets for these victims because just about everything that adulterers and adulteresses do is legal. A woman can move in with a child's father and become his legal heir. A second wife's children with the child's father are allowed to replace the children of the first family and become heirs to everything that the child's father has. Our victimized children cannot complain because all of this is legal. If they take a stand against this practice, we have lawyers and law enforcement officials that will uphold the laws that are written in the best interests of the adulterers and their children, the children of men.

Paul upheld the laws of the lords in his time by bringing "Christians" to the judges for sentencing. The lords, who are like our lawyers and judges, created these laws. Paul was like a bounty hunter or a police officer helping to enforce the laws of the land. For anyone that did not agree with these laws, there was punishment and even death. Those in disagreement most likely would be considered evil because they refused to accept things for face value and just say it is "okay". Judah's two sons were considered evil by their father. These two sons were killed by God scripture tells us, but I think that it was a "lord" that enforced the laws of the lords which resulted in these young men's death. Judah's sons were powerless against their father because of "laws". Judah even commanded that one of his sons have intercourse with his own brother's widow. This son was killed for ejaculating on the ground while he lay beside his brother's widow. It is much like our children of today. Our laws are written in favor of the grown-ups and it is

What About the Step-child?

perfectly legal to abort a child, put a child up for adoption, marry another woman and make her the heir, and replace the children of the first family with the children of the second family. In Judah's case, he thought he could even control his adult children and make them do his bidding.

My husband's life is only one part of the puzzle. I have sons, and do you really think that a son that has been treated badly by a selfish step-mother, an absent father, an abandoned mother, and a step-father that really liked the idea of marrying into some money will be a good parent himself? No. Unfortunately, our problems started with two people. It didn't start with my husband who is the victim of four adulterers and their six children. It started when one decided to commit adultery with another person. My husband's father and stepmother are where it started. My husband grew up with adultery all around him and in the most confusing of circumstances for a child to endure alone.

Late one night, the step-mother called to talk to me. My youngest son and his wife had been having marital problems, which she knew about because I had told them. She asked about them because she wanted my youngest son to come and see his "grandfather." She was hoping that my youngest son had done what his grandfather, her husband, had done. I told her that my son had "made the right decision—he went home to his wife, which is where he belongs." I was not chastising her. I was merely stating the truth. When I said those words, the step-mother gulped the biggest gulp that I have ever heard. It was as though she had eaten those words. This must have touched very close to home with her. This woman did not love my husband's father, my husband, or his family. She saw an opportunity and took advantage of it.

One of my husband's father's relatives, the one that helped to reunite us the second and last time, told me that my husband's father was "such a good man that he would let anyone take advantage of him." I don't think that it is a good thing for us to let others take advantage of us and use us. Later, I told a family friend to tell him that if he was indeed such "a good man that 'he would let anyone take advantage of him,' then he must be living with the first person that took advantage of him." The first person that took advantage of him was the woman that snagged him when he was "alone."

I grew up so backward and poor. I honestly believed that my husband grew up in the better home at first. I was so wrong! It is better to be poor and loved than to grow up with money and isolated from the family by adult competition—adultery. I thought that he would be a better parent than me. I know now that he grew up in a home that was very unhealthy when compared to the home in which I grew up. I may have been poor, but I was loved. He was not loved as much as his three half-brothers and three half-sisters. The poor don't need a lawyer, doctor, or minister to define their family. Because they love, they automatically know. The ones that do not love are the ones that need a lawyer, doctor, and a minister to explain these complex rules.

My sons have grown up with a father that was neglected, abused, mistreated, ignored, unappreciated, isolated, separated, used, taken advantage of, replaced—the list could go on and on. This is the product of full-blown adultery. Why is it that we expect these children to be better parents than the adulterous ones that raised him? The only answer to this question is that adultery is our most sacred sin. Most people never think about the abandoned or abused child or the abandoned or abused mother or father. They just look at the surface. They see a man and a woman. It doesn't matter if it is their tenth marriage as long as it is just "one man and one woman" standing side by side and smiling.

These are the exact terms that many people use to define "marriage" today. They want it to be "one man" and "one woman." All that a man or woman has to do is eliminate their first spouse, and then he/she is single again and can go on and marry someone else. Unfortunately, though, "one man" and "one woman" do not define a family. A family is everyone with whom we have been intimate. God does not give us the freedom to eliminate people from our families unless they try to break up the nucleus of the family. They are family whether we like it or not!

What About the Step-child?

In this case, the "step-mother" and her "oldest daughter" will always be members of our family. This daughter would love to eliminate me from "her family," though, but she can't! She is not the family even though she would like to think that she is! But like Judah and his brothers, she does have her own family separate from the main family. The biggest problem is that my husband's father moved in with her mother.

I do not like a lot of the things that my husband does, but he is still and always will be a part of this family. I detest what his father and step-mother did, but my husband's father will always be his father. I do not like the decisions that my husband's mother made, but she will always be my husband's mother and my children's grandmother. I will never call my husband's step-mother his mother or my children's grandmother because she is not. And yes, my husband's father will always be my children's grandfather, even though he never did anything for them. I guess that we could refer to this man as a "sperm donor" or a "deadbeat dad and granddad."

My oldest son was the most confused about these relationships. He was born into the family at a time when the adultery had evolved into full-blown adultery. He did not understand that his father's step-parents and their children would be the heirs in our family. Children naturally know their positions within the family, but I don't think that he ever expected to have grown-ups taking what was naturally his and his father's and giving it to the children of the second families. He thinks that he is solely responsible for the way that things turned out. But unfortunately, his grandparents and step-grandparents are the ones that cursed him and his father.

My oldest son is most likely the most talented of all of the grandchildren. He is the firstborn son of the firstborn son, my husband, and the firstborn son, his grandfather. His position is very significant in family vines. My husband, who is my sons' natural father, even treated our oldest son like a step-child sometimes—the way that the step-father had treated him. The step-father did not love my children as his grandchildren because they were not his grandchildren. My husband had no choice but to call his step-father his dad because his father never acted like a father. Then, there was the step-mother that didn't want to be a step-mother. She only wanted to be the mother of this man's children with her. She did not want anything to do with my husband. She wanted my husband's father and my children's grandfather, but she did not want my husband or our children except for them to carry the "Frizzell" name forward. She wanted to be this man's only wife at the expense of my husband and his mother. Last of all, there was my husband's mother, who never stopped being a mother but was torn between her firstborn son and her children with another man.

All of this misery and suffering is so that two people can pretend that they are something that they are not. It is so that a man can play house with another woman. Judah fixed things so that the man did not have to kill his first wife and/or her children in order to move in with another woman. His solution was to divorce her and her children and move on. All marriages are based upon law. All of us, including our children, are replaceable. Judah did this for his mother, Leah, who wanted Jacob to move in with her and leave Rachel. They hated Rachel's son Joseph, too.

In this country, women benefit from these legal family laws just as much as men when they eliminate their first spouses for someone else. It was Leah that wanted Jacob. Jacob did not want Leah for his first wife. If another man had married Rachel, if Jacob had left her for Leah, he would also be the one that benefitted the most. The couple from the first marriage are the ones that are the most likely to be taken advantage of and used in the second marriage. Our laws are hostile toward the man and the woman of the first marriage and their children. Our laws bless the new spouses of the second marriage and their children by giving them the privilege of replacing the former spouse and the children of the first family.

Even Jesus' disciples had difficulty with the idea that a family was permanent. They thought that putting their wife away was okay. Jesus told them that if they could not respect this, it was not meant for them (Matthew 19:12). The "it" in this case, I firmly believe, means Heaven. Jesus understood the damage that adultery causes. He knew that children are mistreated and killed. Children, even in this country, do not have a voice. Adults make most

What About the Step-child?

decisions for them every day—most with the help of a lawyer. They even decide that it is more important for another woman to inherit everything and leave nothing for the children of the first family. This is the price that must be paid so that a father can play house with another woman.

If you want to see mental illness in families, let a step-parent work over the child, and then this confused adult will work over his/her own children. Mental illness will become even more obvious in the children of this child. This child's love is incomplete. The bonding and trust that comes with normal families is incomplete in broken homes because there is at least one step-parent that does not want the child. They will both have to make compromises with this child that they do not like. This child will have to give up everything that was his/hers so that the step-parents and their children can have it all.

Based upon study after study, children under the age of three are much more likely to be abused or killed by a step-parent in their home. Researchers have found that parents that abuse and kill their own children actually had diagnosable mental health problems. These step-parents did not abuse the step-children because of mental health problems but rather because they had a problem with the step-children themselves. Step-parents are much more likely to hit step-children more frequently than a parent normally would for "discipline" purposes. Step-fathers are more likely to abuse step-children rather than kill them. A step-father is much more likely to use a step-child as a "sexual object" than the child's own father.[15] A step-father will normally take the side of his child over that of a step-child.[16, 17]

With these odds, what is the likelihood that the step-child will grow up and abuse his genetic children? I will venture to say that the odds are exponentially greater. We have a pandemic of epic proportions coming our way!

I do not know that all physical punishment is harmful, but the biggest problem that I see comes from having step-parents replace a parent and administer punishment. These individuals are the ones that start an unnatural cycle of abuse within the home and family that may go on for generations. Many will physically mistreat the step-child. Then, the step-child perpetuates the problem by imitating the same confusing behavior in his own home with his own children. The root cause of the problem is bringing a step-parent, an unrelated stranger, into the family home that does not belong there. This is the reason that a man is never supposed to marry another man's wife and move in with her. And a father is never supposed to move in with another woman and play house with her. He can have another woman on the side with his wife's approval, but he can never move in permanently!

Jesus said in Matthew 18:6, 7, "But whoso shall offend one of these little ones which believe in me, it were better for him that a millstone were hanged about his neck, and *that* he were drowned in the depth of the sea. Woe unto the world because of offences! for it must needs be that offences come; but woe to that man by whom the offence cometh!"

Our children are our future. We wonder why we are falling behind in fields such as science and math. Children growing up in the fear of step-parents and their children will never reach their full potential. Their growth will be forever stunted. This will also have a serious impact on their future generations. It will almost seem that the glass ceiling is within the family home itself. Step-parents will invest their time, energy, and money in their own children while neglecting the older step-child. There will be no conceivable way for this child to escape from this situation and rise above it because we have grown-ups working against a child. This child, when he is grown, will experience resentment when his own children try to climb past him on the road to success, especially his oldest son. Instead of being excited for his children, he will feel threatened at their success. Our parents and grandparents are cursing their future generations by permitting strangers to live with their children, discipline their children, and become the family heirs.

What Happens to Painful Emotional Memories?

One of the worst things that can happen is for the step-child to grow up and then treat his own children—especially his oldest son—as step-children, just as his step-father treated him. This is very possible because the oppressed frequently become abusers in turn, perpetuating a pattern of abuse. The root cause is the unjust use of a false sense of authority among step-parents and childhood oppression, which involves the taking of everything from our children for the step-parents' and their children's gain. All of this goes back to a false interpretation of scripture within the Bible itself. Instead of reading about what sons of God wrote, we are reading and following the teachings of men.

These little children that were abused are thought to have felt no pain. Their cries went out to deaf ears. These little children must deaden the pain that they suffer in order to survive. As a result of being unable to express their emotions about the humiliation and oppression, they will hurt or injure others because they cannot feel the pain of others or understand their own pain as children. Fear has long ago replaced love; therefore, they find it difficult to feel genuine empathy and pity toward others.[18]

When this environment arises, the adult step-child will leave his children—especially his oldest son—vulnerable to physical and possibly sexual abuse by third parties. These step-sons are missing the "soul" connection with their fathers. This "soul" connection would help them to better understand themselves and to be better fathers. It will be obvious to these third parties that this adult step-child is not there to protect his or her own children, but instead to ensure that his or her spouse and children serve him or her exclusively. He or she will distract the other spouse by constantly demanding the attention that the children need. The children will suffer because there is competition for the love and affection that naturally belongs to them and that they so desperately need to thrive as children.

This adult step-child can be very demanding and narcissistic as a parent. He or she will be an "energy leach" to this family, as Dr. Paul Pearsall describes them.[34] All that this grown step-child will care about is what he or she can get or take. He or she wants to get from the current family what they think was taken from them as a child. Perhaps they are trying to fill a void or emptiness from their childhood, unresolved issues of which they have little to no understanding. This is insanity at its peak. Beware of the damage that step-parents do to our children and, in turn, the damage that our step-children as adults can do to our children.

I believe that when early abuse occurs and the child doesn't understand the "sin" for which they were punished, the memory is stored in the brain for later consideration. It is like a latent effect since the memory can arise at any time in adulthood, especially following betrayal by a spouse, family member, or friend. Often, it manifests itself as a mental illness (as we call it) of some type or another. It could happen in peacetime, or it could happen on the battlefield. What is not understood today is that it is a requirement for the child to go through this in order to become complete. This is why Christ told us to turn the other cheek and to love the sinner. We are supposed to encourage repentance because it helps them to work past these issues. The strange behavior illustrates just how incomplete their learning was when the abuse began. The main problem at the root of all mental illnesses is fear, and it goes back to childhood when their parents or step-parents abused them.

Let's take a minute and examine a specific example of this: the young woman who remained on the toilet seat for such a long time that she had to be surgically removed from it at the hospital. There is no doubt in my mind

What Happens to Painful Emotional Memories?

that this young woman experienced abuse during childhood. She may have been punished for not having learned to control her bladder and digestive system. Or she could have been sexually abused and sought refuge on the potty for protection. She may have found in early childhood that it was safer for her to remain on the toilet. Or perhaps her "parents" had insisted that she stay there in order to prevent accidents. This memory may have resurfaced during some event of betrayal with her "boyfriend." Perhaps she realized that she was not loved but was being controlled and used in the relationship. This was the only way that she had learned to protect herself from abuse. Her response was to return to the only safe place that she knew: the toilet. Hopefully, she will be allowed the time to consolidate her memories instead of being placed on psychiatric medications for the rest of her life and told that she is defective.

A child that has experienced abuse early in childhood will often appear to remain "fairly balanced" until additional betrayals occur in adulthood. This is when the stored emotional memory will rise to the surface so that, eventually, memory consolidation can occur. The memory is actually from the past but will be relived in the present. An unsuspecting bystander may be the recipient of this "child's" self-protective measures. It could be the woman to whom he is married, his child, or someone on the streets of town. These are the ones that pay the price for adultery within the family and the home.

My husband's father had a relative that was hanged because he killed his wife. I theorize that this man grew up in some confusing circumstances. Perhaps he grew up with a father that was living with another woman. This woman may have had children herself prior to her marriage to the child's father. Either way, he grew up with little respect for women, perhaps because of the way his step-father or father treated his mother or because of the way that a step-mother treated him. Or the problem could have gone back another generation to where adultery can be found. Unfortunately, this woman became the recipient of the anger that was directed the wrong way. She paid the price for someone's adultery.

In a culture that embraces adultery, it is hard to blame adulterous parents because it is socially acceptable. For this reason, in many cases, the anger gets directed toward the immediate family instead of in the direction that it belongs.

The "ego," the part of the brain that causes us to worry about ourselves and what we receive, when stroked properly with rewards and recognition, will allow the wisdom of the logical side of the brain to flow through. But when betrayal occurs, the "ego" side of the brain takes over and locks down. This is when the adrenalin starts flowing and we go into self-protective mode. Tremendous strength can be released as a result—enough to even kill someone.

This is also the reason that Jesus told us repeatedly not to commit adultery because step-parents do not love someone else's children like their own. Furthermore, children need to grow up with their own parents, not step-parents. They learn about themselves through their parents, and their parents learn about themselves through their children.

These separated and abused children will not connect naturally. The child will not have the "awareness" of those around him. He will swing objects and hit someone without realizing that someone is nearby or throw something and break a window. The root of the betrayal is the fact that the very people, the ones that he should have been able to trust totally, have hurt him instead of loving him. Each fresh blow as an adult, years after the original event, risks further damage to the psyche. This is why Christ told us to love the sinner. Such survivors of childhood abuse may even experience memory losses as a result. The more that children are hurt, abused, and betrayed, the wilder they will become.

Just as a ram will dash madly into the fence time after time in a futile attempt to escape, so, too, will the adult child become irrational and do things that they would normally not do when placed in a stressful situation. Our sons will run from the police instead of facing the consequences of their decisions because fear has taken over and they have shifted into self-protective mode. During such a period of instability, they need peace and quiet, as well as time to work through the issues about which they may not be aware. They are wild men and women that are very scared.

I doubt that the woman that sat on the toilet for two years remembered exactly what happened in her childhood. She most likely had little understanding at the time that the events were stored in her hippocampus and amygdala for later processing. As that memory rose to the surface, she was forced to begin dealing with her past fears, including possible childhood molestation, and the presence of her current "boyfriend" was the emotional trigger. She may have realized that he did not love her except for, possibly, what she could give to him. What she did not understand was that the present situation was the impetus for the emotional upheaval and not the actual cause. The root cause was the incomplete childhood memory that rose to the surface as a result of the betrayal of love. The betrayal of love was the trigger that caused it to surface from the distant past.

I experienced a period of instability in my life following a betrayal by my husband. He broke a very important promise that he had made to me. I profoundly remember a certain scary place in my mind. I knew it was there, but I also made the conscious decision that I wasn't going to it. I maintained my faith until it went away completely. This didn't happen in days but over several months. Who knows what this memory was about? I don't know, but I strongly suspect that it happened when I was much too young to understand. But I blame no one, and I thank the Lord that I had the faith to stay focused and walk right past it. Faith is truly the rock.

Also, when this period of emotional instability began in my life, I distinctly remember that I had forgotten something that I had learned my senior year in college that was important for me to remember. I could remember that the thought had been there, but I could no longer access it. My brain must have developed new neurotransmitters around this emotional event. Hence, I bypassed it and left it behind.

I have learned so much more since that time. My faith is stronger than ever. I believe that what Jesus said is true. I trust Him. My love and compassion for others has grown, especially for our children when they grow up with adulterous parents and step-parents. I understand just how damaging this is to our families and what they have to endure. Wisdom and understanding are truly more valuable than silver or gold!

I wanted a much easier life than the one that I have had, but I truly love my husband. But I also love my sons. I am caught in the middle in many ways. My husband's step-parents and parents are responsible for him. I am responsible for my children. But someone has to speak up, otherwise this cycle will never stop. If these women and men were not heirs, they would think more carefully before jumping in bed with a married man/woman or someone's father/mother. They might even leave them alone for a while so that they can learn something. Our men and women need time to mend and to think about the consequences of their decisions. Another man or woman, in most cases, is not the answer to their problems. These people will only complicate matters more.

There are many aspects of our society in which these repressed memories can cause harm. How many of our military personnel go to war with latent memories like that stored in their brains? I believe that these personnel are the ones most likely to experience Post Traumatic Stress Disorder (PTSD) after release from the battlefield. We have people that are compulsively drawn to speed, steal, smoke, use drugs, drink excessively, eat excessively, starve to the point of malnourishment, etc. We also have husbands and boyfriends that reach a point in relationships where they break and either seriously harm or kill their partners. As though they were still a small child, they will fight back without thinking of the one that they are harming.

I also believe that early damage to the emotional centers of the brain is what causes the onset of illnesses like Parkinson's disease. I also believe that through damage to the emotional centers of the brain early in childhood, we may develop illnesses such as heart problems, and adult onset diabetes among others. Our children are the ones that are abandoned so that their fathers and mothers can move in with another woman or man. Their fathers break their children's hearts—it is little wonder that our children, especially our sons, will have heart problems during their lifetimes. Doctors

What Happens to Painful Emotional Memories?

will make lots of money off of them and, possibly, their children when the health problems are passed on to the next generation.

This is because our brains are functioning in a dysfunctional state, which, over time, results in illness. The hippocampus and amygdala both play important roles in the regulation and modulation of brain chemistry. It is with early damage to these areas because of emotional events beyond their understanding that we gradually become sick in adulthood. For some, merely a trigger of betrayal will be enough to suddenly change the health of the individual.

Let's take a minute to examine hyperactivity in children and adults. Hyperactivity manifests itself in many ways in our children and adults. Some have excessively strong emotional outbursts, compulsive or impulsive behavior, and attention problems whereby the individual will have trouble staying focused on a problem long enough to solve it. I once talked with a young woman whose sister could not stop stealing. She confided in me that her sister had been to jail numerous times but could neither control nor resist the temptation to shoplift again. I believe that compulsive behavior of this sort also has its root in an early childhood experience.

Paul also described his early life as an adult as knowing what he should do but, instead, doing what he knew he shouldn't (Romans 7:15).[19, 20] I theorize that the sister who could not stop herself from stealing may have been punished when she took something without permission, perhaps another child's toy. Instead of her parent or step-parent allowing her to learn from the mistake, she was most likely harshly corrected. Or worse still, she could have been blamed for taking something that was really hers. A step-parent quite often falsely believes that everything belongs to them and their children instead of to the children of the first marriage.

As a result, she never was allowed to gain understanding and closure in childhood. Even worse, she had a painful emotional memory stored away for later processing. So, here she was as an adult trying to learn something that she was not given the time to learn as a child. And the sad thing is that the same problem would come rising up in her life until she finally gained mastery in adulthood. As a child, she knew it was wrong to take the toy because one of her parents told her so, but she did not understand why, and furthermore, she was denied the opportunity to try again without fear in order to learn.

This is the reason why we have adults suffering from self-destructive behaviors such as speeding, drinking and driving, drinking in excess, lying, stealing, eating disorders, and other impulses. They were denied the opportunity to learn as children to find balance in their childhoods; hence, we have adults forced to face these relatively simple tasks. They were controlled instead of loved. They were made to finish the food on their plates because their parents were afraid of waste.

Step-parents would not be very forgiving about any of these self-destructive behaviors. Most would very likely blame the step-child. I doubt that in this country any step-parents would have any compassion for these children. Adultery is a very sacred sin. You may wonder how I could possibly call it a sacred sin, but it is the one sin that is freely accepted in this country. There is little to no stigma for committing adultery by divorcing and marrying for a second time. No one seems to care if the adulterers are the heirs rather than the children. Most think that adultery occurs only when someone has a secret liaison on the side while married to someone.

Hyperactivity also results from a lack of trust in the very people that we should be able to trust: our family. Why should a step-parent or parent forgive another man seven times seventy times as Christ commanded and yet abuse a child for something about which the child does not understand? I know why—it is because the man doesn't like to be inconvenienced. He wants to control his little "perfect" kingdom on Earth to his own satisfaction and not God's satisfaction. Any man that condones the "spare the rod and spoil the child" mentality will be the abuser in the home.

Furthermore, we don't forgive our adult counterparts seven times seventy times either. Many of these people are still children trying to learn to find balance in their lives because of what they were denied as children. And if they repent of their sins, which is the way to get in touch with their

What Happens to Painful Emotional Memories?

souls, we send them to prison as their reward. Many a man and woman have gone to prison without the opportunity to repent. And many that desire to repent to their victim are not forgiven and go on to prison. This is just like the parent that doesn't forgive but, instead, physically punishes the child. Jesus was physically punished Himself.

Christ was hung on the cross along with two thieves. But before He was crucified, He was beaten with a whip, or something similar. The purpose of the whipping was to inflict pain and make suffering on the cross even worse. Crucifixion was punishment for sins. When the suffering people asked for something to drink, they were given vinegar on a sponge that was stuck to a long stick. People came by and mocked them as they hung on the cross. Christ and the other two hung on their crosses for around nine hours or longer. If they didn't die fast enough, someone would come around and break their legs so that they would die faster.

We punish sinners with jail time and the death penalty. But you will never hear about an adulterer or an adulteress being punished. That will never happen in this country. We reward the other women and men and make them and their children heirs to everything. Thank goodness for jails and prisons so that we can eliminate these unwanted children and grandchildren. These men and women, the step-parents, must have it all.

Our government has a system for controlling our citizens. It seems that everything is about control. Our country's laws are based on control. They desire to control everything through lawyers, law enforcement personnel, doctors, and pharmaceutical companies. Our people need the freedom to govern themselves. They don't need a lawyer to solve their problems. They need for their yes to be yes and their no to be no. (Matthew 5:37)They need the freedom to learn from their mistakes. They need to know genuine love. Could it be that our laws are set up the way that they are because of the lack of love that grown-ups have for children, especially step-children and unborn children. I think that these laws are actually set up to benefit the second wife and the children of the second family.

Doctors need a certain amount of sick people to get rich. Without sick people, they could not live lives as well as most do. Doctors are required for the elimination by abortion of the children of the first family—the cornerstone that ties a man and a woman together. Our police and jailers are dependent upon the sick to support their wife and children. Our psychiatrists need sick people to support their lifestyles. Our pharmaceutical companies need sick people so that they can sell their drugs, make money, and conduct additional research on more drugs.[21] Our lawyers are dependent upon families with adulterers and adulteresses so that they can do their job of protecting the wife and children of the second family. This helps to ensure that the second woman and second man get it all. In turn, the lawyer will make some money to support his lifestyle. Other people need lawyers so that they can sue someone and try to solve their problems with money.

But what if parents loved their children enough to let them be their natural heirs instead of letting a grown-up become the heir through a second marriage? I can't think of any mothers and fathers that would not want their children to be their natural heirs. It is only when we bring in an unrelated adult that everything shifts to the second family and the second spouse. The second family in this country replaces the first family. All of this happens when the mother and father decide to play house with someone else.

We are doing a terrible injustice to Christ's creatures on Earth. We are denying them the opportunity to grow and learn. These are the very things that they were denied as children, and we make sure that we deny it to them as adults, too. Of course, again, this goes back to maintaining the kingdom on Earth, where the very people sitting on the juries consider themselves to be without sin. In today's times, we can be certain that probably at least half of these people have committed adultery, plus a myriad of other sins. The "commandments of men" matter more than the commandments of God.

We want the perfect country, the perfect world, and the perfect society based on man's rules. We don't want to be bothered with sinners. We do not want to be bothered by the children of the first family. We shoot our guns at them, imprison them, and kill them rather than fix the problem

What Happens to Painful Emotional Memories?

at the root. We even encourage their parents to commit adultery and give everything that belongs to our children to another man or woman. Instead of giving them our cloak when they ask for our coat, we call the cops and send them to jail. This is not love.

I once knew a woman that had adopted a son because she had given birth to only girls. When her husband died, instead of giving her husband's tools to this adopted young man, she fought to keep the tools for herself. I told her that if that little boy, who was a grown man now, was really her son that she would have given him those tools. She told me that her husband had been "disappointed" with that little boy. I wonder where that little boy's mother and father are living and why they decided to do a live abortion and give him up for adoption.

It is not normal for any human being to lack the ability to love. Our men seem to love women through their penises and love men through their brains. This is a prejudicial way of living and thinking. On the one hand, they love and are reverent to men but are discriminatory in their love toward women. They think that they are equal to other men but superior to women and children. We even have churches today that encourage frequent intercourse so that man and wife can "connect." There is much more to love than connecting through a little piece of flesh called a penis. There is great confusion in our country about what love actually is and how it should be displayed.

Adultery is the root cause of our nation's ills. Our fathers are with another woman instead of with the children of their first family. Our mothers freely open their doors to another man. Our nation's laws are set up for the destruction of our first families and not the maintenance of our families. The ones that benefit from these laws are the other man, the other woman, and the children of the second family. We are cursing our children of the first family and our first spouse. It is little wonder that our children have painful, repressed emotions and memories from their broken families and homes. All of this is so that a man can play house with another woman. This other man and this other woman are not worth what they have cost.

How Does Abuse Affect Us?

As early as 1888, studies were being performed on the brains of monkeys with behavioral problems.[22] Later studies have produced evidence that damage to the temporal lobe within the brain of monkeys can cause excitability to virtually everything to which they are exposed. In addition to excitability, they also found that these study monkeys also participated in the following activities: placing inappropriate objects in their mouth, promiscuous sexual activity, and taking extreme and dangerous risks without displaying fear of any kind.[23] They also discovered another very important finding: female monkeys had difficulty nurturing and loving their infants. Based on the statistics from a previous chapter, we know that abuse and neglect are the way that this type of early injury manifests itself in the care of the next generation.[24]

In many cases, the pattern begins with a step-father or a step-mother that has difficulty loving another's child. The step-father or step-mother does not have mental illness, but he or she will, in many cases, emotionally damage the step-child. Then in turn, this step-child will damage his/her children as a part of a generational curse. These step-children are separated early from their family. There is no soul connection. Confusing messages are sent at a time when the child is too young to understand what has happened or what is going on. These little children will formulate conclusions based on the limited knowledge base that they have. These conclusions will have a tremendous effect on the decisions that they make as adults. They create a religion that is not based on love, forgiveness, and repentance. It is a religion, in most cases, based upon punishment because punishment is all that they know. Hence, they will punish their own children for wrongdoings.

Recently, I was in the grocery store buying groceries when I met a young man, his "girlfriend," and his son from a previous marriage. The little boy was crying while his father tried to comfort him. It seemed as though they were not in touch with the little boy. But when I approached and began to talk to them, the little boy turned to me and ceased to cry. This little boy, even though too young to talk, was fixated on me. I felt that this little boy sensed the soul connection and love that I have for others. Our small children need this soul connection for the "soul" parts of the brain to grow so that they can love more completely when they grow up. Unfortunately, with a broken home that includes a father and another woman, this little boy may never have the opportunity to know genuine love.

A study was conducted in 2003 on patients with borderline personality disorder, and they found increased activity in the left amygdala. These dear patients did not trust even a face without expression—neither smiling nor frowning—in pictures that they were shown. They were filled with fear because of a general lack of trust in mankind.[25] Then, a study in 2006 came up with similar findings: the test subjects exhibited fear when shown pictures of individuals with aggressive facial expressions and when encountering fearful experiences. Antidepressants appeared to reduce the test subject's fearfulness. I would guess that if antidepressants eliminated the feelings of fear, alcohol, tobacco, and drugs would have a similar effect. It was found that the greater the behavioral problems, the greater the response in the amygdala.[26] Studies have also indicated that the hippocampus and amygdala were smaller in people that were described as having bipolar disorder.[27]

If an adult sees neutral faces as threatening, it is because they saw what they thought was a loving parent or caregiver that was actually a step-parent or an unrelated adult very early in their lives. This adult child knows from childhood experience that adults cannot be trusted no matter what their facial expression. They will speak loving words and then reveal their true hearts which are full of anything but love. The amygdala stores these painful

How Does Abuse Affect Us?

memories from childhood and even from before the child understood what was actually happening. The more emotionally stressful and complicated the event, the more likely it will be stored for later processing. Individuals, especially adults, experiencing phobias, paranoia, personality disorders, and the like, are considered defective in our society. These are merely symptoms of a problem, the problem of abuse in early childhood. Again, we have a group of professionals that is placing the entire burden upon the individual. The actual responsibility should be placed on the "step-parent" that took over the child's family. This could be one or two generations back.

Adultery is at the root of this problem. Our family is based upon a structure that encourages adultery. In years past, only the rich could afford a divorce. Today, almost anyone can get a divorce. It is so commonplace that I doubt there is one family left that has not been affected by adultery in one way or another. This social tradition of taking a stranger into a child's home and making them into a permanent member is ridiculous. Children should never be placed into such a hostile environment whereby a grown-up man or woman becomes the heir to anything and everything that ever belonged to the little child. Grown-ups should never be permitted to compete with children for things that naturally belong to a child. This hostile structure creates unnecessary stress that children should never have to bear at any age. It is little wonder that we have chaos everywhere these days.

Learning is impaired because the individual starts to imitate what is expected and avoids taking risks that would aid in learning. The amygdala is smaller for this reason. They are not putting oil into their lamps. They do not have a good foundation of understanding of what has been happening. They are confused and separated. They will imitate the expected behavior but will learn little and will become whitewashed tombs full of dead men's bones if nothing changes. Furthermore, if individuals are fearful of faces it is because they cannot associate love with humans that hurt them when they were small. They learn that someone can smile and still be capable of causing injury to them. They have learned that they cannot trust people behind the smile. Step-parents, in most cases, are the ones that start this vicious cycle. Their step-children carry it into the next generation.

As these children grow in size, they mask their fear because they have grown large enough to where they can dominate others in order to keep themselves from being hurt anymore. They can even run to escape the abuser, unlike an infant that is totally dependent upon the care provided. They become adult bullies. They fight back and attack before someone threatens their authority and power. They will eventually bully their own wives and children.

These children have spent most of their lives worried about themselves and their own safety because of an abusive and unloving step-parent or a parent that has given them away like an animal to another unrelated adult. They will constantly be on the defensive. Accepting responsibility for mistakes that they have made will be extremely difficult. According to studies, step-parents are less forgiving of mistakes made by step-children than they are of their own children. And in many cases, the step-parent will blame the step-child for things that the child did not do. In a normal home, parents will take the time to talk to their children and guide them with love, forgiveness, and understanding. Unfortunately, this is not always the case with step-children. These grown-ups will compete with step-children until they get it all. In Jacob's family it was the children of the second family and their mother that wanted it all.

Other individuals, rather than becoming bullies, give up themselves totally to become what the abuser wants them to be. This is why we have adults that go through mental challenges. By mental challenges, I mean that they may have problems with accepting responsibility for what they do. They may grow up and become a distant parent with problems connecting with their own children and others. Situations like these finally manifest themselves and become genetic. As a result, we will have children, especially sons, that are autistic. These fathers lost the essence of love way back in childhood because of an adult that dominated them and, most likely, abused them. The abuser, many times a step-father, realizes that he made a giant mistake when he committed adultery with the child's mother. Adults know and sense when something is awry in their choices, but the temptation to take over God's kingdom will normally keep them from doing the right thing. Also, they are worried about their own children that they have produced with the child's mother or father. They look forward to inheriting the property of the mother or the father.

Some children are even raped by an adult "caregiver" or other trusted adult. These children will avoid relationships with others. Some will have frequent sex with multiple partners. Others will rape. Some will become pedophiles and revert back to the childhood age at which they were abused. They will use a child of that age to replay the event that caused them to feel ashamed when they had little to no understanding.

Again, this is the very reason that Paul said, "Be ye followers of me, even as I also *am* of Christ" (1 Corinthians 11:1). This was in the hopes that they could learn proper behavior. In essence, this attempt by Paul only prolonged the problem. Just as children are trying to learn when small, we have adults still trying to learn about things which they were not allowed to learn as children. This is why Christ said to turn the other cheek and forgive seven times seventy times. We must love our neighbors as ourselves and permit them the opportunity to learn from their mistakes. But we must forgive and rebuke and forgive and rebuke until they reconnect with us once more.

It is so unfortunate that our adult children have to go through these growing pains and suffer the humiliation that goes along with their lack of self-control. They bear the burden themselves. Their fathers are with other women. Their mothers are with other men. These adult children have no place to call home. And we look around us and wonder why we have so much chaos in this country. All we need to do is look at the adulterers, and it is easy to understand where the problem lies.

Now, I want to take the time to address the abusers that separated our little ones from us, those who are actually responsible for much of the sin that is happening in our world today. Christ said in Matthew 18:6–7,

> But whoso shall offend one of these little ones which believe in me, it were better for him that a millstone were hanged about his neck, and *that* he were drowned in the depth of the sea. Woe unto the world because of offences! for it must needs be that offences come; but woe to that man by whom the offence cometh! Wherefore if thy hand or thy foot offend thee, cut them off, and cast *them* from thee: it is better for thee to enter into life halt or maimed, rather than having two hands or two feet to be cast into everlasting fire. And if thine eye offend thee, pluck it out, and cast *it* from thee: it is better for thee to enter into life with one eye, rather than having two eyes to be cast into hell fire.

This is not a call for others to remove these parts from our bodies—it is our own call. Lusting on another man or woman, putting our hands upon another man or woman, and using our feet to walk over to another man or woman can all destroy our chances of going to Heaven.

Anyone that believes in the "spare the rod and spoil the child" mentality had better think twice; they may have destroyed their hopes for eternal life. How many adults are in our jails or prisons for committing a great sin because of what a "parent" did to them as a child? We had all better think twice before we raise a hand or a foot to one of these precious little ones!

According to a British study, the most likely way (57 percent) that a small child would die as a result of maltreatment by a "parent" was by hitting or kicking. Of killings by a step-parent, 79 percent were performed by hitting, kicking, or using a blunt object of some type. This study also reports that there is a much greater likelihood for step-parents to kill step-children than their own children. U.S. data reports that small children (newborn to two years old) have a hundred times greater risk of lethal abuse than children living with both of their parents. A Canadian study reported a risk seventy times greater. It is also reported that these assaults by step-parents continued over a prolonged period of time until the child finally died. In many cases, the step-parent reported that the child "wouldn't stop crying" and that this led them to continue the beatings. In most cases, the step-parent was a step-father because it is rare for a step-child to reside with a step-mother. The one thing that was not noted in this study, which I think is extremely important, is whether the genetic parent that killed his own child was raised by a step-father. I believe that adultery is the precursor to this generational curse. Adolf Hitler was the outcome of adultery by his grandfather and Adolf's genetic father abused him.[28]

Now, I am going to attempt to explain what I just said in the above paragraphs. It is complicated, but I must as it is the most important part of this book. Small children are very vulnerable to adults such as their father, step-father, step-mother, or their mother's boyfriend. These were all, at an earlier point in their lives, someone's child themselves. The way in which they were brought up is profoundly important to you and your child. Almost daily we read in the newspaper about a man—a father, step-father, mother's boyfriend, or father's girlfriend—who killed or severely abused a child. Sometimes, even a mother is caught up in this disaster. Countless other children are also abused to a lesser extent, either physically, emotionally, or both, every day!

"But Jesus said, Suffer little children, and forbid them not, to come unto me: for of such is the kingdom of heaven" (Matthew 9:14).

During the early years, a child's only way to notify an adult of their needs is to cry. A man brought up under the rule of law, where punishment was administered rather than forgiveness, will treat the child as he was treated. If he was spanked early in life, he will measure out to the child what was measured to him, having been brought up under the "spare the rod and spoil the child" rule of the Old Testament. The abused becomes the abuser, and the dominated becomes the dominator. This is how the kingdom of men is transferred from generation to generation. But in order for their personal kingdom to meet their own satisfaction, they must have a totally submissive wife and children that have been beaten into subjection. Such a man is so weak that he cannot accept any challenges from anyone within his family. He must maintain his position on the throne. He will get angry if his wife questions his interpretation of the scriptures. Dictators are actually nothing but weak bullies.

We have men that minister in our churches today that are strong proponents of the "spare the rod and spoil the child" mentality. That is how they were raised, and that is how they want their children to be raised. Woe to any children who have sinned because of the sermon ministry, by which I mean a minister encouraging a father or a step-father to abuse children. Then, the child grows up and commits sin trying to overcome the problems of their childhood, and the minister who encouraged that mistreatment may be in for a grievous judgment.

The best opportunity for such a man to revert back to his past unfortunate experiences would be when he is left alone with a child as caretaker. A man of this type will deal with the child's perceived misbehavior, no matter how minor, rather harshly. Children of this age do not willfully sin; they are innocent in the eyes of the Lord. They are trying to learn about the world into which they were born. The infraction could be as minor as soiling a diaper, peeing on the floor, spilling their meal, pouring out their drink, throwing their cup onto the floor, crying out of hunger, or playing with their own feces. These men will spank the children with their belts or use other means of discipline. And if the children are not wearing diapers, they will spank their little bare and tender bottoms. For some men, this isn't far enough; the screaming child may interfere with their peace of mind, drown out the words of their television program, or make them concerned about what other men may think should they hear the child's cries. Many of these men will spank the child again to make them stop crying.

My husband was brought up with this mentality by his step-father. He was taught that grown men don't cry! My oldest son was also brought up to think this way by his father. All of this happened so that a step-father could marry another man's wife, live with her, and become her heir! Adultery is not worth the cost. Adultery has hurt my family, especially my oldest son, very much!

How Does Abuse Affect Us?

Christ said in Matthew 18:10, "Take heed that ye despise not one of these little ones; for I say unto you, That in heaven their angels do always behold the face of my Father which is in heaven."

If we want to know why we have hard-hearted men, this is where it starts. It starts with a step-father and a step-mother that do not want to hear someone else's children cry. When we demand that children suppress their emotions, expect them to imitate us for our own self-seeking benefit, and use force to this end, we create a terrible problem. I believe this is the root of what we call mental illness or sin. Suppression of such emotions robs small children of the ability to express their needs and feelings. Later in life, while trying to live without expressing emotion or self-expression, they will experience great difficulty in living the lives that God intended them to live. They fail to love in their marriage, becoming takers and not givers. They experience serious illnesses. I think this is the reason so many of our men die before their wives with heart attacks, etc.

If we look around us in the natural world, we may also note two types of animals, just as we note two types of people: the separated, the wild, and the connected, the tame. Our children are much the same. Just as with animals, it matters a great deal the age at which they become separated. The earlier the separation, the more severe the behavioral problems and the more difficult that it will be for these children to trust and love others. Animals become fearful after abuse by man and become separated from us. Children become fearful after abuse by man and become separated from us in the same way.

The earlier that the cycle of emotional development is stopped, the greater the psychological problems will be for them as adults. In times of extreme difficulty and betrayal, the resulting problems will manifest themselves most clearly. If the expression of emotions—especially tears and crying—is discouraged, there will be no emotional outlet. The individual will become separated, hard-hearted, and unable to display the loving characteristics expected of human beings.

The Step-Father's Step-Son

Crying is a natural human emotion. Men and women, both being from the same body, each have tear ducts. Men may want us to think that they have none, but they do. Crying is a way of expressing a variety of emotions: sadness, repentance, joy, and thankfulness among them. If our children fear making mistakes, parents will discover those children telling lies to protect themselves rather than telling the truth about what actually happened. Repenting is the key to our souls. It teaches us how to self-correct. We teach ourselves through repentance. We verbalize the mistake that we have made; hence, we begin to teach ourselves. Most men have trouble admitting that they have ever done anything wrong; this inability to repent is the reason that they cannot grow. Men and women who refuse to grow create a huge burden for their families.

I believe that a shift in perception occurs when our children are punished for trying to learn during childhood. Parents and step-parents who operate under the "spare the rod and spoil the child" mentality may cause our children to become fearful and separated. It will not be obvious to most observers when this shift occurs because the child will continue on in much the same way.

The key change is that the child will not experiment in order to learn but rather will imitate and do what is expected—just as Paul said to imitate him. Paul understood the environment in which these men had grown up. He also knew that it was very important to these men that they have power over someone—their wives and children. This was important because as children, just as their mothers did, they experienced powerlessness since all authority was retained by their fathers. Essentially, this ensured the transfer of the kingdom of men on to the next generation.

As I have mentioned in previous chapters, this is the kingdom that Jesus came to abolish. Christ saw these men and recognized that they were empty vessels that looked good to everyone but had no substance on the inside, as if the essence of their existence had been removed. This is what happens when our children experience abuse at the hands of their caregivers: step-fathers, step-mothers, fathers, and sometimes even mothers.

How Does Abuse Affect Us?

Our children become robots, devoid of feelings, first concerned about pleasing the abusive male step-father and then, when they grow up, pleasing men. They become self-centered or self-focused, ensuring that they do the right things to avoid further abuse or ostracism. The feelings of others are of no concern; only their own feelings matter. If they cry, they fear that they will be abused by the controlling step-parent.

All of these problems are unmasked in the home. There is no other outlet because adultery is not considered adultery in this country. It is legal with a lawyer. Furthermore, if women do as Paul commanded and keep silent and submit, nothing will ever change. We will cry after we marry them, and then we will cry when our children grow up and have so-called mental and behavioral problems. We must stop this terrible insanity and travesty. We must remember that we are not less than man just because we are small. We are his equal; his job is to become a servant in the home while we become stronger there.

By becoming a servant and serving as Christ served, he will be lavished with love far beyond his imagination. It will happen in the bedroom, at the table, and other places when he least expects it. In turn for the wife's increased strength, she will have respect from her husband, peers, and children. She will move naturally into the role of loving wife, no longer being forced to give what Paul commanded but rather because of what Christ did. There must be balance; otherwise, we have complete and utter dysfunction. Furthermore, we must keep the commandments in every possible way that we can. It will improve our health and longevity, as well as protecting our children and future generations.

Think back to Abraham, Sarah, and Hagar's relationship and the chaos created in its wake. Believe me, it is not worth it. By following our Lord and Savior's commandments, we can experience the richness of life as God intended. More blessings will come our way. We will see a drastic change in our prosperity, too, but in a way which does not always mean money! Just remember that miracles happen every day. All we need to do is look around us!

The Old Law Is No More!

Jesus said, "No man putteth a piece of new cloth unto an old garment, for that which is put in to fill it up taketh from the garment, and the rent is made worse. Neither do men put new wine into old bottles: else the bottles break, and the wine runneth out, and the bottles perish: but they put new wine into new bottles, and both are preserved" (Matthew 9:16, 17).

These are specific instructions from Jesus concerning His new covenant. Our country today, over 2,000 years after the death of Christ, is a mixture of the old and new law. The new covenant and the old have been applied to women, while men have risen above the laws and placed themselves into the position of god on Earth. Because men have done this, our problems are worse today instead of better. Our children are suffering because of poor parenting by their fathers. Our fathers are distracted by another woman. Our mothers are distracted by another man. In turn, their children are suffering because of our children. This is a problem that is going to keep getting worse until our men start living as Christ told them to live. Instead of listening to Christ, they have remained deaf to women in order to do their own will on Earth. They love their kingdoms more than they love God. They want to rule anywhere and everywhere that they can. They prefer arrogance over humility. They prefer to be served rather than to serve. This is why most are last in heaven. They have received their reward on this Earth.

Jesus said, "And this is the condemnation, that light is come into the world, and men loved darkness rather than light, because their deeds were evil. For every one that doeth evil hateth the light, neither cometh to the light, lest his deeds should be reproved. But he that doeth truth cometh to the light, that his deeds may be made manifest, that they are wrought in God" (John 3:19).

Paul raised men above the law—the Ten Commandments—into the realm of the law of the Spirit, which is love. But he left the Pharisees' leavening in its place. Christ warned that we could not have both and that if we tried to honor both the old and the new covenant, things would get worse. Our society is a living example of how this huge mistake has been manifested. We must move past the Pharisaical teachings and laws and move into the law that Christ laid down for us! The Ten Commandments apply today just as much as they did in the past.

Jesus said, "No man also having drunk old *wine* straightway desireth new: for he saith, The old is better" (Luke 5:39). And in John 14:6, "Jesus saith to him, I am the way, the truth, and the life: no man cometh unto the Father, but by me."

> Then said Jesus unto them again, Verily, verily, I say unto you, I am the door of the sheep. All that ever came before me are thieves and robbers: but the sheep did not hear them. I am the door: by me if any man enter in, he shall be saved, and shall go in and out, and find pasture. The thief cometh not, but for to steal, and to kill, and to destroy: I am come that they might have life, and that they might have *it* more abundantly. I am the good shepherd: the good shepherd giveth his life for the sheep. But he that is an hireling, and not the shepherd, whose own the sheep are not, seeth the wolf coming, and leaveth the sheep, and fleeth: and the wolf catcheth them, and scattereth the sheep. The hireling fleeth, because he is an hireling, and careth not for the sheep. I am the good shepherd, and know my *sheep*, and am known of mine. As the Father knoweth me, even so I know the Father: and I lay down my life for the sheep. (John 10:7–15)

The hireling is the step-father and the step-mother. They are the ones that come to steal, kill, scatter, and destroy. They will not protect someone else's children like they would protect their own because this child is not their child. They care not for the child but rather for what they are going to receive or already have received. Jesus gave His life for these "step-children." He commanded their parents not to commit adultery!

Jesus said, "And ye shall know the truth, and the truth shall make you free" (John 8:32). He also said, "A new commandment I give unto you, That ye love one another; as I have loved you, that ye also love one another. By this shall all *men* know that ye are my disciples, if ye have love one to another" (John 13:34, 35).

Adultery has nothing to do with love. The second wife and second husband do not love the first wife, the first husband, or the children of the first family. Our families are most beneficial to these two individuals because they become the heirs. It is very lucrative to take a woman's husband, a man's wife, a child's father, or a child's mother.

> He answered and said unto them, Well hath Esaias prophesied of you hypocrites, as it is written, This people honoureth me with *their* lips, but their heart is far from me. Howbeit in vain they worship me, teaching *for* doctrines the commandments of men. For laying aside the commandment of God, ye hold the tradition of men, *as* the washing of pots and cups: and many other such like things ye do. And he said unto them, Full well ye reject the commandment of God, that ye may keep your own tradition. (Mark 7:6–9)

Paul said in 1 Corinthians 14:34, 35, "Let your women keep silent in the churches: for it is not permitted unto them to speak; but *they are* commanded to be under obedience, as also saith the law. And if they will learn any thing, let them ask their husbands at home: for it is a shame for women to speak in the church."

This is the reason that women are denied the opportunity to learn to read and to attend school and college in some countries. It is about maintaining the old law, the old covenant that is centuries old. Their husbands are considered the experts in all things and are above reproach and questioning. He was trying to encourage everyone to keep the laws of the lords.

This is how we get homosexuals. Our children watch their mothers slave and their fathers do as they please. For boys, it must be especially confusing because they are without guidance on how they should behave and how they should treat their mothers and other women. They love their mothers, but their fathers do not love their mothers. They witness silent chaos. They associate serving as a female characteristic and taking as a male characteristic. If they choose to do anything other than take, they are associating with the female gender and begin giving. Perhaps they choose to take but decide that it is inappropriate to take from a female, as their fathers have done. Their solution is to associate with males and take from other males. Alternatively, the son could identify with the mother and become submissive. He decides to become submissive to his father and later is submissive to other males in his sexual relationships. Daughters experience the same confusion in early childhood. Our parents and step-parents are leading the children astray. Paul's teachings are unnatural. During his time, homosexuality was common just as it is today. If we go back in time and look closer at the book called the Song of Solomon, we can very likely get more insight into homosexuality. In Luke 12:27, Jesus said, "Consider the lilies how they grow: they toil not, they spin not, and yet I say unto you, that Solomon in all his glory was not arrayed like one of these."

Solomon was the son of Bathsheba, the woman with whom King David committed adultery. Solomon must have dressed very flamboyantly. I think that Solomon grew up in some very confusing circumstances because of the adultery that occurred before, during, and after the time of his conception.

In his book, the Solomon Song, he said some very revealing things. In the beginning of Chapter 5, Solomon speaks very lovingly for his wife before going to sleep. But then when he awakens he says, "My beloved put in his hand by the hole of the door, and my bowels were moved for him. I rose up to open to my beloved; and my hands dropped with myrrh, and my fingers with sweet smelling myrrh, upon the handles of the lock. I opened to my beloved; but my beloved had withdrawn himself, and was gone: my soul failed when he spake: I sought him; I called him, but he gave me no answer. The watchmen that went about the city found me, they smote me, they wounded me; the keepers of the walls took away my veil from me. I charge you, O daughters of Jerusalem, if ye find my beloved, that ye tell him, that I am sick of love." (Solomon's Song 5:4–8)

Paul spoke of homosexuality as a sin because he did not understand its roots—adultery. He said in I Corinthians 6:9–10, "Know ye not that the unrighteous shall not inherit the kingdom of God? Be not deceived: neither fornicators, nor idolaters, nor adulterers, nor effeminate, nor abusers of themselves with mankind, Nor thieves, nor covetous, nor drunkards, nor revilers, nor extortioners, shall inherit the kingdom of God."

Romans 1:25–28, "Who changed the truth of God into a lie, and worshipped and served the creature more than the Creator, who is blessed forever. Amen. For this cause God gave them up unto vile affections: for even their women did change the natural use into that which is against nature: And likewise also the men, leaving the natural use of the woman, burned in their lust one toward another; men with men working that which is unseemly, and receiving in themselves the recompence of their error which was men."

God gave us Paul and his teachings because he knew that men would prefer the old wine (laws) before they would move to accept the new wine (laws) that He presented during Jesus' walk on this Earth. Most men today accept that Jesus was the Christ, although they do not follow His teachings. This was God's purpose in using Paul. Just as Christ predicted, they would choose the Pharisaical teachings over His teachings. Few men live as Christ commanded them to live. Few men love as Christ commanded them. Perhaps it is now time for the Spirit of truth to correct their faulty thinking. God is in control, and His timing is always perfect. He has a plan.

The Brain and Our Nighttime Dreams

The amygdala has been found to serve as a repository for incomplete emotional memories. The amygdala stores important information about events which occur in our lives, even in early childhood before we have a complete understanding about what this world and life is all about.[29]

    I have a half-brother, and when I was about five years old, I remember that I loved to kiss him. He was grown and probably in his early 20s. I remember him sitting on the sofa, and I would come up to him from behind and shower him with kisses on his cheek. My mother interrupted me one day and told me that it was not appropriate for me to kiss him, most likely, because he was my half-brother, or maybe it was the sheer number of kisses that I was giving. (Based on what I know now, I could have married this guy when I got old enough. He was my father's oldest child with his first wife. I was my father's oldest child with his second wife, my mother.) When she told me this, I felt somewhat ashamed of myself and stopped cold turkey. Once I grew up, I remember thinking that it seemed unnatural for me to kiss him.

    Without realizing it, I had an incomplete emotional memory about wanting to be kissed on the cheek by my much older half-brother. At a very turbulent time in my professional career—I was being unfairly challenged by men in a male dominated profession—I had a dream that a man that had come to my rescue had kissed me on the cheek. Following the dream, I experienced an almost irresistible attraction to this man. It took a lot of thought and discipline to overcome the attraction. Only recently did I make the connection that the dream and the incomplete emotional memory were connected. The dream was the way that the incomplete emotional memory surfaced. The strong spiritual man who came to my rescue in my adult life was like the strong half-brother that I had when I was five years old. Both of them took care of me in a very special and important way during my life.

All of these experiences gave me the opportunity to complete another portion of my learning that had been delayed during my childhood. But instead of coming with closure, it came as a profound temptation, one like none that I had experienced before. There was nothing sexual about either event; the strong spiritual man was married with three daughters, and I was married with three sons. It was only about expressing my love. I loved the man's strength and courage. I did not keep the temptation to myself, though. I talked to a priest about it, and I have talked about this experience with others. It helped me to get a grasp on the situation; talking about it helped to bring the temptation to light and helped me to overcome it. Once that was accomplished, I became more emotionally complete than ever before.

Parents need to be careful with children. What adults consider inappropriate may not be inappropriate for children. We must not impose adult laws upon our children. Think about a young boy who is exploring a girl's body or a young girl exploring a boy's body. There is nothing sexual about it. What happens when a parent or "step-parent" yanks out a belt and stops them in their tracks before they have gained any understanding of the situation? What kind of emotional memory is stored for future processing? What happens if the desire to be with a woman in adulthood results in someone being raped or a child being molested? What about the girl? Could she become a prostitute? Who do we hold accountable? The grown child, of course! But who planted the seed? The parent or step-parent! A step-parent protecting their child would most likely have a big problem with this type of childhood play from a step-child. This is why Christ told us to love the sinner and to forgive. But what I do not understand is why do we hold children to such high standards when most of us can never obtain the same perfection ourselves? If children are properly raised, they will not hurt others as adults. Christ also told us that whoever uses his hand or his foot to cause one of His little ones to sin would suffer great consequences.

I am not condoning sin. I have experienced the suffering that sin causes in so many ways in my life. Most people that sin think that they are doing the right thing at the time. It is only after sinning that they begin to realize they have made a big mistake. When they come to this realization, they have grown one step further. Furthermore, all sin is about self and is done for selfish reasons. We want something. Some will steal to get it; others will lie. Some will commit adultery to get something that they want.

But adultery is the one sin that most adulterers desire to never change. The only change that most adulterers want is the ability to erase the memories of every man, woman, and child that was a part of the family before them. They will use manipulation, control, and the full extent of the laws of our lords to make certain that they benefit.

What about Peter? He was tempted three times to deny Christ and succumbed all three times. Had he not done this, he could very likely have been hung on the cross because he was one of Jesus' accomplices. Try to imagine the guilt that he must have experienced. Christ came after His death to work things out between them. Jesus forgave Peter. He asked Peter if he loved Him. When he said "Yea, Lord," He told him to tend His sheep. Then, He asked Peter again to get His point across. Again, Peter said, "Yea." Christ told him to feed His sheep (John 21:15–17). Christ used His life as an example of how we should go to those that we have wronged and ones that have wronged us and work it out. If Peter had devoted the remaining years of his life to guilt, he would not have produced much fruit for the Lord at all. By working past the guilt, he was a great servant.

I remember a man that I met while serving in Iraq. I was the only woman at an all-male camp—at least on the civilian side. There were a few women on the military side at the same camp, but we had no interaction with them. It was obvious that he was tempted to have sex with me. My job was safety, and one night, he came to the hooch where I slept and knocked on the door. Since he was a man of high position, number two in command at the camp, I opened the door to see what he wanted. We talked about safety issues, but I knew that he wanted more.

Later, he asked me in front of other men how I overcame the temptation. Referring back to my experience with my temptation, I told him that I had tested myself before and had overcome the temptation. He yelled in excitement. He never bothered me again. My only hope is that I helped him to learn how to manage his temptation. I want to believe that I did. And furthermore, I believe that he did.

I could have had him written up for sexual harassment and who knows what else, but the guy did not do anything wrong except to ask non-verbally. I could have chosen to sleep with him and cheat on my husband and his wife. He was attracted to me but went no further. It is very likely that he would have been attracted to any female, because I am not the cutest thing on two legs. I forgave him. I cared enough to help him. I would like to believe that I helped him to become a better husband to his spouse, who was at home in the USA, and a better man. This man was alone, and I did nothing to interfere with his relationship with his family back home. I wish that my husband's step-mother and step-father could have loved and respected my husband's family in this manner.

Going back to my childhood experience, I am no longer dependent upon my husband or my father for love. I have a more mature love for others than I have ever had before. It is beyond body; it is in spirit that I love others. And it is the reason that I am writing this book.

I remember one time when our family—my husband, three small children, and I—had flown across the Atlantic from Germany back to America after being overseas for three years. We retrieved our car from the nearby port, and then we drove from the East Coast to Texas. Upon our arrival, my husband's step-father demanded that my husband mow the grass immediately after he got out of the car. My husband did as he was asked without question, as he had probably done one thousand times before. This step-father told my husband's younger high-school-age half-brother to go visit some friends while we were there. I never wanted to go to back to this house ever again. This was the promise that my husband made to me and then later broke. I remember him saying, "We'll see how it is next time." I truly never wanted to see these people again.

In our country, children are adopted out with the help of a lawyer. Lawyers can create laws to eliminate children by abortion. They can eliminate children by adoption. They can break up a family with a piece of paper. These lawyers are like God. They have the power to do things that God does not even authorize. As long as we submit to their laws, they can retain their power.

If only our parents and grandparents could love our children enough to keep their adulterers on the side and not bring them into the family household. It is unfair to punish our sons when the actual problem is the other man and/or the other woman. What a terrible travesty that we have going on in our country! It is little wonder that the victims are the ones that hurt someone else as they were hurt. This is all that they know. And then, in the end, another innocent person is hurt and will ultimately pay the price for what the step-parents did. All of this is because these little children had little to no understanding of the grown-up laws that were being applied to them! Even more shameful is the fact that there is no punishment for adultery. These individuals walk around like nothing happened and, in many cases, are highly respected within the community. In actuality, their condition is so bad that most will not make it to Heaven, and yet people just adore these sick individuals without considering the children and others that they have profoundly hurt.

Adultery is a sin that can shake up a family for generations. In our culture and society, it is very appealing to commit adultery, and most people do not even think of it as a sin. Adulterers' hearts are so hardened that most do not waste time thinking about the family members that will be hurt by their choices and decisions. Eventually, the children of the kingdom (the children that are the product of the adulterous relationship) have no problem with adultery at all. It is as though no one is hurt, and everything turns out the way that it should—at least as long as no one does unto them what their parents did to the step-child. Adultery is very beneficial for the children of the kingdom because they become the heirs to everything that once belonged to the first family.

Human Development

Life is a journey. As we travel in our continuum, we evolve. Our evolution takes us from total dependence to as close as we can get to total independence—from freedom to bondage, from bondage to freedom, from heavenly spirits to earthly bodies, from earthly bodies to heavenly spirits, from health to illness, from illness to health, etc. For some, the journey is fast, and for some, it is slow. For some, it is long, and for others, it is short.

Child development researchers Frances Ilg, Louise Bates Ames, and Sidney Baker published a book in 1992 entitled *Child Behavior: The Classic Child Care Manual from the Gesell Institute of Human Development*.[30] I am providing a brief summary of their findings and associating those findings with what I strongly believe to be "the shift in perception."

Let's move back in time together to the point when we were newborns and attempt to retrace our evolution. I think that by studying the developmental stages of children, we can understand the developmental age of many of our adults. In many cases, I believe that it will be possible to determine the age at which "the shift in perception" occurred and mastery was not accomplished. When disruption occurs during the learning process, our children grow up to become adults that still have not mastered important personal skills.

Initially, we were totally dependent upon our mothers and fathers for survival. Mom provided the life-sustaining milk perfectly prepared for our little bodies, and Dad provided the shelter to keep us warm and dry. But this is the ideal way for a child to start out. Today, many of our fathers and even some of our mothers have left us and moved in with another woman or man. In many cases, we did not even make it this far because they aborted us with birth control pills or by abortion. The breasts, uterus, and vagina are reserved for the entertainment and stimulation of another man and may never be available for a child. The penis is reserved for the stimulation and entertainment of another woman. The hands and arms will never be used to cradle a small child.

So, if we were safe and secure in the beginning, our brains mastered things like heart rate, blood pressure, and muscles for coordination. How many of our men and women have heart problems and blood pressure problems? Heart attacks are one of our most probable causes of premature death. Blood pressure problems are common. Many people have difficulty with hand-eye coordination, and some are even clumsy with their leg movements.

If we have made it this far without a shift in our perception, we should be mobile, spiritually connected, and able to hear, see, speak, and love. Children around the age of eighteen months will often do the opposite of what is requested by their moms and dads. How many adults do you know that still do the opposite of what is expected? Paul even had a problem with this one.

Children around the age of two and a half years will normally be somewhat selfish, demanding, impulsive, and emotional. We have many adults today that appear to be stuck in this stage. There will be some that won't master it before they exit this world. My husband's step-mother could possibly be the perfect example of this age. She admitted that she was selfish. I think that my husband's father most likely found her to be controlling and very demanding. It is sad that he did not love her enough to kick her out. Then, she most likely would have grown past this selfish stage.

If we have survived the "shift in perception" to the age of three, we will be able to love enough to share and even to use the word "we" instead of "me," "my," and "mine" most of the time. There are many adults today that have difficulty with this one. Laban, Rachel and Leah's father, seemed to have difficulty with this concept. He seemed to think that everything was "his."

By three and a half, children may experience hand tremors and even crossed eyes. Hand tremors are most likely associated with fear. Some children may also state that they can't see or hear. I believe that these are the symptoms of a shift in brain dominance, a "shift in perception." Later in life, these adults will most likely develop Parkinson's disease or other similar ailments. My husband's hands are very shaky and he has been an insulin dependent diabetic for many years.

At around four years, our children—even girls—may use foul language, tell tall tales, ignore family members and friends, and talk highly of themselves. Many parents will use harsh punishment and even wash their mouths out with soap, as was the practice in past years. All harsh punishment will do at this age is to harden these precious little hearts even harder than they were before. Our children will learn nothing with punishment. They need to be loved enough to make mistakes and to know that they will be forgiven. Step-parents do not like the mistakes of someone else's child.

Children need to have the opportunity to gain an understanding about why cussing is not good. I knew that the words were dirty words, but I didn't know the meaning of many of these words until after I married my husband. He is the one that had to explain their meanings to me. You can know that if I didn't know, children do not have the slightest idea either. They are using these words just as they would many of the other words that they can speak. The only problem here is that grown-ups impose adult rules upon children. Adults don't get spanked for using foul language, but many believe that it is acceptable to punish a small child that has no understanding.

Around the age of five, children develop a strong appreciation for their mothers. They begin to realize how much her life means to them and how much she actually does for them. Many of our men in prison acknowledge their love for their mothers, but many are plagued by the regrets of a grandfather and/or a father that abandoned their family for another woman.

Five year olds like to win. They enjoy competing with others in order to win. Everything seems to be about winning, and if they don't win, they will accuse the "competitor" of cheating them. Blame becomes a big part of their thinking. They have difficulty accepting responsibility. We have many adults that appear to be stuck in this stage of human development.

By age seven, children may be really separated and generally feel unloved. They withdraw as they begin to realize that there is no hope.

By eight years of age, their focus is still on themselves. Children at this age try unsuccessfully to accomplish new things by themselves. Failure is difficult to accept. Parents make them do what they think that they should do rather than children doing what they want or need to do.

At around nine years of age, children begin to realize that their family members hurt them, but others do not. Children of this age may begin to worry about things. Some will rebel against authority figures.

There is no doubt in my mind that fear replaces love and limits our ability to truly enjoy being with other people. We are forever worried about ourselves and how others see us. And while we are busy worrying about ourselves, we miss out on opportunities to extend ourselves freely in order to be closer to the people that are a part of our lives at work, at play, and at home.

By ten years of age, many have given up. They know that there is no hope. They submit to servitude and imitate the expected behavior. They have officially become whitewashed tombs at this early age.

Many young adults have little respect for authority. They want to dominate the world. They have little respect for girls, young women, other men, and women. Their irrational behavior causes problems.

None of us should spend our lives fearful of authority figures. We must not let ourselves become fearful of police officers or others in similar positions. Their job is to be public servants. We are not called upon to respect each other. We are called upon to love each other. There is a big difference between love and respect. Respect is about fear; it could be the fear of being rejected and abandoned if we do not do as they demand. Love is the higher standard; love is what would require the adulterers and their children to change their lives instead of them expecting the step-child to change their life.

As adults faced with spousal betrayal and/or extreme difficulty in making life's plans come to fruition, some experience a breakdown or commit a serious crime and end up in jail or prison.

At this last stage, during our adult years, we have adults that encounter childhood problems that rise to the surface. We can see that many of our men's and women's personalities were formed long ago. It is also obvious that they are stuck in the past. Unlike a child growing through the cycles, these men and women retain characteristics that have become so engrained that we actually believe are normal traits.

Our men's need for competition is a strong indication that many have achieved the emotional maturity of a five year old. Success has nothing to do with competition. Instead it has everything to do with discovering ourselves and how well we can do something without worrying about competing with others. Everyone has different talents and abilities. We each need to give ourselves the opportunity to explore and fully utilize our talents without trying to walk all over everyone else in the process. There is plenty of room out there for all of us.

Left-eye/right-brain dominance is not normal in human beings. The most important aspect of left-eye/right-brain dominance is when it initially occurred. Some children will be born with this shifted brain dominance because it has become genetic. The earlier that the shift in brain dominance occurred and remained, the more debilitating the results will be for the child and his family once he or she matures into adulthood. There will be a time when he will have to deal with the underlying emotional injury. The emotional issues can be bypassed provided the individual has adequate faith and understanding and is able to maintain right-eye/left-brain dominance—to walk by faith.

Jesus said,

> The light of the body is the eye: therefore when thine eye is single, thy whole body also is full of light; but when *thine eye* is evil, thy body also *is* full of darkness. Take heed therefore

that the light which is in thee be not darkness. If thy whole body therefore *be* full of light, having no part dark, the whole shall be full of light, as when the bright shining of a candle doth give thee light. (Luke 11:34–36)

Eventually, the emotional problem will just disappear and will not resurface again if they do the work required.

The primary purpose of depression is to give up one piece of ourselves at a time. It is the shedding of self in order to reveal the kingdom of God within us. It is a signal that it is time for a change. Thinking back, I have realized that the things that I was depressed about were all about me. It was always about things that I didn't get and thought that I should have received. Or it was the way that I was treated or wasn't treated. It was always about me worrying about myself.

Conversely, I have realized that the more I have shed myself to serve and love others, the more I have come to find genuine peace and happiness. Our trials on Earth are blessings because they lead us along this amazing path and cleanse us of these often painful memories that do little except restrict our growth. Problems stop us from thinking about ourselves too much and help us to focus on other issues in the bigger world.

Our society has actually come to conclude that depression is not normal. I want to challenge that notion; I think that it is a normal part of our growth process as spiritual beings. Each time that we shift back to left-eye/right-brain dominance and shift to thoughts of ourselves, depression returns. Over time, we train ourselves to stay steadfastly right-eye/left-brain dominant, utilizing both sides of the brain but with the left brain in charge. Once we have done this, depression will be short and, eventually, nonexistent. But until we reach this point, Christ gave us some very good instructions.

Here are two of His lessons for us on the subject. When we give up a portion of ourselves, we mourn its death. For instance, we may mourn the fact that our father was never there for us. This mourning leads to the death of this self-centered desire and leads us to rely on our Heavenly Father more fully. Furthermore, if we can gain an understanding of why he was not there, it will help us even more. If you can do this, you will learn to love him more fully than you ever thought possible. This is about gaining wisdom and understanding, which are more valuable than silver or gold. I am hoping that this book will help you to gain at least some understanding.

In Matthew 5:4, Jesus said, "Blessed are they that mourn: for they shall be comforted." And in Luke 6:25, Jesus said, "Woe unto you that are full! for ye shall hunger. Woe unto you that laugh now! for ye shall mourn and weep."

If there is trauma during birth or infancy, the individual may experience difficulty moving, talking, etc., if there was a permanent shift to left-eye/right-brain dominance. If the individual is allowed to remain stuck, we will have a physically handicapped individual as an adult. Christ was able to correct this problem.

A child fifteen to twenty-one months old is abused for playing with feces. If the adult experiences betrayal by a close relative, he will revert back to this experience for closure. There are adults in mental hospitals that play with feces. My brother told me that after touring one during his college training. I believe that it is true!

A child is abused during potty training. The child will be afraid to leave the seat for fear of a beating. It obviously is the only place where the child feels safe. Recently, we had a young woman that grew into the toilet seat and had to be surgically removed. This woman went back to her "safe" place. What she did was perfectly normal considering her childhood.

A loving and peaceful child is abused at around two years of age while doing nothing wrong and then is spanked for crying. Following betrayal, the adult will experience withdrawal and revert back to a silent eighteen–month-old. These individuals will have difficulty with self-expression and caring for themselves for a while until they grow past it.

A child that is neglected and abused, especially by a step-parent of the same sex that obviously cares more for his own biological children, leaves the child with no social standing within the family. The adult may develop adult onset diabetes. He will be separated from his wife and children even after marriage. Diabetes is a problem that deals with difficulty with food. Food has everything to do with our survival.

If a child is abused during the self-centered period of the "terrible twos," he will not grow out of that age. He will become stuck. As an adult, the child may be extremely self-centered and narcissistic. Perhaps this was the step-mother's problem. She wanted to have things her way, and my husband's father let her have it all. He should have sent her away with her three children. She might have learned to trust in God more fully.

If the small child is harshly corrected for stealing something from another child or adult, an incomplete emotional memory will remain. This child may be faced with the temptation to steal as an adult. And if the temptation is not mastered the first time, they may become compulsive shoplifters for a while. Also, this could be a byproduct of a step-parent that took things from a child that actually did belong to the child.

If a small child is harshly corrected for exploring another child's body parts and not permitted to gain an understanding, again an incomplete emotional memory will remain. This adult may be faced with the temptation to succumb to pedophile activities and possibly even child rape. They stopped maturing emotionally at an early age.

If a young girl is sexually molested as a child, she may be withdrawn from men or become promiscuous as an adult. This woman will be fearful of a relationship with a man if she was in a stable age at the time of abuse. If she was in a demanding, self-centered stage, she may become promiscuous or a prostitute.

If a small girl witnesses her mother being used by her father for his purposes, she may start to identify with her brothers. This woman may become a lesbian—butch-type.

If a small boy witnesses his father shirking his responsibilities to the family and his mother, he may start to identify with his sisters. This man or his child may become a homosexual—female version.

All sin has its root in our childhood. It is during this sensitive period that adults transfer problems to their children. The last thing that children need is to have a stranger, a step-parent, living in their homes. The earlier that the shift in brain dominance occurs in the child, and if left-eye/right-brain dominance was maintained throughout adulthood, the more likely the adult will transfer his emotional condition to his children and grandchildren in the form of autism, childhood cancer, childhood diabetes, physical disabilities, mental disabilities, and other serious medical conditions.

Autism, in my opinion, is nothing more than extreme self-centeredness and an imbalance in thinking, whereby one side of the brain—the right side—is used almost exclusively. Furthermore, it appears to be occurring earlier and earlier in our children. Our self-centered men are at the root of this problem because this undesirable characteristic is being transferred genetically to our children as a result of our men's self-centeredness.[31] Their parents did not create this problem. Step-parents that are living in the family home are causing this problem. When I speak of the "family home," I don't just mean the present generation. Grandparents that have invited a stranger into the family home are, in many cases, where the problem began.

Many assume that autism is caused by childhood vaccines, and in some ways, this notion is plausible. But because the child is already self-centered, the injection and the resulting fear tend to increase the child's isolation and separation from those around and closest to him or her.

Left-eye dominant men are more likely to develop post-traumatic stress disorder, high blood pressure, heart problems, and other ailments. These individuals are very focused on details and problems and not the bigger picture. If left-eye dominance continues for a lifetime, Alzheimer's disease is also very possible because right-brain dominance is dysfunctional. Again the severity and age of onset will vary depending upon when the shift in brain dominance occurred. Alcohol, tobacco, and drugs will delay the individual's ability to work through the stored emotional memories to permit a natural shift in brain dominance back to our natural state: right-eye/left-brain.

By two and a half years, we were rigid. We wanted things the same. Decision making was difficult. We thought mostly of ourselves. We used the word "I." This self-centeredness describes the autism that we are seeing in our children, and unless mothers recognize this correlation, we will be creating a lot of opportunities for men to build their kingdoms. First, they created a condition; now, they can treat it with expensive drugs and conduct expensive research on a myriad of topics looking for a cure without truly understanding the cause. All the while, they are actually working on creating more fear in the hearts and minds of mothers everywhere.

The Origins of Narcissism

Right-brain dominance appears to predispose individuals to narcissistic tendencies. The more our women and men cease to love others and obey God, the further they drift into darkness. This darkness will lead them into a fearful and irrational state, one in which they will make poor decisions regarding the lives of their family and the lives of others. Satan loves to find our men isolated and alone in this place. This is a state of sin. All sin is a form of mental illness in adults. Our right-brain dominated men and women are the ones most likely to become involved in drugs and alcohol, to get speeding tickets, commit adultery, and to have car accidents. This is where they do things that others usually don't understand and quite often find frightening.

The earlier that our men become emotionally and spiritually separated from others, especially women and children, the greater the darkness will be. In many children's lives, this darkness begins even before they understand what is going on in this world. Hence, they have no recollection of what it is like to love and trust for they have been brought up in the dark world of fear. Then, they grow up emotionally immature and make poor decisions as adults because they have spent their entire childhood worried about self-preservation. The only way for a child who is now an adult in size to leave this state of darkness is to "return to love," as Marianne Williamson so eloquently stated in the title of her book *A Return to Love: Reflections on the Principles of "A Course in Miracles."*[32] All humans, including our men, were created to love and not to fear. We are different than animals, especially the wild ones. Even animals can trust totally if they are brought up by a loving and caring human being.

Because of early abuse, we have many hard-hearted men and women today. It is because they have been taught to fear their abusive mothers, fathers, step-mothers, and step-fathers rather than to love and trust. Learning for children is risky, especially in the presence of a man or woman that is dominating and wants to rule over children so that they are in total control. If mistakes based on adult standards result in abuse, the child will be careful about taking chances. They will play it safe and learn to imitate the expected behavior rather than learn by doing. These children may also create their own unique set of commandments separate from God's because they are not old enough to understand them. Then, when our children mature, they will find it difficult to establish a close relationship with their spouses and children.

This problematic childhood will render this man or woman immature in love, especially in regard to a spouse and children. This is a double blow, and it will draw strength and energy as time goes on.

In an adulterous relationship, the divorced spouses will very likely become servants to the people that they marry the second time. This will send a very confusing message to our children. The child will see both of his parents serving another man or woman instead of God. God's greatest commandment is to love not only Him but others as well. But God comes first. The call is to obey His commandments and never ever put the commandments of men first in our lives.

Yet our men and women have such difficulty in loving their spouses and their children. Over half of our marriages end in divorce. The problem is our spouses did not love before we married them; hence, they will not love in marriage. If they were spiritually separated from their families during childhood, they will gradually slip further from their own families. They will dominate in order compensate for their weakness in loving. This is not normal behavior. It is only by loving that we are forgiven and get oil for our lamps, as Christ told us to do. And in doing so, our faith increases and the

The Origins of Narcissism

left side of our brain—the rational, spiritual side—becomes stronger and more dominate. From here we can begin to find ways to tap into our talents using the logic and wisdom that God has given to us. The right side of our brain is our creative side, but without love, logic, communication, and the development of the left side, we are like fools walking blindly in this world. Many and probably most of our criminals are right-brain dominant. These men and women are brilliant, but they just need a "shift in perception." If professionals were to test those in our mental hospitals, jails, and prisons, probably at least 95 percent of them would be found to be right-brain dominant at the time of admission for the first time.

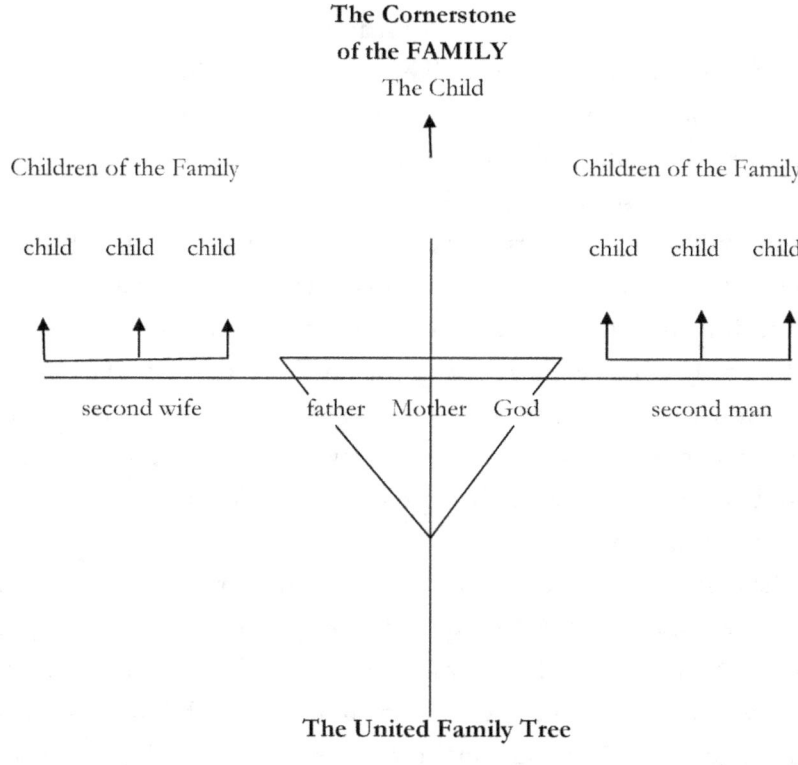

A COMPLEX FAMILY TREE

Narcissism has been a subject that has interested me for a very long time. At the beginning of my search for answers, I could not understand how someone could become so self-centered that they could not think of others.

The first clue that I found was in a book called *The Power of the Family*.[33] In that book, Dr. Pearsall mentioned the "energy leech." There wasn't much information about how an energy leech was created, but I soon linked it with a narcissist.

After many years of searching for answers, I have finally reached a startling conclusion based on Matthew 18:6, 7, "But whoso shall offend one of these little ones which believe in me, it were better for him that a millstone were hanged about his neck, and *that* he were drowned in the depth of the sea. Woe unto the world because of offences! for it must needs be that offences come; but woe to that man by whom the offence cometh!"

I believe that small children, like domesticated animals, if raised in a loving environment, will grow up to be loving, trusting, and caring adults. But the opposite effect occurs if the child is abused, in many cases even before they understand what sin is about. Then, compound this problem with an adult who, after abusing the child, is further abusive in order to get the child to stop crying. This suppression of emotion will cause the child to have difficulty with the self-expression of needs and wants when the child is small and when he or she grows up. They may put others first to the point where they neglect their own health, finances, etc. Or they may become an angry and bitter child and grow up to become a demanding, selfish bully in the home—bullying their own spouse and children while taking from the family.

The child becomes fearful of the abuser. The abuser believes that he or she is teaching the child to fear God, but instead, they are teaching the child to fear him. This is how our men grow up to be men-pleasers, while they have no love or respect for their own wives and children. This is all about kingdom building and transfer of power from one male generation to the next. This is very damaging. Quite often, the child will grow up to be worse than the abusive father or step-father. The grown-up adulterers and adulteresses are the ones that should fear God. Our children only need to know love, not fear. Fear is reserved for the ones that have committed adultery, failed to accept responsibility, and done nothing to correct the problem!

Once the child's shift in perception from love to fear has occurred, he or she begins to focus on self in order to try to ward off future abuse, to please a man, and to ensure that his or her own emotional outbursts do not occur. I shudder at the thought of an adult step-parent, boyfriend, or girlfriend living in a home with a child that is not loved. These little children must think constantly about pleasing the abusive parent or step-parent. They don't learn to love because they have become fearful and are focused on protecting themselves and their interests. Once they grow up and are free of the controlling parent or step-parent, they have problems with compulsive behavior. They will be concerned about their own self-interests and will neglect their own families. Their hearts became hardened long ago. But just think of how many women, wives especially, that have been blamed for not pleasing these men after they leave them for another woman.

The reason for this compulsive behavior is that from very early in their lives, the wrong side of their brains became the dominating factor in their lives. Like Paul, they know what is right, but the irrational, selfish side of their brain overrules the logical, loving side, and they end up doing what they know that they ought not to do. Once the first sin is committed, it becomes a compulsion to do it again and again in repetition, just as Paul enjoyed collecting and bringing true Christians to justice. Another example could be gambling, or the alcoholic who drinks and drives, or promiscuous sexual activity. They may repeat the same behavior hundreds of times in their lives before they gain understanding.

The earlier the shift in perception from love to fear occurs, the less understanding that the child will have. And the child as an adult will experience dysfunction and extreme self-centeredness. They can't control the speed of their cars and get frequent tickets. They can't stop stealing and end up in jail time after time. They can't stop themselves from drinking and driving and end up causing terrible traffic accidents or end up in jail.

The Step-Father's Step-Son

They can't stop eating and become obese. They may starve themselves to unhealthy standards. They drink to the point of drunkenness and even death. They may have sexual intercourse with numerous women and even cheat on their own spouses. Could it be that their childhood was based on control and that they never had the opportunity to learn self-control themselves?

Notice in all of these situations how the adult is unaware or unconcerned about how their behavior affects others. Their hearts have been hardened. They do not love anyone but themselves. But in actuality, they don't love themselves either, because if they did, they would not do the things that they do.

I like to think of Adolf Hitler as the epitome of self-centeredness. Adolf Hitler's paternal grandmother supposedly became pregnant while working for a Jewish family. This Jewish family most likely honored laws written by lawyers more than they honored the family or God. I feel confident that because Alois, Adolf's father, was an illegitimate child, they did not feel responsible for him. Just like I have said before, the woman and the child bear the responsibility for the pregnancy and not the man in most cases. This Jewish family betrayed a member of their own family. It may have been that Alois was this man's firstborn child that he betrayed.

For the first thirty-nine years of his life, Alois bore the surname of his mother, Schicklgruber. At age sixteen, he dropped out of school. In 1876, he took the surname of his step-father, Hiedler, which was also spelled Huetler, Huettler, and Hitler. In 1909, he lived in a shelter for the homeless. In 1910, he moved into a house for poor working men. Alois married twice and had two living children born to his second wife. Each of Adolf's father's wives died of supposed health problems. Then, he started looking for a woman to care for the children of his previous marriage. Alois met and later married Klara, who was twenty-nine years younger than he was. Adolf was a product of that marriage. Biographies relate instances of abuse for both Adolf and his mother. He was the fourth child of six children of whom only he and a younger sister survived into their adult years. I do not know what his childhood was like, but I shudder at the thought.

The Origins of Narcissism

Adolf once confided to his secretary that he had found a way to totally disconnect himself from the pain of his numerous spankings and actually counted all thirty-two blows that he received on one occasion without shedding a tear.[34, 35] Many people suffered for the things that he did. How much responsibility did his grandfather and his father's step-father have in this vicious cycle? We can be certain that our Lord knows exactly what happened. It is ironic that Adolf disliked the Jewish race because he was actually a Jew himself. But because of the Jewish religion that is like our own, he was isolated and separated from his family through lawyers and their laws. His own Jewish family rejected his mother, his grandmother, his father, him, and his children. Should we hate Adolf or love him for the sinner that he was? What about his grandfather—how much credit do we give to him? What about Saul who later became our Paul? There are countless others raised in this type of environment. In actuality, Adolf was a victim that became a bully. His children and many others paid the price for the decisions that his grandfather and his grandfather's family made that excluded him and his mother.

Adolf found the way to overcome the fear of his beatings. He used the left side of his brain to rise above the pain. This was how he could count all thirty-two blows and not cry. He used the left side of his brain to see the big picture and to walk by faith, but he ended up using his faith in the wrong way. He used it to strengthen his desire to conquer—his plans were broad. Christ said that "if thy right eye offend thee, pluck it out" (Matthew 5:29). In this case, Adolf should have done just this. This is never a call for others to decide which body part should be removed—except maybe the testicles. Some people actually cut off people's hands for stealing. This is a call for the individual that could potentially lose their salvation for committing adultery, etc. This is a calling for the person. None of us must ever cut off someone's hand. Nor should any of us vote in juries to have someone put to death or given a lifetime sentence in prison in a cage. Only God has the power to deliver punishment not us. An ounce of prevention is worth a pound of cure. If only their family—and most especially their fathers—could have been there for them from one generation to the next.

Adolf is only one example of a man that used right-eye/left-brain dominance as a way to build a kingdom. Plenty of our men are doing this today. Where you have mega stores you also have kingdoms. All of these men are taking more than their allotted portions, and they are cheating other men out of the opportunity to use their own creativity.

Christ told us in Matthew 5:29, 30,

> And if thy right eye offend thee, pluck it out, and cast *it* from thee: for it is profitable for thee that one of thy members should perish, and not *that* thy whole body should be cast into hell. And if thy right hand offend thee, cut it off, and cast *it* from thee; for it is profitable for thee that one of thy members should perish, and not *that* thy whole body should be cast into hell.

If only Adolf had known of Christ's words and followed them. Adolf was a man that was obviously dominated by the right side of his brain but used his left side for his own personal gain without loving others. The right hemisphere used and dominated his left hemisphere. He had a plan with a very large scope to dominate mankind. He was in the process of dominating as much of the world as he could take.

Ladies, we've got to see that this cycle ends. It hurts us too much to have our children hurt. Believe me, Adolf was a mother's son, and I wonder if she lived to witness the atrocities that he committed. Lord, help us to find the way, the strength, and the voice to take a stand before we marry and, most importantly, in our homes once we marry. We must not stand back, silent and submissive, and let our children be damaged by step-parents. This world is bad enough without the burdens put upon our children by abusive males and step-parents who have grown up under Pharisaical teachings! But most importantly, our sons must be very cautious of the women that they marry. The daughters of men must be avoided. Our men are the ones that have moved in with and married the other woman while abandoning the wife and children of the first family. The daughters of the other woman are the ones that should be avoided. These are the women that will hurt our sons of God. She will dominate them just as her mother dominated the child's father.

Adultery is the root of this unnatural cycle that pervades our entire country today. Step-parents punish rather than forgive. Our laws are based upon punishment rather than forgiveness. It is obvious that this country was set up for step-parents and their children. Step-parents, their children, and their grandchildren primarily run this country. They are the lawyers, doctors, law enforcement officials, and politicians – our lords—that we know and see every day. They are the ones that grew up in two-parent families. Overall, they will make a lot more money during their lives than children of the first family and choose career fields which dominate and imprison the children of the first family.

The only question that remains is this: To whom should we give the responsibility of perpetuating this generational problem . . . our children of the first family? Of course not! The responsibility must lie with "the adulterers" that started the cycle within the family—the one that willingly moved into the family home and took over the family; the one that became the family heir; the one that did not love the first spouse and the children of the first marriage. But the primary responsibility rests with the father that let this woman move in with him or that moved in with the other woman. This man never repented his errors, lifted up his cross, and began to correct the mistakes of his past. As one of my supervisors in Iraq once said, "Hoist acre!" We know this saying as "Hoist anchor"—get the anchor out of the water and move the ship. Either way, we get off of our asses and fix the problem. A man will never make the adjustment, but a son of God will. My husband's father was nothing but a man. He never "hoisted his acre" on behalf of his firstborn son!

Unfortunately, in many cases, there is no way to change what has transpired. Time is time, and there is no way to go back. Our only option is forgiveness. Christ said, "Father, forgive them; for they know not what they do" (Luke 23 34). They crucified Him! There is no way to go back and change that. Adulterers usually have a long time to think out and plan the way that they want things to go. Also, mothers are very protective of their children. A second wife will do almost everything in her power to bless her children and only her children. This is where a strong man is needed to put her in check. He is responsible for making decisions to protect the entire family and not just her and her children. He may even have to kick her out in order to protect the "family." I wish our men could be more like Abraham, Isaac, and Jacob. We need a strong son of God, not a man that submits to his second wife and makes her and her daughter the heads of his household!

It is unfortunate that the children of the first family will be so damaged by these confusing circumstances. Sometimes, we will have no choice but to leave these men who are the fathers of our children. Growing up in such an unnatural environment was not of his own making but, instead, that of his parents and grandparents. This man will need room for growth, and sometimes, he must do it alone in order to find the answers. We must have the patience to wait, and our family is only as strong as its weakest link. This weak link will need time, and sometimes, he will need an entire lifetime. These men, like Noah and Laban, will be forgiven for much more than a man or a woman that left their family for another woman or man.

The sad thing is that if we need to leave a man of this type, there will be plenty of women willing to commit adultery with him. The second marriage and subsequent children complicate the situation to the point where it is difficult to have closure or resolution. Everything is turned upside down. This man will never have the opportunity to grow because he has committed adultery with another woman. The father will never be there. The child will grow up without his father and will most likely feel little obligation to be a father himself. These unfit men pass the same problems on to their children. They are improperly socialized males who don't have the slightest idea what love is all about. They will blame their first wives or a family member for their decisions. These women will have to bear the burden as the men refuse to lift a finger to help.

I believe that the "spare the rod and spoil the child" mentality was replaced by the New Covenant that Christ offered us. If Christ told Peter to forgive seven times seventy times, why is it that an adult male must beat a small child for the smallest of infractions? It is absolutely absurd! Children who grow up under the rule of law will need the rule of law to keep them under control as adults. They fear authority figures, and as crime increases, we must have more police to control our adult population.

Step-parents have great difficulty disciplining step-children properly. They will demand respect because there is an absence of love. I think that this is where the "Mr. and Mrs." terminology began. It puts pressure on the children of the first family and others to respect a man's wife even though she may be his second, third, fourth or fifth. It puts emphasis on the one man and one woman concept that is so important to adulterers. These men and women expect to be the heirs rather than our children; they are, in actuality, competing with the children of the first marriage for everything that is rightfully theirs. We have grown-up adults in competition with little children. Respect is earned with a beating if their demands are not met.

Once the adult starts abusing the child and the child becomes fearful, dysfunction within the home starts manifesting itself. It will be harder and harder to halt the dysfunction as it courses from one generation to the next, much like a familial curse. The child has become spiritually and emotionally separated from the rest of the family. They are on their own. They are there to receive life-sustaining needs, but they will be afraid to give of themselves for fear of abuse. This is how they become takers and not givers. This is the root of hyperactive behavior. It is like a dog that has been on a chain since it was a puppy: when taken off the chain, it will run and run and run without control.

Some of our children do not become hyperactive. Instead, they become complete and total servants to their parents, especially their dominating father or step-father. They will be model children throughout their childhood. Then, when they become adults, they will get into trouble with the law, drugs, or alcohol. They are much like the puppy that grew up on a leash.

Also, we take our small animals away from their mothers much too soon; thus, they aren't learning love either. To learn love, they need to be with their mothers for at least the first six months of their lives. Six weeks is much too short for a small animal to gain a clear understanding of their role in life. This is especially true if they are dealt harsh, unfair retribution, like when a dog urinates on the floor and its owner rubs the dog's nose in it.

In the same way, the six weeks given for maternity leave isn't long enough for our small children to learn about love, patience, consideration of others, etc. Just as animals need time with their mothers, so too do our little children. But we must remember that only mothers can breast feed! This is important to our small children's growth and maturation. They need their mother's closeness and nourishment for at least one year and possibly two years. We are the vine—we must be there for our children! Otherwise, it is a very good possibility that our children will become white-washed tombs! We must be there for our children—they need us. Daycare centers are not the answer.

Most of our men are operating in this mode. How sad it is for all of us ladies. It is an empty vessel of a man that lives in your house. You are the head of the house, and he will hate you for it, but there is no one inside him to fulfill the responsibility. You will have to fill the void. You will have to take most of the responsibility. And when you don't need to accept additional responsibility, he will pass it on to you when there is an important failure, just as Adam did in the Garden of Eden and Paul did. Such a man will worry about maintaining his good looks before men. Therefore, he must blame you in order to maintain this false image. Don't think for a minute that Christ doesn't know. He saw the emptiness in our men even 2,000 years ago. I only wish that I could say, "Lord, things have changed. Our men love their wives and their children now." Unfortunately, I have to say, "Lord, our men are in love with themselves, they don't care about us or the kids. They are only concerned about what they get and receive."

Abusers want to rule over others. They will use force to gain control if necessary. They will especially resent a small child for getting in their way. Pregnant women are especially at risk because of the care and attention that they receive from others. This child and mother have become competition for the abusive man. He will have to fight to get back what he perceives that he has lost, even to the point of killing the child and possibly the mother, too. The mother is at the greatest risk during the later trimester when it is difficult to miss the fact that a child will be interfering and changing his "special" life very soon.[36] Furthermore, the smaller the child, the more likely they will be abused. In order for a man's ego to be satisfied, his ego must receive the good things to which he believes that he is forever entitled. Some of these entitlements are three good meals a day, a clean house, a woman that can work a full-time job and care for the children, a woman that is devoted to him more than to a child, sex when he wants it, a wife that submits to him in everything and never questions him about anything, and a wife and children that will accept the blame for things for which they are not responsible. These entitlements satisfy his ego. The number one cause of death for pregnant mothers is automobile accidents. The second leading cause of death is "partners." Some partners! Step-parents seldom love someone else's child as their own and this is especially true if they have given life to their own children with the child's mother or father.

Autism is the same manifestation of entitlement. The only difference is that it starts in early childhood and gets worse with each generation.[37] Back in the 1980s, it was thought that one to five children per every ten thousand children had autism-like symptoms. Now, in today's times, it is thought that one in every one hundred-fifty children have autism. Boys are being diagnosed four times more frequently than girls. Most believe that there is a genetic basis for this, too. I, for one, think the same way. Just as talents can be passed from one generation to the next, so, too, can undesirable traits be passed from father to son and daughter. Some think that older fathers and exposure to pesticides, vaccines, and toxins contribute to the problem. I agree with the older father issue because separated men become more separated over time. Older men who have maintained a self-centered lifestyle will be much more likely to transfer autistic tendencies to their sons.[38]

I believe that it is transferred by left-eye/right-brain dominant men. The longer the dysfunction has been passed between generations, the earlier the dysfunction will appear in our children and the more likely that it will become a genetic link until the cycle is broken. In other words, at first it starts with early abuse, most likely with a step-parent, which causes the child's unnatural shift in perception. Then, the child grows up and abuses his son, who grows up and abuses his son, and so on. At some point along this insane line, unfavorable traits are beginning to be transferred genetically to the man's children.

The brain controls the genes that transfer talents and unfavorable behaviors. Look around you at those men who have children with physical and mental disabilities. In many cases, it is easy to see that the father is not all there himself. It makes me so angry to have something so foolish passed from one generation to the next. And if a child, especially a son, does not shift perception early enough to satisfy the father, then we have football to knock it into them and make them into hard-hearted rogues at a later date. In this way, women and children will forever be denied the opportunity to mother in a home created with God as its foundation and with a son of God present that can fulfill the obligations of a real father and help mate! The more self-centered our men, the more they will operate without a conscience.

I once visited a family in Austin, Texas, that had a grandmother with auditory (hearing) problems. She produced a son that was mostly deaf but who could hear with a hearing aid. This man, whom I tested and found to be left-eye dominant, produced a son that was totally deaf. This is an example of how our problems become genetic and are passed from generation to generation. I was fortunate to test this man's son for eye dominance. What amazed me was that I found that this young man in his early twenties was right-eye dominant and what I consider walking by faith. I will hypothesize based on my studies that this young man will produce children that will not be deaf.

"And as *Jesus* passed by, he saw a man which was blind from *his* birth. And his disciples asked him, saying, Master, who did sin, this man, or his parents, that he was born blind? Jesus answered, Neither hath this man sinned, nor his parents: but that the works of God should be made manifest in him" (John 9:1–3). This blind individual had no choice except to walk by faith.

God builds stronger families through our children. When a child is born blind, sick, etc., it is a calling for the family to rise to higher heights of faith. A problem is being brought to the attention of the parents and other family members. A correction needs to take place so that the family can be strengthened in faith and in the ways of the Lord. Today, we have a great calling as parents as many of our children are being born with autism, cancer, and other diseases. Our husbands have extreme difficulty in loving. Our seniors develop Alzheimer's disease late in life. All of these are times of reflection and awakening for us all. God is calling us to awaken from our slumber and serve Him more fully!

In our society today, we read a lot about testosterone and its effects upon our males. Studies have shown that males congregating in groups have testosterone levels that are similar. But testosterone levels begin to rise when one within the group starts to exhibit aggressive behavior. Football should boost all of their testosterone levels. Hence, it is the behavior that causes the change in testosterone levels and not the other way around. We have used testosterone as a crutch to explain away bad behavior among our males. We have been misled. Most importantly, other males have fallen prey to these false teachings. They simply do not believe that they can rise above and overcome certain behaviors. How very sad![39] We can't blame testosterone as the root of this problem. The brains of these men and the way that they perceive the world and others are the problem. But the problem goes even deeper. All we need to do is look at our laws and examine the way that our sons are treated. Our sons grow to become men, and our men are responsible for the physical needs of the family. In our culture, rather than making our sons our heirs, our fathers prefer to make another woman the heir.

This is where self-centeredness begins. It all starts when the abusive and controlling adult takes over the child's life by introducing fear. The normal behavior of an eighteen-month-old child is handled badly by an adult male who is forever concerned with himself and about fulfilling what he perceives to be his authority as a male: to bring his children up in the "strictness of the faith." This is because he was brought up this way. It is much like passing a baton. He wants his son to be just a calloused and selfish as he is. He also wants to ensure that his son does not receive more than he did, and that includes the kingdom of God within. If he received abuse, he will want to ensure that his son also receives it. Furthermore, by doing this, he is teaching his child to fear him. This further puts him in the place of god on Earth—first, a servant wife, and now, a servant son. How appealing it is to him! Our God is about love and not fear. When these men teach their children to fear them, they are turning their children's world upside down.

In Matthew 23:13, Christ said, "But woe unto you, scribes and Pharisees, hypocrites! for ye shut up the kingdom of heaven against men: for ye neither go in *yourselves*, neither suffer ye them that are entering to go in." And we read in Luke 1:16, 17, "And many of the children of Israel shall he turn to the Lord their God. And he shall go before him in the spirit and power of Elias, to turn the hearts of the fathers to the children, and the disobedient to the wisdom of the just; to make ready a people prepared for the Lord."

Now is the time for our men to turn their hearts to their children and away from their second wives so that we can prepare ourselves for the return of our Lord and Savior on the clouds. I want my husband, my four sons, their families, and myself to make it to Heaven. I want all of my brothers and sisters and their families to be there. He is coming. Let's start getting ready!

Christ emphasized love and the rule of the Spirit. A child brought up in this environment will understand how to love someone other than just themselves.

The Origins of Narcissism

However, the earlier the abuse occurs, the more dysfunctional the child will be as an adult. There are clues to help with determining the age the abuse caused them to stop trusting and start fearing.

1. Does the child dress like a left-handed person or a right-handed person? Which arm do they put in the sleeve first? Which leg in the pants?
2. Are they left- or right-handed?
3. Which hand do they use to hold the spoon?
4. Are they left- or right-eye dominant?
5. Do they hold their phone to the left ear or the right ear?

Parents can encourage the use of one hand over the other. But if an adult dresses as a left hander, putting his right arm in the sleeve first, then that could indicate the child's perception was shifted around the time he learned to dress himself or before he learned to dress himself.

Jesus sits at the right hand of His Father. God looks upon His Son with love as we do with the right eye/both eyes working as one approach. Our sheep are flexible, loving, caring, and forgiving. Goats are rigid. These are our separated and wild left-eye dominate adults that can only see the gnat on the windshield. They want to do their own thing. They neither love nor trust. They have trouble with forgiveness. They frequently abuse alcohol and drugs during their journey to try to find the way. They are searching for the "something" that is missing in their lives, something that they cannot ever remember having tasted.

Our children remain frozen at the age at which the shift in perception occurred. They may be self-centered, uncaring, hard-hearted, unloving, etc. Who is responsible when this adult harms someone seriously? Who remembers the fearful event that caused this child to see his father or step-father from the different perspective? How old was the child when the shift occurred? The child's father or step-father is responsible, but the child also bears responsibility for what he does. Furthermore, the father

The Step-Father's Step-Son

and step-father had better be very careful, for the Lord said it would be better for them to have a noose around their neck and drown than to cause this to happen.

This is a primary example of why the rule of law was supposed to be abolished when Christ served His Heavenly Father here on Earth. Christ went to great lengths to tell men about the importance of love. But because of the fact that the rule of law was brought from the Old Covenant into the New, it is still applied to men, women, and children today all around the world. Men, even in this age, do pretty much whatever they please within the confines of their homes with their wife and children present. Most of the major religions around the world have accepted a prophet that came after Christ. They want to rule in their kingdom on Earth. Jesus came to break up man's kingdom on Earth and replace the commandments of men with the commandments of God. Christ intricately described the commandments in great depth and detail so that little confusion would remain concerning what was expected. Men want to rule more than to obey. But He did not tell them outright. He told them with parables—ones that were complex enough to require them to put oil into their lamps in order to understand what He was saying. Christ said, "Inasmuch as ye have done *it* unto one of the least of these my brethren, ye have done *it* unto me" (Matthew 25:40).

Women and children are both smaller than men. We are least in many men's eyes. The homeless, poor, and sick are also least in many men's eyes. Many think that the homeless and the sick did something to cause their own poverty or illness. What about the father or step-father? What about the step-mother? Where was the father? Was he even present at all during our children's childhoods? Did his father give everything to the other woman? And if he was present, did he love his children or did he abuse his children?

It is obvious because they respect women so little that they want us to submit to them in everything, stay silent, and not ask questions, and if we do have a question, we must ask our husbands. Women have been silenced throughout history. We do our jobs without expecting much in return, and that includes equal pay, too. Women are following the example of Christ, while our men follow the opposite example themselves.

Ladies, it is time that our silence ended. God did not create man to dominate women.[40] He created man to tend and keep His garden, just as He created women to do the same. We are both help mates. Men have overstepped their authority and created their own kingdom on Earth. We have also let them because of their size and their voice, which sometimes overpower us. Can you imagine how their size must impact our children, especially when they abuse them? Through our silence, they can maintain their kingdom. Certainly, we all would like to have a servant or a slave, but our purpose on Earth is to serve the Lord God Almighty! We must let ourselves experience the freedom associated with the rule of the Spirit. This is where we receive strength, knowledge, and power from God, the Lord of Heaven and Earth. We must do it for the benefits of our children and our future generations.

Even Christ recognized a woman for speaking up despite her low position given to her by men. Here is what was said in Matthew 15:21–28:

> "Then Jesus went thence, and departed into the coasts of Tyre and Sidon. And, behold, a woman of Canaan came out of the same coasts, and cried unto him, saying, Have mercy on me, O Lord, *thou* Son of David; my daughter is grievously vexed with a devil. But he answered her not a word. And his disciples came and besought him, saying, Send her away; for she crieth after us. But he answered and said, I am not sent but unto the lost sheep of the house of Israel. Then came she and worshipped him, saying, Lord, help me. But he answered and said, It is not meet to take the children's bread, and to cast *it* to dogs. And she said, Truth, Lord: yet the dogs eat of the crumbs which fall from their masters' table. Then Jesus answered and said unto her, O woman, great *is* thy faith: be it unto thee even as thou wilt. And her daughter was made whole from that very hour."

The Shift from Love to Fear

When our children begin to have problems as adults, we have many that are willing to place the whole blame and responsibility on our children. They will be happy to say that no one knows what caused it and no one knows what caused our son or our daughter to be this way. In this way, the abuser doesn't have to accept any responsibility. (Just remember, the abuser doesn't necessarily have to be someone from this generation. Victims can also abuse, but the adulterer is usually our first abuser, the one that sets this whole domino effect into motion.) He can just say that the doctors don't even know. It is a great secret. But God knows what happened before the child even understood why they were being spanked so harshly. Then, these "children of men" are more than willing to provide counseling to parents and our children in order to convince us that he or she has some incurable man-named mental illness.

If it were not for the children of the first family, many of these "children of men" would not have the high-paying jobs that they currently have. These "children of men" are literally using the children of the first family to make money. Most of these jobs pay very well and are used to deal with and treat the abandoned children of the first family. If the children of the first family were treated as God intended them to be treated, very few of these "children of men" would have these high paying jobs. The children of the first family are being taken advantage of by the "children of men" in this country, and most people don't even seem to notice or care!

In actuality, the "stage" that the child is going through is perfectly normal and is a required "stage" for correction and further growth. And if we are foolish enough to believe them, we will accept something curable as something that is forever a disability. We are way too willing to allow our children to be labeled for life by the "children of men."

All of this happens because the right side of the brain is in control. The right side is our creative side, but we need the logic on the left side to help us to make good decisions and to fully utilize the talents that we have been given.[41] When the right brain rules over the left side, we will have people that decide to drink and drive, speed, use drugs, and take other extreme and dangerous risks. They are operating in a state of busyness that has little purpose or connection to life. There is darkness all around them. We have many brilliant people locked up in our jails and prisons. If only their grandfathers and fathers could have loved them enough to leave the other woman alone long enough to give them some quality time. Love is the bridge to learning. Without love, none of us can ever reach our potential. Love is soul food. Studies also demonstrate that intellectually gifted girls develop faster than intellectually gifted boys. By age six, girls are about a year ahead of boys. Three years later, they can be as much as eighteen months ahead of boys. The study also found that boys tend to be right-brain dominant. Just think, if girls are eighteen months ahead of them by nine years of age, what will it be like when they are twenty, then thirty, then forty, then fifty?[51]

It is easy to understand why our men would be on the road to ill health and Alzheimer's disease. Our men have always been more prone to heart attacks than we are. They don't live as long either. They became separated early and have experienced dysfunction in their lives ever since. All of these are the complements of a father, mother, step-mother, and step-father that are involved in adultery. That also includes grandparents and their adultery; adultery is a generational sin because of what it does to the family structure and the family tree.

Studies have proven that the dominant side of the brain will have control over the decisions that we make.[42] Brilliant people will make terrible personal choices. It is as though they have no common sense. They are like a ship without a rudder. Many of our so called professionals operate in this mode continuously. They are disconnected from the spiritual aspects of life. They may have extreme difficulty connecting with anything but a textbook and facts. Here are some examples. Richard Feynman, Albert Einstein, and Bertrand Russell were all promiscuous. Albert Einstein had trouble managing his money and lost most of it in bad business dealings.[43]

I believe that right-brain dominance is abnormal in humans. Love is a natural part of our existence, males and females alike. We should not fear each other nor should a child have to fear his father or mother and most certainly not a step-mother or a step-father. Just like adults, children learn best when they don't have to fear abuse for making mistakes. When children fear abuse more than making mistakes, they start imitating the expected behavior and stop learning. The earlier that this happens, the more damaging it is to the individual and to the future generations. In such instances, the father or step-father will appear favorable because the child will obey out of fear. The problem is that when they grow up, the cycle starts over where it stopped. When they first make mistakes as an adult, they may react out of shame, jealousy, and guilt. They will make bigger mistakes as they lose control. They may start to compulsively steal or binge-diet. Some people may suddenly "snap" when faced with situations in which they are caught off guard. When this happens, they may kill or seriously injure their friend, spouse, or child. Other children, instead of becoming the perfect child, will become angry and take their problems out on the world around them. They will bully others.

Christ instructed us to love each other. He did not say that children should fear their fathers as grown-ups should fear the Lord. Instead, we are to love the Lord our God with all of our soul, heart, and mind.

Women have to deal with a person in the house who appears to be an adult but, by all practical purposes, is really just a child on the inside. The earlier the child stopped walking by faith and started fearing, the more confused they will be. They will establish rules that don't apply. They will see opposites in everything. They mistake love and concern for control and domination, especially when it comes to women. The wife will have to mother not only her own children but also this man-child. This man-child may not be willing to be taught by his wife. He "thinks" that he is grown up and knows everything—pretty much like an adolescent. He may also fail to listen to his wife after having been taught by his dominating father or step-father not to value words spoken by women. Again, this is contrary to Christ's teachings.

He will ultimately do pretty much whatever he wants to do if it is good for his perceived benefit and the gratification of his ego. He will put himself first. He will, in most cases, never consider the needs of his family when making decisions. When he fails to receive what his ego holds to be important, he will revert to abuse, anger, or even murder in retaliation. This is because his ego has dominated his entire life. If the ego stays fed, the individual will cooperate and appear to be the model citizen. Beware the minute that an individual like this fails to receive what he wants; that individual will become your archenemy. Osama bin Laden is an example of this type of individual. He was friends with the United States until we stopped making him the center of our attention.

The biggest problem of all in this is trying to help someone overcome something about which they have little knowledge. We may not know anything except for the few snippets of information that we have overheard about our husband's childhood. The burden of responsibility lies on the parents' and step-parents' shoulders. Unfortunately, the woman and her children will inherit this mess. This is an unfair burden that adulterous fathers, mothers, step-mothers, and step-fathers place upon our families. This is why the ounce of prevention is more important than the pound of cure.

We have fathers who don't even take the time to see their own sons at all during their childhood and sometimes even into adulthood. Essentially, they abandon their own children for an adulterous second union with what is actually a mistress, although they may be legally married according to this country's standards. Adultery is adultery no matter what earthly laws say. God has established rules, and unfortunately, we have almost fifty percent of our population divorced or remarried, in many cases multiple times. Whatever wounds may exist from his absence will be ones that are transferred to the woman and children. She will have to try to teach her husband what this absent father did not. In other words, our wives are having to mother and wife these men-children because of another man's apathy. How very sad for a useless father to transfer such responsibility to a woman and her children! The Lord will one day deal with this man's foolishness.

Jesus said, "Strive to enter in at the straight gate: for many, I say unto you, will seek to enter in, and shall not be able" (Luke 13:24).

The straight gate is one in which we keep the commandments and our generations perfect! The earlier the shift to left-eye dominance without correction and the return to right-eye/left-brain dominance, the greater the likelihood that the individual will transfer undesirable characteristics, including birth defects and illness such as childhood cancer, diabetes, muscular ticks, etc., to their children. This includes behavioral problems as well.

We have children who, early in life, become self-dominated and primarily use only the right side of their brain. Unipolar is a good description of the condition. It is not a chemical imbalance causing this but, instead, a serious thinking imbalance between the two sides of the brain. The wrong hemisphere is dominating!

The self is like a prison. The earlier that the shift occurs, the stronger the self, or "ego," will be and the more difficult it will be for the young adult to escape its clutches. Alcohol and drugs—both legal and illegal—will relax the right side of the brain enough so that they can have a taste of love, God, and others. This may be the reason why alcoholics tend to sing hymns when they are drunk, but the feeling is good only as long as the drugs stay in the system. When the drugs are eliminated, the person returns back to the state where they were before. There is a feeling of hopelessness because there is no escape. They cannot remember a time in their lives when they were not in bondage to self, or "ego." They live in darkness. If only their parents had allowed them to experience love and forgiveness. Then, they could have tasted the freedom that is associated with true love.

We are supposed to go after our lost sons and daughters. Instead, most parents today just let them go their way and wait for them to come home. How many of our church members will wait for people to come to them instead of them going to the people? Paul had it backwards. We don't exclude sinners from our lives; we include them. Christ never excluded Judah! In Matthew 18:12–14, Jesus said, "How think ye? if a man have an hundred sheep, and one of them be gone astray, doth he not leave the ninety and nine, and goeth into the mountains, and seeketh that which is gone astray? And if so be that he find it, verily I say unto you, he rejoiceth more of that *sheep*, than of the ninety and nine which went not astray. Even so it is not the will of your Father which is in heaven, that one of these little ones should perish." We must live by Christ's example and go after our lost sheep, especially those in our family.

In the book *Return to Love* by Maryanne Williamson, the author speaks about a "shift in perception" that saved her life. She had reached a dead end and had no options but to make changes in her life. Out of desperation and love for her mother, she picked up a copy of *"The Course in Miracles"* by The Foundation for Inner Peace and began reading. This is how she turned her life around. This book reprograms our false beliefs about religion and love. It corrects our faulty thinking and the false religions that we formulated in childhood.[44]

I know now that the shift in perspective that she spoke of—was actually a shift in brain dominance. I did not understand this at the time. I learned about this "shift in perception" during a leadership course while working for the Department of Defense as a safety officer. It was not until much later that I understood fully what was actually happening.

Christ said in Luke 9:27, "But I tell you of a truth, there be some standing here, which shall not taste of death, till they see the kingdom of God."

Christ said let your eye be single. That means both sides of the brain working together but with the right side primary. This is how we experience the kingdom of God. This is what it means to walk by faith. We walk through life looking at the big picture, not focusing on details or problems.

My husband's father was busy watching the ship disappear over the horizon and out of view. He had a very limited perception.

Again, in reflection back on my life, I remember the time when I had been betrayed by my husband—when he told me that I would have to go back to his step-father and mother's house. I trusted this man, and the fact that he broke this promise hurt me terribly. I remember finding a scary place somewhere in my mind. I knew where it was, and I knew that I did not want to go there. So, what I did was walk on water and bypass it. I maintained my faith in God, put one foot in front of the other, and went on until the scary place disappeared completely. I believe that had I gone there, I would have reverted back to some stage in my early childhood when something happened that was extremely frightening to me and about which I had no understanding. Faith is truly a rock to our mental and emotional stability. I do not know what occurred, nor do I know how old I was at the time. I do know that I had an alcoholic father and a brother and sister, twins, who were born within thirteen months of my arrival. I am sure that it was a trying time for my mother and father, especially my father, who had committed adultery by marrying my mother. My mother may have been caring for the newborn twins when my father may have done something which he should not have done to me. I will never know; it is forever gone from my thoughts. And whatever it was, I have forgiven him completely. I just wish that he could have been there for my family in a more productive way. But for reasons about which I can only guess, he was consumed with alcoholism almost until his death.

The longer the dysfunctional state exists, the more likely that illness or disease will strike. Right-brain dominance is an unnatural, irrational state in which an individual deals with fear at many different levels. Until the shift back to left-brain/right-eye dominance and equilibrium occurs, the individual will experience depression and other fearful states of mind. Once the left-brain/right-eye equilibrium is developed and maintained along with a strong faith in Jesus Christ as our rock, depression and the temptation to sin will disappear. The individual will no longer experience depression or fear if they can remain left-brain/right-eye dominant. But they will experience depression each time that they return to this right-brain/left-eye pattern. The longer they stay there, the longer the depression will linger. If the right-brain/left-eye dominant state is the only one that the child has ever known, he or she will learn to develop defensive mechanisms to keep from sliding into deep depression and returning to that point where the early interruption of their left-brain/right-eye dominant state was interrupted and they started fearing for the first time. These defensive mechanisms will become "entitlements." Alcohol and drugs may become entitlements. They are an adaptive and protective barrier to more injury and hurt.

DEGREE OF DOMINANCE

Separation	Connection
Left-eye Dominate/Right Brain Dominant	Right-eye Dominate/Left Brain Dominant
Fear/Paranoia	Love
Self-Centered	Faith
Mental Dysfunction	Ability to Heal
Autism	Telepathic
Physical Dysfunction (Illness)	Health

And Peter answered him and said, Lord, if it be thou, bid me come unto thee on the water. And he said, Come. And when Peter was come down out of the ship, he walked on water, to go to Jesus. But when he saw the wind boisterous, he was afraid; and beginning to sink, he cried, saying, Lord, save me. And immediately Jesus stretched forth *his* hand, and caught him, and said unto him, O thou of little faith, wherefore didst thou doubt? (Matthew 14:28–31)

And Jesus answering them said, They that are whole need not a physician; but they that are sick. I came not to call the righteous, but sinners to repentance. (Luke 5:31, 32)

The Shift from Love to Fear

The earlier the shift to left-eye/right-brain dominance, the more severe the disability will be for the grown-up child and the less likely the child will see the world from the perspective that the other side of the brain has to offer. Just as Peter had the faith to walk on water, he also shifted his perception and started fearing the wind and waves.

Alcohol, tobacco, cussing, stealing, adultery, and promiscuity are all examples of rigid, impulsive, and compulsive behavior.

The Betrayal

Jesus said, "And ye shall be betrayed both by parents, and brethren, and kinsfolk, and friends; and *some* of you shall they cause to be put to death" (Luke 21:16).

Each year, we abort thousands upon thousands of babies because they are unwanted. And each year, we abort living children from our lives for our own convenience through live abortion. Some of the living children are murdered, some are abused, some are forgotten, and some are given up for adoption. We have decided that there are degrees of neglect. It is acceptable to murder unwanted children if that child has not yet been born into this world and no one knows about him or her except the mother and possibly the father.

We have decided that is it all right to put a child up for adoption so that we can go about our lives as though the child never existed. Young women especially are encouraged to do this so that they can continue on with college and not have the responsibility of dealing with a small child. In our society, this act is highly encouraged.

When the union of two adults—one male and one female—occurs, our Lord expects them to stay together. They can live apart if need be for growth, but no one is ever allowed to move in and separate them! Furthermore, when a child is created, our Lord expects both parents to be present for that child. It is in the second wife's best interests to separate the father from the child of his first marriage. This way she doesn't have to be reminded of the first marriage. Christ said in Luke 12:15, "Take heed, and beware of covetousness: for a man's life consisteth not in the abundance of the things which he possesseth." In this case, the new wife will covet the man that she "got" from the child. I consider this to be stealing. She is taking the life of the father completely away from the child or children of the first marriage.

The step-father will ensure that the child's mother devotes most of her time to him and his children. They may even change his last name to avoid confusion with two blended families, especially when the child's father has abandoned him.

This child will never belong to either of these two new families; this child is the only living representative of a family that two people failed to honor. This child is left holding the bag alone.

God's covenant is with the child of the holy union. Because of this one child, who has been beaten, abused, adopted, and betrayed, all four adults and their offspring are interrelated. That child is the one who ties everything together. This is most likely one of the greatest reasons that this child is at risk for abuse and death at the hand of the step-father and step-mother.

Furthermore, God's covenant is with this child, the product of a holy union which no man or woman can separate. That child is a constant reminder of what was and what most people incorrectly believe is no more.

> Jesus saith unto them, Did ye never read in the scriptures, The stone which the builders rejected, the same is become the head of the corner: this is the Lord's doing, and it is marvelous in our eyes? Therefore say I unto you, The kingdom of God shall be taken from you, and given to a nation bringing forth the fruits thereof. And whosoever shall fall on this stone shall be broken: but on whomsoever it shall fall, it will grind him to powder. (Matthew 21:42–44)

People of today are cursing the children of their holy union and blessing the children of their adulterous union. We are told in Jeremiah 3:1, "They say, If a man put away his wife, and she go from him, and become another man's, shall he return unto her again? shall not that land be greatly polluted?

The Betrayal

but thou hast played the harlot with many lovers; yet return again to me, saith the Lord." As a result of many adulterous unions, our entire land is being greatly polluted. We are to leave sin and return to God. In the same way, we are to leave our adulterous relationships and return to our first wives and children. We need to put our family back together.

My mother is a wonderful example of this. My father encouraged her to leave because of his abusive actions, and my mother did it because she knew it was best for all of us. When she left and took us with her, it freed my father to go back to his first family. I don't know if his wife took him back, but I do know that his children did. When I visited with one of his daughters (my half-sister), she told me about how they had lovingly arranged his burial. This family was blessed with his coming home.

One night during my mother's struggles to support all five of us children on her own and without welfare, she saw a vision. She saw stairs leading up to a golden throne that was empty. I have no doubt that this throne was reserved for my mother because of the great thing that she did for us and for our Lord and Savior. She freed my father so that he could return to his first family—the one where he belonged. She obeyed the commandments of God. I doubt that she knew at the time that she was keeping the commandments, but she did it naturally out of love. She did not put herself first in life but, instead, her Heavenly Father.

Something as simple as the taking of a child's teddy bear by a step-parent could be a great indicator of the place that the child holds within the home. This is symbolic of the position he would hold within the family. The step-father was sending a subtle message that the child, my husband, would hold no position within the family. His own firstborn son would be first in his life.[45]

This action is significant. It indicates two things: 1) that the child had some understanding that things were amiss, and 2) this is how things would be handled in the future. The fact that his teddy bear was taken away predicted that he would hold no position within the family. He was not the cornerstone of anything. And since his half-brother's teddy bear was bigger, this signified that his half-brother would have greater standing in the family. Then, let's take a look at the other side of the family, the one where no one acknowledged that the child had ever been born. The child is totally isolated from his father's side of the family as though he was never born or never existed. How old must the child be before they will tell him that he is adopted? How much guessing must the child do when things seem strange? Isn't the truth better than a lie? When will the parents and step-parents accept responsibility for what they have done?

Morals to the Story

First of all, the biggest danger is when there is only one child. It is much easier to take advantage of one child than two or three from the first marriage. Also, there is no one for the child to confide in if things are amiss.

Secondly, the step-parent will not let the step-child fill the social position of "oldest" in their brood. They will either covertly or overtly save that position for their own firstborn child.

Thirdly, if there is only one step-child, the step-parent will permit the step-child to fill the position, but only as a servant to the other children. If it is a girl, she will be responsible for the care of their children both physically and financially. If it is a boy, he will be responsible for caring for the children, doing chores to help them, and giving up his inheritance. If they do not serve in the proper way, they will be abused.

Fourthly, each step-parent will be determined to survive the child's natural parent to ensure that the sum of the estate is controlled by them and their own children, not the step-child.

Lastly, the earlier that the step-parent enters the child's life; the greater the likelihood that these behaviors will be repeated during the child's adult life. He will attempt to dominate his wife and children in the same way that he has witnessed in his life. This will make for a very bad marriage. He will take everything that he can from his wife and children and claim it for his own, just as the step-parent did during his childhood. He will deliberately try to force his own children into failure in order to get even for his losses. Also, if his children fail, it will make his accomplishments appear to be greater than they actually are. The children of the first family are usually not as successful as the children from the second family. This adult child will feel inferior to his half-brothers and half-sisters from the second marriage. This adult child has been defeated.

The "children of men" have little understanding about adultery. They were fortunate to grow up with a mother and a father, while the child of the first marriage had "none." The "children of men" in this country get just about everything. It is little wonder that our sons and daughters have problems with adultery of this magnitude going on legally in their own homes.

Testing for eye dominance is never to be used to identify someone as defective. It is merely a test to provide information to others so that their lives can be restored and recovery can be accomplished. These children have endured much for the second family. Their suffering needs to be recognized and more completely understood so that responsibility can be placed upon the appropriate individuals. There needs to be some good, wholesome judgment here whereby we actually call adultery "adultery" for the first time in this country's history! It is long overdue. It is no longer acceptable to just to say that "it is okay."

How Is Eye Dominance Determined?

Most of us are born with two eyes. Of those two eyes, one will usually in most cases be more dominant than the other. Also, during the course of a day, we may shift eye dominance several times. For example, when we become fearful, the left eye and right brain usually become dominant. This is the eye that focuses on problems and in many cases causes the problem to appear larger than it really is.[52] For this reason, it is important for us to have a greater understanding of ourselves and the way that we think. Once we begin to realize the difference in the role that the two sides of our brain play in our lives it will help us to better understand why we behave the way we do. We will find that it is the way that we think that affects our lives and our outcomes.

With right eye and left brain dominance, stress will be reduced. Our blood pressure and heart rate will be more consistent. We will walk by faith.

With left eye and right brain dominance, our lives will be very stressful because little problems will appear to be mountains that we cannot overcome.

The only reason that I am sharing this is because it has made a difference in my own life. I have practiced it and I know that it works. I am just thankful that I was able to attend the Leadership Development class where it was first introduced to me. Just remember though, that at the time, I did not fully understand the significance. I have taken this information and tested it and practiced it in my own life. It works! Furthermore, I believe that this has everything to do with what Christ was trying to tell us when he talked about letting your eye be single and walking by faith and not fearing. He repeatedly said, "Do not be afraid." He is with us always!

A single test is required to determine eye dominance. All that is required is an 8.5 x 11 inch piece of paper and an index card, envelope, or a piece of paper of similar size.

The first thing to do is to take the 8.5 x 11 inch piece of paper and fold it in half. Then, fold it in half again. Find the center point of the fold and tear out a small hole. When you unfold the paper, you should have a small hole in the center of the page. See the example below.

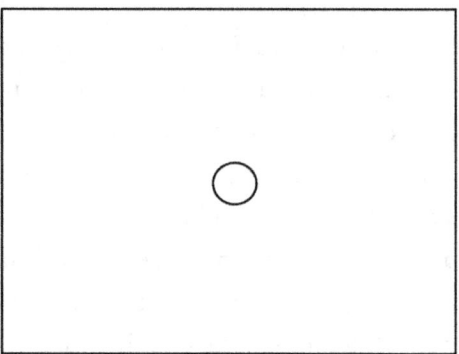

Now, you are ready to test your family members. Here is how to do it.

First, have them stand or sit. Next, find a small object for them to focus on that is across the room, across the street, etc. Ask them to take the piece of paper in their hands and stretch out their arms, holding the paper with both hands.

Then, ask them to focus on the object with both eyes open (no squinting) and through the hole in the piece of paper. Stand on their right-hand side, and gently take the index card or envelope and place it in front of their right eye. Ask them if they can see the object with their right eye covered. Note their answer.

If they can see the object with their right eye covered, this means that they are left-eye dominant. If they cannot see the object with their right eye covered, this means that they are right-eye dominant.

How Is Eye Dominance Determined?

Repeat the test. This time, stand on their left-hand side, and gently take the index card or envelope and place it in front of their left eye. Ask them if they can see the object with their left eye covered. Note their answer.

If they can see the object with their left eye covered, this means that they are right eye dominant. If they cannot see the object with their left eye covered, this means that they are left eye dominant. Note the dominant eye on the chart included in this book.

To further help us prove the theories, hypotheses, and conclusions that have been written about in this book, and for the benefit of others, I would like to encourage your participation by mailing a copy of your family study to the following address: Family Matters Publishing, 614 S Business IH35, Ste C, New Braunfels, Texas 78130. A copy of the research template and consent form are available for down-load at www.stepfathersstepson.com or by sending a stamped self-addressed envelope to the address listed above.

Why Is Eye Dominance Important?

These are my conclusions based on my research and testing. Note that the capital letter in the diagram denotes the dominant eye: R = Right-eye dominant, and L = Left-eye dominant.

Here is what happens when we get two sheep together in a marriage. They are both servants and give in order to receive. They are both genuinely interested in caring for each other. They are connected and intimate. The two will be able to communicate without talking. The circle of communication is complete.

Functional Relationship

Servant Leaders and Partners in Marriage

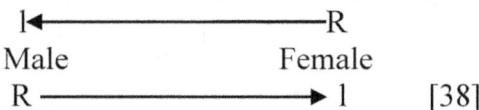

[38]

The Step-Father's Step-Son

This is the strongest of all relationships and the most ideal. These two will be able to communicate without speaking a word. These partners will accept responsibility, be independent while being dependent upon each other, trust, serve, love, and tend to God's garden and their family.

This couple, two goats in the workplace and at home, will see everything in reverse—the separate or opposite perspective of the truth. Where there is love, care, and concern, they will see something other than love, care, and concern. They will blame someone or something else, like Adam and Eve did, for their problems. They are experiencing a major dysfunction. There may be sin, waste, self-indulgence, crime, etc. The condition of their property may be in disrepair. These individuals will have the greatest likelihood of experiencing some type of serious illness during their lifetimes. This couple has the greatest potential for passing birth defects on to their children and grandchildren.

These two will have specific traits such as dependency, controlling natures, blaming, a desire to rule over family members, fearing, and dominating. This will be an extremely confusing and chaotic relationship. Whoever tries to follow the other's lead will be met with failure. We have the blind trying to lead the blind.

Blind Leading the Blind

Self-Centered Man   Self-Centered Woman

L ──────────▶ r

Male   Female

r ◀────────── L   [38]

How Is Eye Dominance Determined?

We see this arrangement with people that join gangs. They instantly recognize and identify with others like themselves. When people like this leave alcohol or criminal or drug groups, the temptation will linger to return. They feel a strong sense of belonging. They will want to associate with people with a similar perspective. It can be dangerous in gangs; despite their similar way of thinking, members have been known to kill each other if proper control is not maintained over each member. Violence also happens in the home when one member feels threatened and is unable to maintain what they perceive to be proper control over the other spouse or child. Also, in organizations and businesses that are run by individuals of this type with the bulk of power, there will be chaos, waste, and an atmosphere of fear. They will blame the employees, but the real problem is the leadership.

In this example, he—the goat—will see the opposite in everything. He will be on the defensive and put himself first. Communication will be incomplete. She, the sheep, will make good decisions, but the man will undermine her. Similarly, he will make poor decisions. Despite the differences of which he is well aware, he will still try to overrule and dominate her. This happens quite often in the home and the workplace. This is the very reason why it is so difficult for women to succeed in the workplace. Women must suffer much to accomplish anything. When problems arise, they will blame the woman. They will not see the plank in their eye and remove it. If she makes a mistake, they will make sure that her splinter is addressed as though it were a plank. She will have to work harder to prove herself than a man would. Even then, they still will not respect her because they have little respect for women. If he is in charge, he will change the rules to his advantage. When you think that you have figured out the rules, he will change them again. There will be much confusion in the workplace, home, etc. He will be a poor manager. Life will be difficult for his family and his employees.

The woman will accept responsibility for her mistakes, be independent, trusting, serving, and loving, and tend to God's garden and family. The man will be self-centered. He will be controlling, dominating, fearful, and blaming.

The Step-Father's Step-Son

This woman could also be a goat, even though she is right-eye dominant. She very well could also be the adulteress in a marriage and use manipulation and control to keep her man. In this case, she will overrule him who used to be a sheep and dominate him. He will become a broken man in this relationship.

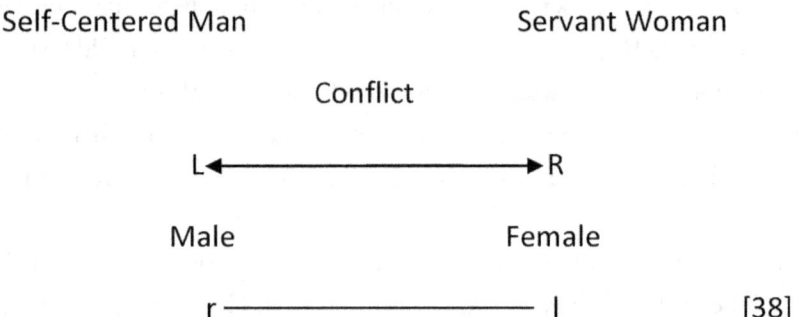

[38]

This is the Pharisaical relationship. The servant woman does most of the work of caring for the business, the home, the family, the finances, the customer, etc. The man will want her to serve and worship him. This man will feel threatened by the female if she is strong and independent. She is the most likely to experience abuse. The man's desire will be to dominate the wife. He will expect her to be submissive, and if she is not, he will feel threatened. He does not desire intimacy for he prefers to get things the easy way: to take them. Women will be falsely accused. In the workplace, there will be attempts to have her removed from her job.

He will still see the opposite in everything. If his wife is weak in her faith, she will put him first in her life. She will worship him and serve him. He will be a whited sepulchre full of bones, just as Christ described them. He will look good on the outside, but his heart will be as hard as a rock.

Since she does most of the work in caring for the family, he will have keen awareness of her value. When she grows tired and tries to leave him,

How Is Eye Dominance Determined?

he may seek her out and attempt to kill her. Any man that tries to fill his shoes he will also seek out and attempt to kill.

In this relationship, the man—the sheep—accepts responsibility, is independent, serving, loving, tending God's garden, family, and trusting. The woman, the goat, will be one of two types. She can become the person the man wants her to be—a follower or she will be very self-centered. She will do her own thing without considering his needs or the needs of the family.[46]

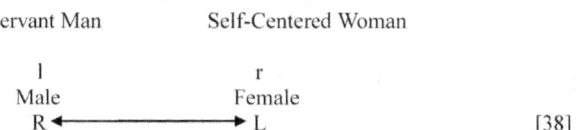

This man, if he is spiritually strong, will lead this woman. If he is not strong, she will dominate him. She will want him to serve and worship her.

People who are left-eye dominant are much more likely to suffer from dyslexia than others because they see the mirror image of the truth and of what actually exists. Instead of seeing love in a good deed performed, they may see something other than love, for example, manipulation or control.

We must also remember that many of our children are born with this left-eye/right-brain dominance. It is not something that they had any control over. They were born this way so that the glory of God could manifest itself as Christ said. With each step, these little children are walking by faith. The only difference is that they are doing it the hard way because of family members and "step-parents" in the past that took something from one of their family members that was not theirs to take. It could very well have been a great-grandfather that took something from this child's grandfather who, in turn, had difficulty loving the father who produced this beautiful child with difficulties using the right side of his body.

Left-brain dominated individuals will search for the deeper meaning in what is said and experience greater awareness of those around them.

In Matthew 6:1–4, Jesus said,

> Take heed that ye do not your alms before men, to be seen of them: otherwise ye have no reward of your Father which is in heaven. Therefore when thou doest *thine* alms, do not sound a trumpet before thee, as the hypocrites do in the synagogues and in the streets, that they may have glory of men. Verily I say unto you, They have their reward. But when thou doest alms, let not thy left hand know what thy right hand doeth: That thine alms may be in secret: and thy Father which seeth in secret himself shall reward thee openly.

In summary, Jesus said, "Do not let the right brain (left hand) know what the left brain (right hand) doeth."

I have read studies that indicate that left-eye/right-brain dominance is on the increase. Back in the 60s, it was estimated that roughly 98 percent of the population was right-eye/left-brain dominant. Today, we are at about a 50/50 ratio by some studies. It may be much higher than a 50/50 ratio for men. While I was in Iraq, I was astonished at the number of left-handed people. I have never seen so many in one place at the same time. I believe that this is the cause for our increase in crime and illness. Dysfunctional thinking leads us to dysfunctional lifestyles and bodies. It is not a chemical imbalance that we need to be concerned about but rather a thinking imbalance. In order for humans to survive, we must be spiritually connected to others. When we get a whole cross section of our society, especially the majority of our men, that is left-eye/right-brain dominant, selfishness will dominate our families, businesses, and societies.

Jesus said in Matthew 6:22, "The light of the body is the eye: if therefore thine eye be single, thy whole body shall be full of light. But if thine eye be evil, thy whole body shall be full of darkness. If therefore the light that is in thee be darkness, how great *is* that darkness!"

Methods for Shifting Eye Dominance and Perception

Study after study reveals that our human language center is primarily located in the left hemisphere of our brain.[47] Language is one way of reaching outward and connecting with others. Yet we have known for quite some time that many of our men and women have trouble with communication and with loving others, especially their spouses and children. For these men and women, sex is the only type of love that they seem to desire—love in the physical sense—while abandoning the spiritual totally. They remain distant and aloof. And they will be quite content in a relationship of this type as long as their wives or husbands are very giving and they get what they want most of the time. When their spouses stop giving completely, they will become very dissatisfied.

And if our language center is located on the left side of our brain, it would make sense that the dominate side of our brain would also be the left side. I spent over a year working in Iraq as a contractor with Kellogg, Brown, and Root. It was the most amazing opportunity to study men. I even had an opportunity to study some of the men more closely. I tested some for eye dominance. Following the study and a brief explanation of what I had learned, some of the men experienced jealousy and others experienced disdain. You might have guessed that the right-brain dominant men were the ones that felt left out. The left-brain dominant men expressed disdain for the right-brain dominant men. It was like light and darkness being separated for the first time within that office.

The Step-Father's Step-Son

In my research for writing this book, I have concluded that there are many bridges to "faith," to left-brain dominance. Books that have been written and movies have been produced about the "shift in perception," but little is understood beyond that.

One example is Dr. Lester Fehmi of Princeton University who wrote of shifting focus from the ship to the lake in a technique which he refers to as "open focus." Using the technique, the subject switches from focusing on the ship in the middle of a lake to focusing on the lake, the bigger picture.[48] There are other people that have written about similar but different techniques.[49, 50]

You might recall from an earlier chapter in this book that my husband's father focused upon the ship as it disappeared over the horizon. He is a good example of a man that missed out on the fullness of life and lived a very limited one. I think that he shifted his perception after committing adultery and giving up his wife and firstborn son. These are all life-changing choices, especially when we do nothing to correct the situation.

I also think that my husband's step-father lived a similar limited existence. He married into a family that already existed rather than building his own family.

There are many ways of training ourselves to shift back to our natural loving and trusting state, that which we left behind during our childhood. One way is to use divergent/convergent thinking. I learned about this during a leadership course while working for the Department of Defense as a safety officer. Clearly, there are two perceptions of our existence and experiences. Convergent thinking focuses on problems. These individuals will have much trouble multitasking. They will focus on one problem at a time without seeing the big picture. With divergent thinking, we recognize that there are problems, but we will find a better solution by looking at the big picture. With this perception, we will be better able to understand how our actions to correct the problem will affect others and the larger scope of our existence.

I recall that it was shortly after a leadership development class that I and most of the hospital staff attended that I was having difficulty juggling all of the projects for which I was responsible. I stopped into a head nurse's office and discussed this problem with her. Immediately, she reminded me of the training that we had both received. While I sat in her office, I shifted my perception from focusing on the problem to looking at the big picture. After that meeting, I started practicing what I had learned more completely, and it really did help me to manage my job more successfully.

It was not until much later that I understood fully what was actually happening. I was driving on I-10 toward Houston with a large truck in front of me. I noticed that I became fearful because I could not see traffic beyond the truck. Immediately, I shifted to the other eye, using my right-eye as my dominant eye. It was then that all of my fears disappeared, and I realized what was actually happening with divergent/convergent thinking: it is actually a shift in eye/brain dominance. Furthermore, the side that dominates, affects very strongly the way we think and reason.[51] Ultimately, the dominating side will lead us to make good or bad decisions and to walk by faith (love) or by sight (fear).

Divergent vs. Convergent Thinking

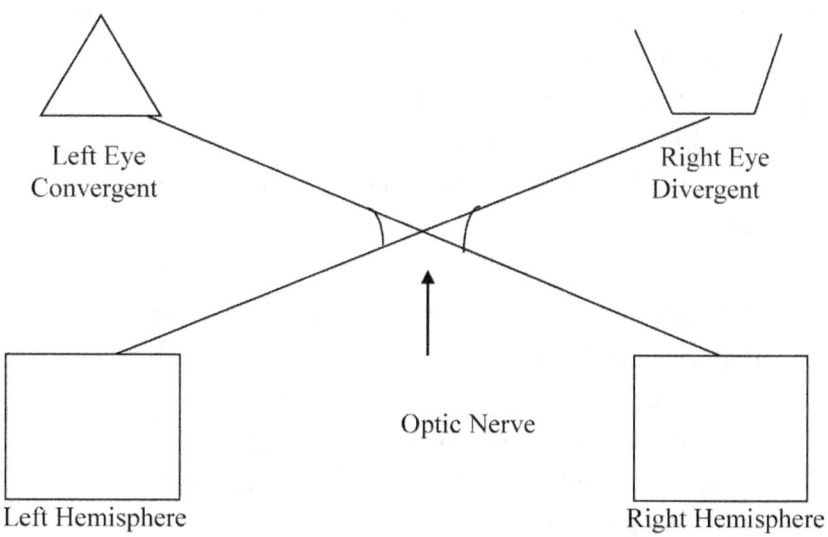

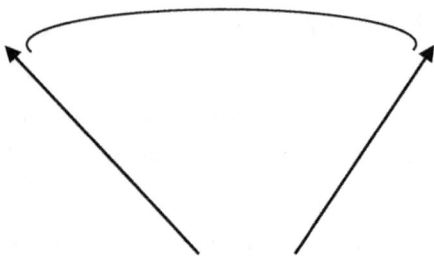

Convergent thinking involves focusing on problems such as the little fly specks on the windshield. It causes us to fear because the little grain of sand or the fly speck will appear larger than life.[52] As a result of this type of focus on life, many problems will appear to be insurmountable, and because we lack faith, we will fail at accomplishing our goals in life. Studies have demonstrated that left eye dominance does indeed cause images to appear larger than they actually are.[52] In this mode, we are gambling with our safety, finances, and lives.

Divergent thinking involves taking in the entire panoramic view in front of us. The problems are there; the only difference is that they don't seem as ominous. We are able to love more completely and our lives are richer and fuller. We are free to take prudent risks. Our blood pressure should be lower, and our health improved.

Many books have been written about this "shift in perception." Here are a few:

- *A The Course in Miracles* by The Foundation for Inner Peace
- *Brain Magic* by Neil Slade
- *The Frontal Lobes Supercharge* by Neil Slade
- Matthew, Mark, Luke, and John written by the disciples Matthew, Mark, Luke, and John. These men were witnesses to Jesus' life and the words that He spoke.

Methods for Shifting Eye Dominance and Perception

- *Getting Unstuck: Break Through Your Barriers to Change* by Dr. Sidney B. Simon
- *A Return to Love: <u>Reflections on the Principles of "A Course in Miracles"</u>* by Marianne Williamson
- *The Road Less Traveled: A New Psychology of Love, Traditional Values and Spiritual Growth*, M. Scott Peck, M.D., Sept 15, 1988

There are many movies that have been produced about the "shift from fear to love." Here are a few:

- *9 to 5*
- *The Ultimate Gift*
- *The Game*
- *It's A Wonderful Life*
- *Fireproof*
- *Flywheel*
- *The Ultimate Life*
- *Fly Away Home*
- *Welcome to Mooseport*
- *Overboard*

Be aware that some of these movies promote adultery and other sins. There are some individuals who do experience a shift in perspective in these movies. You must look deeply enough to find them. If you have not experienced the shift in perception yourself and joined the "club," as it is considered in *The Game*, then you will not understand. I am a member of that club myself, but I cannot explain it because it is something that you must experience yourself.

Recently, the state of Texas executed a young man. As he lay on his death bed, with leather straps buckled around his body, he expressed repentance of the things that he had done. Then, he said something that I will never forget and still rejoice about today. He said something like, "I will see you on the other side!" This young man was, and is, also a member of the club. This young man died a son of God. Had they forgiven this young man instead of killing him, he could have been a testament to others, but the judges, lawyers, and jurors wanted him to die. This man was a better man than a lot of men outside of prison. There are few men that are willing or have the courage to learn what this young man learned. This young man was a great man. This is exactly what Jesus was all about.

I believe that incomplete emotional memories are stored in the left amygdala. When we succumb to the temptation associated with the incomplete memory, we experience guilt, pain, and further separation from God. We shift eye dominance and start focusing on the problem—the temptation—just as Adam and Eve did. Jesus came into the world to love us, forgive us, and restore our faith so that we could overcome the temptations. When we start to focus on Him and to trust Him, He helps us to shift our perspective back to faith. Hence, we have the strength to overcome the temptation or fear and maintain our right-eye/left-brain dominance. Faith gives us freedom from the temptation to act out our stored emotional memories.

When we have an imbalance in faith, we are left-eye/right-brain dominant. So we must help each other to strengthen our faith to shift. This is why we must forgive as Christ has forgiven us. This is why we must love as Christ told us to love. It is so very important!

Adultery is one of the most damaging of sins because it splits the family apart. Adultery may very well be a sin for which there is no forgiveness unless corrective action is taken. We know that Abraham, Isaac, and Jacob are in Heaven. Their lives are a testament of the choices and the decisions that they made. Some of those decisions were not easy ones, but they made the decisions that were in the best interest of the whole family and not the part. Christ came to free us from bondage. It is our job to free others from bondage by forgiveness, repentance, and love. It is time that we freed the children of the first family from jail and prison. It is time that their fathers mustered the courage to lift their children of the first family into their rightful places.

Jesus Is the Way, the Truth, and the Life

Christ was a step-child too. The one thing that really stands out here is that God never gave Jesus' inheritance—His thrown at the right hand of His Father—to any of His half-brothers or half-sisters. His Heavenly Father even met with Him, Peter, and others on the mountain top. Jesus did not express concerns about being abandoned until about the ninth hour as He hung on the cross. In Matthew 27:46, He said, "My God, my God, why hast thou forsaken me?"

If God did abandon His Son, He did it so that He could know how it felt for a father to abandon his son during his greatest time of need. There are many of our sons that are given the needle of death with no father there by their side. In most cases, their fathers are most likely with another woman.

Jesus' Father tore the curtains of the temple in half as a way of expressing His dissatisfaction with what our men had done. I think this was His way of telling us that the temple is insignificant in God's eyes. He was also trying to tell us that the teachings within the temple were not something that He agreed with.

But 2,000 years later, here we sit again. Not much has changed since that time. We have cars now and other modern conveniences, but we still have the same problems with mankind. And even today, most prefer Paul's teachings instead of Christ's teachings. They still reject Christ for their own benefit. Our children still suffer through abortion, abuse, neglect, and abandonment. Many of us are still very self-centered and work hard to build kingdoms on this Earth. Most seek the recognition of men but fail to consider God's Son as an example for our lives. Most everyone desires to be greatest in the classroom or office or on the golf course, tennis court, soccer field, basketball court, and football field. Few prefer to humble themselves and serve in the way that honors our Heavenly Father.

Divorce is as prevalent, if not more prevalent, today. In years past, it was difficult for a woman to leave. With a brood of children at her side, she would have to fend for herself and her children alone. The man will go out, get another woman, and start over. But forcing a woman to stay in a dead marriage is not the answer either. Women have gained freedoms, including the freedom to leave and take the children with us. But no woman should have to make such a difficult decision alone. We must realize God's intentions for us and make Him forever a part of our lives.

Our men must find it within themselves to finally give the kingdom back to God. They are humble servants, too. Instead of learning from women, they have used women for their benefit. What a terrible injustice! But we shouldn't feel disappointed. Even Jesus' half-brothers did not believe in Him. It was only after Christ's death that James became a believer himself.

It is amazing that no matter how two people try to blend two distinct and separate families, their children will almost always remain separate. Jesus even gave Mary, His mother, to John instead of to His half-brothers before He died. Mary stayed with her firstborn son, Jesus. This is the only way to keep the family unit intact. Joseph's family became a separate and distinct family within the main family at that time.

God did the same thing with Abraham and Sarah. Jesus endured a very difficult childhood, much more difficult than we can ever know. Perhaps this is the reason God sent His Son as a step-son. God saw a serious problem and came for the children of the first marriage—God's marriage between two people. God sent His Son, Jesus, for the lost children of the house of Israel. God knows that the children of these lost children are being given stones in the place of blessings.

Jesus Is the Way, the Truth, and the Life

In the following verses, Matthew, Mark, and Luke give an eye witness account of what Jesus said when his mother and half-brothers and sisters came to see him. With these three scriptures, he is leading us to look at the big picture. He wants us to see the whole and not focus on the part alone. Rather than referring to Mary and his half-brothers and sisters as the whole, he pulled in all of the souls that were present. He said with the bigger picture in mind, "Here are my mothers, my brothers, and my sisters. Do the will of God and you too can be a member of my "Club."

> Then came to him *his* mother and his brethren, and could not come at him for the press. And it was told him *by certain* which said, Thy mother and thy brethren stand without, desiring to see thee. And he answered and said unto them, My mother and my brethren are these which hear the word of God, and do it. (Luke 8:19–21)

> There came then his brethren and his mother, and, standing without, sent unto him, calling him. And the multitude sat about him, and they said unto him, Behold, thy mother and thy brethren without seek for thee. And he answered them, saying, Who is my mother, or my brethren? And he looked round about on them which sat about him, and said, Behold my mother and my brethren! For whosoever shall do the will of God, the same is my brother, and my sister, and mother. (Mark 3:31–35)

> While he yet talked to the people, behold, *his* mother and his brethren stood without, desiring to speak with him. Then one said unto him, Behold, thy mother and thy brethren stand without, desiring to speak with thee. But he answered and said unto him that told him, Who is my mother? and who are my brethren? And he stretched forth his hand toward his disciples,

and said, Behold my mother and my brethren! For whosoever shall do the will of my father which is in heaven, the same is my brother, and sister, and mother. (Matthew 12:46–50)

But from the beginning of the creation God made them male and female. For this cause shall a man leave his father and mother, and cleave to his wife; And they twain shall be one flesh: so then they are not more twain, but one flesh. What therefore God hath joined together, let no man put asunder (Mark 10:6–9). This scripture tells us that our sons should stay with us until they marry. There are many fathers that will kick their children out of the house that they share with the other woman.

If people kept this one commandment, and cleaved to their first wives as commanded by God, our world would be so different. Furthermore, if other people would respect that union and the children produced, most of our problems would be nonexistent. We would all be living to one hundred and twenty years. Unfortunately, because we choose to live our life differently than God intended, we put our trust in our lords, our doctors and their pills, to give us a chance to live a longer life. A man is not a solution to our problems. A pill is not a solution to our problems. God is our solution! We just keep his commandments and put our faith and our trust in his son, Jesus.

> *For the Son of man is* as a man taking a far journey, who left his house, and gave authority to his servants, and to every man his work, and commanded the porter to watch. Watch ye therefore: for ye know not when the master of the house cometh, at even, or at midnight, or at the cockcrowing, or in the morning: Lest coming suddenly he find you sleeping. And what I say unto you I say unto all, Watch. (Mark 13:34–37)

Are You a Son or a Daughter of Men, or Are You a Son or Daughter of God?

Mothers are the mothers of all living, including Christ. God is the Father of all living. All of our men are step-fathers!

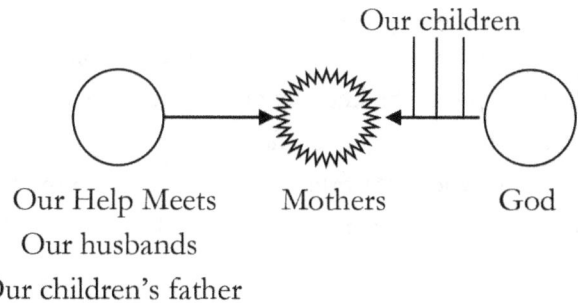

Men are step-fathers: they were created to be helpmeets. The family is leased out to them temporarily under a very stringent lease agreement by God Himself!

All was good in the garden, even after Adam and Eve were driven out. It was not until the remaining sons of God started focusing on the physical instead of the spiritual that God had a problem with our behavior. This was when the sons of God started lusting after and taking the daughters of men for their spouses. Since that time, it has been chaos in the kingdom. No longer do men put the spiritual first in their lives. They take their wives and make them into property along with their children. They raise their borrowed children and make them into sons and daughters of men. They use pornography, sexy clothing, nudity, lust, sin, adultery, and violence to stimulate their physical side, all for the satisfaction and arousal of their penises. They use abuse as a way of maintaining control of God's kingdom (the sons and daughters of God) for themselves. They desire to dominate the kingdom instead of serving within the kingdom. They enjoy creating their own commandments.

They spend most of their waking and nighttime hours thinking about intercourse, both natural and unnatural. No longer is the spiritual important. It has been a very long time since there was less ejaculation and men and women could safely be naked and not be concerned—a time when there was genuine, spiritual love not associated with the physical. It has grieved God greatly since He created the male helpmeet. As the matter of fact, it grieved Him so much that He sent His own Son. That wasn't enough! What will it take to wake these men up?

Here's the answer: you! If you take the information in this book, apply it to your life, and spread the knowledge to others, we can begin to loosen the reign of the commandments of men.

Tell us what you thought of the book. Log on to www.stepfathersstep-son.com and tell us. Thank you.

Index

104 boy babies born for every 100 girl babies 76
"Let not thy left hand know what thy right hand doeth." 161
Abandonment 22
   Mary never abandoned Jesus 57
   reasons for 37
Abortion 22, 255
   family members are not expendable 71
Abraham
   Sarah's half-brother 101
   Son of God 66
Abram and Sarai 62
Adoption 255
   excuse to abandon 42
Adultery 214
   abandoning a natural heir 124
   a sacred sin 48
   cheating on a spouse 38
   definition 20
   full blown 34
   highly acceptable 187
   hogs at the trough 37
   looks perfectly normal with the passage of time 134
   marrying someone that is divorced 29, 30
   move in with the other woman and play house 91
   our land is polluted 257
   Parent's 47
   root cause of our nation's problems 71
   separating a parent from a child 30
   socially acceptable 182
Adultery does not erase or separate 114
A father meeting his adult son 40
Amygdala 134, 209
Autism 223
   statistics 238
A woman supporting two men's children 125
Baggage from the past 57
Bathsheba and King David 63
Beguile
   to trick or cheat by deception 9
Betrayed 41
Body
   focusing on physical form 10
   on display 9
Bringing strangers into the family home 122
Builders
   the mother and the father 72
Burning at the stake 108
Castration 55, 107
   Eunuchs 134
Chaos 193, 195
Children of God
   do not marry 45
   do not need laws to govern or define their family 45
Children of the kingdom 32, 57, 58

keep the laws of this land 50
weeping and gnashing of teeth 49
Child's natural social position within the family 123
Christ
   let your eye be single 251
Circumcision 66, 67
Commandments of men 100, 137
   replacing the commandments of God 205
Competition 219
   Step-parents and a pregnant mother 237
   Step-parents competing with step-children 235
Complex family 104
Cornerstone 41, 72
Covetousness 256
Daughter of God 62
Daughters of men 17, 18
Depression 220
   mourning 221
Despising little children 31
Developmental stage 215
Dinah and Shechem
   bypassed tradition for love 88
Dinah's love
   her brothers killed an innocent man 106
Divergent/Convergent 271
Divorce
   root cause 53
Do not love father or mother more than Jesus! 59
Dream
   became a temptation 210
Drinking and driving 113
Every child fathered by a man is his heir
   His firstborn son with his first wife can receive twice the inheritance of the other children 130
Family
   complex family 98
   forced separation 70
   structure 51
   temporary separation 71
Famous
   let us make us a name 24
Father shall deliver up the child to death 118
Father was alone 58
Fear
   children should not fear their dominating father or mother 14, 197
   jealousy and failure 14
Fertility drugs 83
Finding your father, but letting him go 60
Firstborn son of the first wife 104
Firstborn son of the first wife twice the inheritance 131
Funeral 44
Gathering of the family 112
Generational curse 177, 192
Giants 17
Giving
   out of poverty 14
   out of riches 15
God shortened our lifespan 19
Golden throne
   a vision 257
Grandfather's failure to accept responsibility
   Sons pay the price 12
Hagar 65
   bread and water 69
   Hagar and Ishmael cast out 69
   head of her household 69
   sent away 73
Hard hearted men 199
Harlot 90
Harlots
   Publicans and harlots may enter the kingdom before the man that had intercourse with the harlot 97
Heirs
   women were also heirs 86
Homeless 52, 55, 57, 167

Are You a Son or a Daughter of Men, or Are You a Son or Daughter of God?

Jesus 36
Homosexual
   Soloman, Bathsheba and King David's son 207
Homosexuality
   Paul speaks out against it 207
Homosexuals desire to marry 119
Husbands
   four types 139
Incest
   it is not considered incest for the children of two men's wives to marry 103
Inheritance 74
Intercourse
   love 10
   recreational 25
Isaac
   God transferred his covenant 75
It's all in the jeans 113
Jacob
   became a son of God - name changed to Israel 92
   hired by Leah in exchange for mandrakes 83
   his children's inheritance 130
   Leah's son, Reuben, lay with Bilhah, his father's concubine 93
   Leah wanted him to move in with her 81
   left to escape the wrath of Esau 80
   Rachel and Leah 80
   tricked by Laban 80
Jacob and Leah's sons
   answered deceitfully 89
Jacob's messages to his twelve sons 104
Jacob's message to Judah 105
Jesus on 178
John the Baptist
   not lawful for Herod to have another man's wife, his brother's wife 64
Joseph
   Israel's firstborn son with his first wife, Rachel 94
Joseph's dreams 94
Judah has intercourse with his own daughter-in-law 96
Keep the way of the Lord 67
Law
   Daughter-in-Law, Sarai was Terah's daughter with his second wife 101
   daughters-in-law 97
   Daughters-in-law 103
   fathers-in-law 97
   Judah's laws regarding family 107
   marriage 97
   Wife-in-Law 102
Law-abiding citizen 118
Law of the lords
   benefit adulterers 211
Laws
   break up of the family 24
   imposing adult laws upon children 211
Lawyers and doctors
   job security 188
Lawyers and law enforcement officials 108
Lawyers and their laws 213
Leah's sons made Jacob 90
Leaving children alone with a step-parent 73
Legal heir versus natural heir 31, 46, 56
Legal husband 33
Lords
   actors, presidents, doctors, lawyers, etc. 136
Lost sheep of the house of Israel 99
Love versus respect 218
Man
   alone 84, 100
   becoming the property of the other woman 35
   Bodies similar 7
   Claiming the title 6
   created to provide for the physical needs of the family 49
   human 21
   Male and Female 5

Naming of the animals 6
none good - keep the com-
    mandments 51
things which defile 19
Man's foes
    in his own household 44
Man's responsibility
    protecting the family 11
Marriage
    paper and laws 62
    without paper 74
Maternity leave
    too short 236
Mother of God's children 62
Mr. & Mrs. terminology 235
Narcissism
    self-centeredness 225
Obituaries 43
Offenses
    Using the hand or foot 196
One church 151
Open focus 270
Opposing interests
    between mother and step-mother 35
Original sin
    Unresolved childhood issues 12
Our fathers are with another woman 189
Parthenogenesis
    reproduction without a male 55
    Reproduction without a male 6
Partnership
    balance of power 13
Perfect in his generations
    Noah 16
Peter walks on water 252
Responsibility
    failure to accept 11
Sarah
    Abraham's half-sister and his wife 67
    Daughter and future mother of
        God's child 66
Secret liaisons 72
Self
    like a prison 249

Sexuality
    focus on 143
Sexual reproduction
    Reproductive unit 6
Shift in brain dominance 250
Simple family
    one wife 89
Sin
    root in childhood 223
Sinners called to repentance 252
Son of God 62
    Do not marry the daughter of an
        adulteress 64
Sons of God
    cleave to their wife 155
Soul connections 192
Soul Family
    Sons and daughters of God, Mother's
        of God's children 149
Spare the rod and spoil the child 196, 201
Sperm donor 65, 175
Statistics 197
    Abuse of step-children 172
Step-father's and step-mother's old-
    est child 31
Step-mother head of household 76
Step-parents
    come to steal and scatter 204
Subtle messages from a step-parent to a
    step-child 258
Surrogate mother 65
Tame versus wild 199
Temptation
    Peter denied knowing Christ three
        times 211
Temptations
    Christ was tempted just as many of our
        children are 134
Testing for eye dominance 262
Test tube babies 65
The ass
    The ass's colt and his significance 111
The elimination of family members

our way of keeping generations
    perfect 109
The eye
    the light of the body 220
The firstborn child - the cornerstone
    a threat to adulterers and adul-
        teresses 256
The gathering of the Family 110
The whole versus the part 20
Titles 51, 138
To keep the way of the Lord 62
Treatment of small animals
    separation at six weeks is too early 236
Turn hearts away from second wives
    back to the children of the first
        family 240
Two people can play house 176
Unipolar 249
Victim 12
    paying the price 12, 22
    the one who paid the price 20
Vision
    empty golden throne 75
Welfare 26
Wild West days again
    open carry 155
Winning 15
Witch-craft
    twisting the truth 36
Women
    tending the garden and raising their
        children 19
Work
    toil and sweat 10
You do what you have seen with your
    father 58

Endnotes

1. Sims, Guilfoyle, and Parry, "What Cortisol Levels Tell Us About Quality In Child Care Centres," *Australian Journal of Early Childhood*, 30(2), 1–41, 2005.

2. Juliet Eilperin, "Female Sharks Can Reproduce Alone, Researchers Find," *Washington Post*, Wednesday, May 23, 2007, p. A02.

3. Mahmood Shivji, "Captive shark had 'virgin birth'—Female hammerhead sharks can reproduce without having sex, scientists confirm," *BBC News*, May 23, 2007, 13:09 GMT.

4. Rick Groleau, "Tracing Ancestry With MtDNA," NOVA Online, http://www.pbs.org/wgbh/nova/neanderthals/mtdna.html

5. www.smartstork.com/p11.asp "Natural Gender Selection – How to have a boy or a girl?"

6. Shettles, Landrum B. and Rorvik, David M., *How to Choose the Sex of Your Baby*. Broadway Books: New York, 2006

7. Wilson, Margo and Daly, Martin, "Who kills whom in spouse killings? On the exceptional sex ratio of spousal homicides in the United States." *Criminology* 30 (1992): 189–216. Accessed 7 March 2006. DOI: 10.1111/j.1745-9125.1992.tb01102.x.

8. Wilson, Margot and Daly, Martin, "Lethal and nonlethal violence against wives and the evolutionary psychology of male sexual proprietariness" In R. Dobash, and R. Dobash (Eds.), Sage Series on Violence against Women: Rethinking violence against women, Thousand Oaks, CA: SAGE Publications, Inc., 199-230. doi: http://dx.doi.org/10.4135/9781452243306.n8.

9. Homicide Research Working Group, "Trends, Risks and Interventions in Lethal Violence." Proceedings of the 3rd annual spring symposium of the Homicide Research Working Group, Washington DC: National Institute of Justice, SAGE Publications, CA: Thousand Oaks (1994).

10. Qazi Rahman, "Scans see gay brain differences—The brains of gay men and women look like those found in heterosexual people of the opposite sex, research suggests," *BBC*, Monday, 16 June 2008.

11. "Daly, Margo and Wilson, Martin "Special Issue: stepparental investment," *Evolution & Human Behavior* 20: 365–366 (1999).

12. "Wilson, Margo and Daly, Martin, "Male sexual proprietariness and violence against wives," Psychological Science 5 (1996):2–7, doi: 10.1111/1467-8721. ep10772668.

13. Simon, Sidney B., *Getting Unstuck—Breaking Through the Barriers to Change*. New York: Warner Books, 1988. 1–293.

14. Konner, Melvin, *Why the Reckless Survive and Other Secrets of Human Nature*. New York: Viking Press, 1990. 1–320.

15. Daly, "Martin, and Wilson, Margot, "Evolutionary Psychology and Marital Conflict: The Relevance of Step-Children," in *Sex, Power, and Conflict: Feminist and Evolutionary Perspectives*, ed. David M. Buss et al. (New York: Oxford University Press. 1996). 9–28.

16. Daly, Martin and Wilson, Margot, *The Truth About Cinderella: A Darwinian View of Parental Love*. London: Yale University Press, 1999, vii–67.

17. Dobson, James, <u>Bringing Up Boys: Practical advice and encouragement for those shaping the next generation of men</u>, IL: Tyndale House Publishers, 2001, IX–259.

18. Homicide Research Working Group, "Trends, Risks and Interventions in Lethal Violence." Proceedings of the 3rd annual spring symposium of the Homicide Research Working Group, Washington DC: National Institute of Justice, Sage Publications, CA: Thousand Oaks (1994).

19. Eccle, J.C., "The Split Brain in Man," *Scientific American*, Volume 217, (August 1967), 24–29.

20. Gazzaniga, W., "One brain two minds?" *American Scientist*, Volume 60, (1972): 311–317.

21. Will, George F. "Boys Will Be Boys or you can just drug them." *Washington Post*, 2 December 1999, 39A.

22. Brown, S. & Shafer, E. "An investigation into the functions of the occipital and temporal lobes of the monkey's brain." Philosophical Transactions of the Royal Society of London: *Biological Sciences* 179 (1887–1895) 1888-01-01:303–327.

23. Kluver, Heinrich, and Bucy, Paul, "Preliminary analysis of function of the temporal lobe in monkeys," *Journal of Neuropsychiatry and Clinical Neurosciences* 9:4 (1997), 606–620, dx.doi.org/10.1176/jnp.9.4.606-a.

24. Bucher, K., Myers, R. E., Southwick, Chris "Anterior temporal cortex and maternal behavior in monkey." *Neurology* 20:4 (April 1970), 415.

25. Donegan, NH, Sanislow, CA, Blumberg, HP, Fulbright, RK, Lacadie, C, Skudlarski, P, Gore, JC, Olson, IR, McGlashan, TH, and Wexler, BE, "Amygdala hyperactivity in borderline personality disorder: implications for emotional dysregulation." *Biological Psychiatry* 54:11 (2003): 1284–1293.

26. Nathan, Dr., Phan, Luan, Fitzgerald, Daniel, and Tancer, Manuel, "Studying Brain Activity Could Aid Diagnosis Of Social Phobia." *ScienceDaily*. www.sciencedaily.com/releases/2006/01/060118205940.htm (accessed July 19, 2015)

27. Blumberg, HP, Kaufman, J., Martin, A., Whiteman, R., Zhang, JH, Gore, JC, Charney, DS, Krystal, JH, and Peterson, BS, "Amygdala and hippocampal volumes in adolescents and adults with bipolar disorder," Arch *General Psychiatry* 60:12(2003): 1201–8.

28. Daly, Martin and Wilson, Margo. "Some differential attributes of lethal assaults on small children by stepfathers versus genetic fathers." *Ethology & Sociobiology* 15 (1994), 207–217.

29. University of Idaho College of Science (2004). "amygdala." http://www.sci.uidaho.edu/med532/amygdala.htm. Wikipedia the free encyclopedia.

30. Ilg, Frances; Ames, Louise; and Baker, Sidney, *Child Behavior— The classic child care manual from the Gesell Institute of Human Development*, NY: Harper, 1992.

31. Eaves, Elisabeth, "The Extremely Male Brain –What caused the explosion in autism diagnoses? Why are boys more affected by the disorder?" *Forbes Magazine*, 22 June 2009.

32. Williamson, Marianne, *A Return to Love: Reflections on the Principles of "A Course in Miracles."* NY: Harper Collins, 1996.

33. Pearsall, Paul, *The Power of the Family: Tapping the power of family life to strengthen, revitalize, and heal*. NY: Doubleday, 1991.

34. Miller, Alice, "Adolf Hitler: How Could A Monster Succeed in Binding A Nation?" *Spiegel*, 1998.

35. Miller, Alice, *The Body Never Lies—The Lingering Effects of Hurtful Parenting*, NY: Norton, 2006, 1–227.

36. Melissa Fletcher Stoeltje, "A risk of pregnancy: abuse, homicide—Violence is the second-leading cause of trauma death for expectant and new mothers," *San Antonio Express-News*, July 23, 2007, Section C.

37. Susan DeFord, "Triplets' autism means three times the angst—Parents struggle with the emotional and financial costs," *San Antonio Express-News*, January 14, 2008, 3C.

38. Linda Searing, "The older the father, the lower the child's IQ score," *Washington Post, San Antonio-Express News*, March 30, 2009, Section C, 4.

39. Robert Sapolsky, "Testosterone Rules—It takes more than just a hormone to make a fellow's trigger finger itch," *Discover*, March 1997, 45–50.

40. Martin Daly and Margo Wilson, "Darwinism and the roots of machismo," *Scientific American*, 10:2 (1999), 8–14.

41. Roger Sperry, "Left Brain, Right Brain," *Saturday Review*, August 1975, 30–33.

42. Russel N. Cassel and Susie L. Cassel, "Need Gratification and Brain Dominance—Nucleus for Transpersonal Psychology and Biofeedback Use." *Psychology* 21, no. 2 (1984), 48–53.

43. Rebecca Coffey, "20 Things You Didn't Know About Genius," *Discover*, October 2008, 88.

44. *The Course in Miracles*, CA: The Foundation for Inner Peace, 2007

45. Randolph E. Schmid, "Social rank' in family, not birth order, tied to boys' IQs," Associated Press, *San Antonio Express-News*, Friday, June 22, 2007, 10A.

46. Leger, Frederick J., *Beyond the Therapeutic Relationship—Behavioral, Biological, and Cognitive Foundations of Psychotherapy*, NY: Hayworth Press, 1998.

47. "Gazzaniga, M.S., and Hillyard, Steven A., "Language and Speech Capacity of the Right Hemisphere," *Neuropsychologin*, Volume 9 (1971): 273–280.

48. Fehmi, Les, and Robbins, Jim, *The Open Focus Brain: Harnessing the Power of Attention to Heal Mind and Body*, MA: Shambhala Publications, 2007.

49. Slade, Neil, *The Frontal Lobes Supercharge*, CO: Neil Slade Books, Film, and Music, 2011.

50. Slade, Neil, *Brain Magic 2*, CO: Neil Slade Books, Film, and Music, 2012.

51. "Roubinek, Darrel L.; Bell, Michael; and Cates, Lesa, "Hemispheric Preference of Intellectually Gifted Children," *Roeper Review*, Vol 10, Issue 2 (December 1987): 120–122.

52. McManus, I.C., and Tomlinson, Julia, "Objects look different sizes in the right and left eyes," *Laterality*, Volume 9, Issue 3(2004): 245–265.

www.ingramcontent.com/pod-product-compliance
Lightning Source LLC
Chambersburg PA
CBHW070533010526
44118CB00012B/1123